Producing Hit Records

ZADOC MUSIC BUSINESS SERIES

available

Promoting Rock Concerts
   by Howard Stein with Ronald Zalkind

Getting Ahead in the Music Business
   by Ronald Zalkind

Producing Hit Records
   by Dennis Lambert with Ronald Zalkind

Contemporary Music Almanac
   by Ronald Zalkind

in preparation

Understanding Music Business Contracts, 2 vols.

Financial Planning for Entrepreneurs in the Arts

Writing Hit Songs

Producing Hit Records

by Dennis Lambert with Ronald Zalkind

Foreword by Al Coury

SCHIRMER BOOKS
A Division of Macmillan Publishing Co., Inc.
NEW YORK

Collier Macmillan Publishers
LONDON

A Zadoc Book

Zadoc® is a registered trademark protected by law.

Copyright © 1980 by Dennis Lambert and Ronald Zalkind

SCHIRMER BOOKS
A Division of Macmillan Publishing Co., Inc.
866 Third Avenue, New York, N.Y.   10022

Collier Macmillan Canada, Ltd.

Library of Congress Catalog Card Number:79-91505

Printed in the United States of America

printing number

1   2   3   4   5   6   7   8   9   10

Library of Congress Cataloging in Publication Data

Lambert, Dennis.
    Producing hit records.

    (Zadoc music business series)
    1.   Sound   recordings—Industry   and   trade—United
States. 2. Music, Popular (Songs,   etc.)—Writing
and publishing. 3.   Sound—Recording and reproducing.
I.   Zalkind, Ronald, joint author.   II.   Title.
III.   Series.
ML3790.L35   388.4′7789912′0973   79-91505
ISBN 0-02-871950-6
ISBN 0-02-871960-3 pb'

For "Biggy," whose memory inspires me,
and for Diane and Jody, and Robert Altshuler

Contents

List of Illustrations

Demonstration Record References

Side 1

Recording the drums

Recording the bass

Recording the rhythm guitars

Recording the keyboards

Evaluating the rhythm section

Recording the background vocals

Recording the lead vocal

Side 2

Recording guitar overdubs

Recording guitar effects

Recording solo guitars

Recording synthesizer

Recording percussion

Evaluating final 2-track master

Acknowledgments

Many thanks to Jay Lewis, for preparation of the demonstration record and evaluation of technical material; Matt Hyde, for assistance with recording technique; United-Western Recorders, for generous use of their facilities; Al Coury and RSO Records, for their cooperation and supportive spirit; Player, for hit records and good times; Gordon Bayne and his staff, for artistic assistance; Paul Riker, for information on home studio construction; and Christine Hopkins, for ink drawings made on the finished manuscript.

Foreword

Throughout my years in the music industry working closely with many different artists and many different kinds of music, I have found that the producer is a key element in the success of any musical endeavor. One of the finest producers I have worked with is Dennis Lambert, whose wide-ranging knowledge of every aspect of the music business is an invaluable asset to any project. His flexible talents have led him to work not only with records but also with motion picture and television themes, delivering superb results in all fields. Dennis brings to each project a sensitive awareness of its specific needs combined with the outstanding technical expertise and experience that have enabled him to become one of the industry's most respected producers.

Dennis Lambert and his partner Brian Potter, songwriters as well as producers, have worked with a spectacular array of artists such as Glen Campbell, The Four Tops, Santana, The Grass Roots, The Righteous Brothers, Dusty Springfield, Tavares, and Player. In fact, one of my most exciting memories of Dennis Lambert is his work with Player, when "Baby Come Back," the very first single from the group's first album, became an instant number one hit across the board.

With a catalogue of almost three hundred songs and more than four hundred commercially released recordings, Lambert and Potter are firmly established as a noteworthy and important production team, a fact the music industry has acknowledged with a number of awards over the years. Yet they continue to write and produce hit music with a fresh and timely sound that I am sure will continue to bring them great success in the years to come.

With this book, Dennis Lambert has distilled the essence of his talent and experience into an interesting and illuminating guide to the complexities of recording music. It is a welcome addition to the literature of music, one that I am sure will be helpful to aspiring artists and producers everywhere.

AL COURY
President, RSO Records

1
Getting to Know Me

Record production, one of the most sought after, potentially lucrative careers in the entertainment universe, is something of an enigma. Almost everyone, at one time or another, has wanted to become a producer; almost no one, on the other hand, including successful producers like myself, has taken the time to explain record production in a clear, comprehensive, and realistic way. I hope this book will answer most of the practical questions aspiring producers have about getting into and getting ahead in this creative, dynamic corner of the music business.

My involvement with the record industry grew out of my career as a live performer. Working professionally as a singer from the time I was seven years old, I was lucky enough to be signed by the Tokens to a recording contract with Capitol Records in 1961. The Tokens, who had had hit records in their own name, were operating as independent producers, supplying different record companies with completed masters of artists they found and developed. Although their efforts with me as a singer enjoyed no commercial success, the process of recording captured my imagination. I began to think that someday I could become a good record producer.

In the years that followed I tried several more times to make it as an artist, both alone and as the lead singer in a group, but again, no cigar. Yet the attraction of working behind the scenes was growing stronger, and in a matter of months I forsook the potential glamour of performing for the fascinating, creative role of record producer.

In fifteen years, I have made a lot of records, some good, some not so good. I joined forces in 1969 with Brian Potter, and we are currently celebrating our eleventh year as collaborators and partners. Together we have created enormously successful records that have sold in the millions of units. Where possible in this book, I will make specific reference to some of these recordings.

1

My growth depended in part on luck, which is always the unknown and unpredictable factor in the how-to-become-successful equation. But if you want something badly enough, you tend to make your own luck. In other words, if you want to be a producer, produce. That may mean spending valuable time with your cousin's friend who *thinks* he can sing and play the guitar, but at least you'll be producing, learning, and meeting colleagues in the university of hard knocks.

Most producers I know were involved with music in some other capacity before they were put in charge of a recording session. From the ranks of musicians, audio engineers, singers, managers, and record lovers come producers. Though their backgrounds and qualifications may differ, they have much in common. All are highly motivated, willing to try and try again until they get it right. The more successful ones are able to balance creativity with a sense and feel of the market. They understand and appreciate music on both an aesthetic and a commercial level and can stand back from the tedious and demanding process of recording to shape and judge their own work objectively.

Producers have varying styles, and consequently they work differently. My approach is dictated by my background. I'm a musician, a songwriter, and a singer (as a practical extension of what else I do), but I'm not an engineer. No producer need be a technical master in the recording studio, unless he intends to do his own engineering, which I don't recommend. The president's job is big enough; let somebody else be secretary of labor. Of course, a fundamental knowledge of the equipment and the recording process is essential. But more important is your ability to lead a session, to convey your concepts, and to set the direction a record will take and to keep it on course.

This is a nuts-and-bolts book. There is a great deal of specific information that I hope to impart in a simple, concise manner. Much of it, unfortunately, is technical, so I may, in an attempt to keep us all awake, try an occasional bit of humor or an odd anecdote.

A careful study of the following chapters should provide the reader with a working knowledge of how to prepare for a session; what to look for in a studio; how to get a good sound recording the various instruments, including voice; how to mix and edit multitrack tapes; how to present the product to a record company; and, perhaps most crucial, how to cope with the business world outside the recording studio.

Being able to deal skillfully with artists, managers, publishers, and record companies is becoming more and more important. Having good ears is almost taken for granted today. What really counts (beyond proving, of course, that you do have good ears) is demonstrating an understanding of contracts, artist relations, record industry terminology and practices, and other dues-paying elements. If you don't have a thorough grasp of what else goes on—if you're not a student of the market and of the workings of record companies—you exist on your own island, and it just doesn't work in the end. Consequently, the business aspects of becoming a successful record producer will be dealt with rather extensively in this book.

When I started my career as a record producer, the industry had a mom and pop feel, and people seemed to have more time to devote to new talent. But today it's big business. There are more conglomerates, and they market a much greater volume of product than the smaller, independent record companies used to put out. This greater demand for product has given birth to more encouragement of (though not necessarily more personal contact with) creative talent and more freedom for producers to express themselves in the studio. Now there may be more competition, but the record-buying public is much more interested than it used to be.

Record production is still a wide open, growing industry. If this book serves you as a shortcut in learning how to get ahead, I'll consider it no small accomplishment.

2
What Is a Record Producer, and How Do You Become One?

The purpose of this chapter is to specify what a record producer does; to distinguish the various types of record producers; to identify the supporting players in the record production business, including A&R (artist and repertoire) executives, audio engineers, and arrangers; and then to tackle the sixty-four-dollar question—"How do you get your foot in the door and actually become a professional producer?"

Take heed, those of you who are impatient with the technical material that follows: you may be doing yourself a disservice by skirting this chapter. If you're not 100 percent certain what a producer needs to do in order to become successful—if you're not absolutely clear how the production game is played—the place to begin reading is right here.

THE ROLE OF THE PRODUCER

The biggest misconception most people have about record producers is that they are merely creative technicians—that their job consists entirely of recording, mixing, and editing tape until a finished master is achieved. That, in reality, is the *majority* of what any producer does for a living, but equally important is the *minority* interest a producer has in his profession.

All successful producers have the following in common:
• They have the ability to pick hit songs and hit artists.
• They have a feel for the marketplace.
• They know how to present a new artist or song to a record company.
• They are familiar generally with standard operating procedures within the

4

record business and specifically with production budgets and artist-producer deals.

• They know how to deal effectively with studio and record company personnel.

No professional producer, not even a staff producer on salary to a major record company, lives in a creative vacuum today. Far from being an exclusively musical personage, the successful producer of the 1980s can best be characterized as a figment of his own multitrack recording environment. Here is how a producer's "tracks," if we can call them that, might look under spectrographic analysis:

Track A is the successful producer's ability to recognize that new, unrecorded music has commercial possibilities. All producers, in addition to knowing how to conduct studio sessions, must be skillful talent scouts.

Track B, the ability to feel sympathetic pulsations from the marketplace, suggests that the successful producer must be both business oriented and sales oriented since the producer must sell his concept of a new artist or sound to the record company. The successful record producer, therefore, must also be a gifted salesman.

Track C, the ability to present a new artist or song to a record company, means that the producer must be articulate, courteous, patient, and diplomatic. Henry Kissinger may play this gambit better, but all successful record producers must be clever political strategists.

Track D, which implies that a producer be well versed in what are considered customary practices in the record industry, makes the producer a partner of his lawyer, accountant, and business manager. Indeed, many of my friends tell me that I'm a better music business lawyer than their own high-priced attorneys. What I've learned about contracts, I've learned out of necessity and self-interest.

Tracks E and F, which encompass the producer's ability to record the artist in the studio and to deal effectively with studio and record company personnel, are the more technical end of the producer's talent spectrum.

Recording technique, like dance, acting, or guitar technique, can readily—in fact speedily—be learned. But what also needs to be learned, if you want to be a successful record producer, are the elements covered in tracks A, B, C, and D. This is why I suggested that the place to begin studying record production is not the chapter devoted to getting a good sound, but here. Let it sink in that a successful record producer is more than a music man, more even than a talent scout. As figure 1 shows, he's also a businessman, salesman, politician, counselor, director of operations, attorney, and accountant. The most successful producers also carefully monitor record promotion, public relations, record and tape manufacture, and foreign licensing of product. What happens in the studio, although it occupies the majority of a

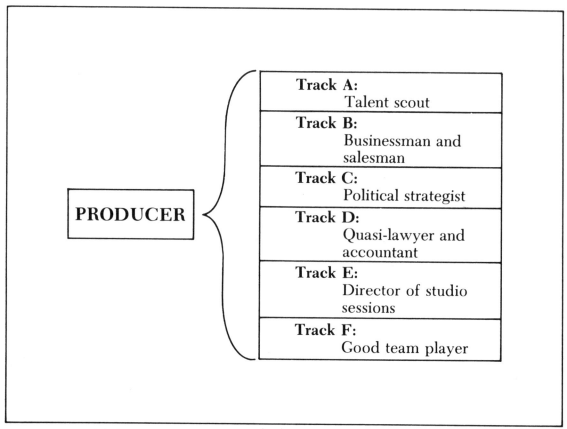

FIGURE 1. Producers do more today than just record music.

producer's time, is but the tip of the iceberg. Today, record production is an all-encompassing creative as well as business endeavor.

These preliminary, state-of-the-production-business remarks lead to some unavoidable conclusions. Nobody jumps into a career as a record producer without having tried something else first. Many producers were originally artists; others were originally audio engineers, songwriters, personal managers, or A&R personnel. Regardless of the road you take, one of the keys to getting ahead in the production business is to find a job with an established, reputable company as early as possible. It can be a record or publishing company, a booking agency, a management office, or even a retail record store. But it's crucial to be visible in some way to the industry, to see who's coming and going, and to learn the best and most inexpensive way possible—on the job.

The next conclusion may be the toughest pill of all to swallow. Although the majority of a producer's time is spent in the studio, it's what the producer does wearing his *minority*-interest hat (tracks A, B, C, and D) that has the greatest impact initially on being able to sign new artists and make production deals. Having an exclusive contract with a new artist, for example, means much more to a record company than a producer's technical qualifications. Business comes before technique; one can always begin on the fringe of production and work up to the ultimate goal of creative control. If you become expert at tracks A, B, C, and D, you may never need to learn how to turn on the tape recorder. You can hire somebody to handle that task, or you may get out of record production altogether and start your own record or personal management company.

Last but not least, the magic key that opens doors in the music business is something highly impersonal. It's called a hit song or a hit artist demo or, less frequently, a hit master tape. The bottom line in this business isn't whether you went to Harvard, whether you wear clean or dirty underwear, or whether you're straight, gay, or somewhere in between. The bottom line, especially for record producers, is, "How good is this demo you brought us?"

I don't wish to belabor this putting-the-cart-before-the-horse point. Let me summarize where I'd like each reader's focus to be now:

1. The term "record producer" is something of a misnomer in that it does not adequately describe the gamut of business as well as creative imperatives demanded by the job.

2. The best way to study record production generally is to plug yourself into a highly visible job within the music industry. Production technique can be studied specifically either by taking a course in record production or by hanging out at recording studios (my production technique was developed through the latter method). Presently, however, there is no college-level program anywhere in the world that even remotely approximates what you will learn in time from working in the music business.

3. Leverage counts much more than knowledge of recording practices. Novice producers are encouraged to learn as much as they can about the use of recording equipment, but their primary emphasis should be on scouting talent and on signing talent to exclusive production contracts. A legally enforceable contract, coupled with a crudely produced *demo* tape of a potential hit song or artist, is worth many times what it will cost to produce a twenty-four-track *master* tape recording of a bad song.

4. Less is best. There is absolutely no need for beginning producers (especially those who haven't mastered tracks A, B, C, and D) to think about producing expensive master tapes. A demo tape will do fine. If a postage stamp can do the job of a long-distance telephone call, use the stamp. In short, saving money makes a lot of sense, no matter how elevated your financial position may one day become.

Having established these general priorities, we're ready to identify the different

7

types of producers, their pecking order within the industry, and their supporting players.

TYPES OF PRODUCERS

There are staff producers, executive producers, and independent producers. A *staff producer* is a salaried employee of a record company. He takes direction from the record company's A&R department, which periodically assigns him to listen to or work with new or established artists signed to the label. Most staff producers earn $300 to $600 weekly and receive incentive production royalties of 2 to 3 percent of the retail list price of the records they produce, less standard packaging deductions. This is quite an improvement over the 1 percent staff producer royalty that was customary a decade ago, and like day to night compared to what was customary two decades ago—at that time, staff producers only received a rather modest salary.

Executive producers are the heads of A&R, or executives functioning in primarily administrative capacities, at major record companies such as CBS, Warner Brothers, and Polydor Records. Unlike staff and independent producers, they work almost exclusively in an office. In the production business, this means that the executive producer directs the flow of traffic—i.e., demonstration tapes, talent scouting assignments, and actual production work loads—to the producers and A&R employees whom he supervises. Executive producers are also in charge of approving production budgets, mediating disputes among artists, producers, and studio personnel, and developing the overall roster configuration for the label (e.g., how many rock, R&B [rhythm and blues], country, jazz, and classical artists the label should have). These jobs pay well—between $50,000 and $100,000 a year, plus bonuses—but they are primarily paper-pushing jobs. The executive producer in the record business has his counterpart in the executive producer of a motion picture or a television series.

Independent producers are people who function pretty much on their own. They work for one specific company, although they may have an agreement to make a certain number of records over a period of time for a given label. For the most part they move from record company to record company, taking on the projects that are most interesting to them and most relevant to their particular style of production. Independent producers make their living through a combination of advances against royalties and independent production royalties earned based on sales. The parameters of independent production advances and royalties depend entirely on how strong the producer is—how much the record company desires his services—or on how hungry he is—how eager to get his foot in the door at a particular label. Advances range from zero to $50,000 per album and higher; royalties are in the range of 2 percent to 4 percent of the retail list price of an album, with the present industry norm being 3 percent. If you're very much in demand, you may be able to get 5 percent.

The logic of which job is most desirable—staff producer, executive producer, or independent producer—can be expressed by simple arithmetic:

Executive producers, as previously stated, make between $50,000 and $100,000 a year, plus bonuses. They receive excellent employee benefits, such as health and life insurance, pension plans, and stock options. Practically all of their business expenses are paid for by their employer, including meals, transportation, and hotel accommodations. Most of their paycheck, after deducting for federal, state and local taxes (and if there's anything left after buying groceries), can be put right into the executive producer's investment portfolio.

Staff producers earn a base salary of between $15,600 and $31,200 a year, plus bonuses. As company employees, they are also entitled to employee benefits and reimbursement of their business related out-of-pocket expenses. Assuming that the retail price of an album is $7.98, which is the current industry standard (soon it will be $8.98), and assuming that the staff producer is involved annually in three different recording sessions (this is a typical work load for an established in-house staffer), the producer, whose current royalty is 2 percent of the retail list price of albums and singles less packaging deductions (which brings the royalty base price down to $6.98 approximately, rather than $7.98), will receive additional compensation as follows:

- $.14 (rounded off) for each album sold through normal U.S. distribution channels;
- $10,500 if, as an example, each of three albums sold 25,000 units;
- $126,000 if, as another example, album A sold 100,000 units, album B sold 300,000 units, and album C "went gold," or sold 500,000 units;
- $420,000 if, as still another example, each album reached the "platinum" album goal of a million units sold. Note that in each of these cases the staff producer's salary may technically be considered either a complete or a partial advance against production royalties, when and if they are earned.

Independent record producers receive advances in lieu of a salary. They usually pay their own way for everything; in addition, the advances they receive are recoupable from the production royalties they will eventually receive. Assuming, however, that an independent record producer is getting a royalty of 3 percent of the retail list price of an album ($7.98) less packaging deductions ($7.98 becomes $6.98 approximately), and assuming that the independent record producer, like the staff producer, is involved in three different recording sessions during a one-year period, his earnings will be:

- $.21 (rounded off) for each album sold through normal U.S. distribution channels;
- $15,750 if, as is the first case of the staff producer, each of the three albums sold 25,000 units;
- $189,000 if, as with the second staff producer example, album A sold 100,000 units, album B sold 300,000 units, and album C sold 500,000 units, making it a gold record;

- $630,000 (plus three platinum album awards from the Recording Industry Association of America) if, as with the third staff producer example, each album sold a million units.

It's quite rare, incidentally, for a producer to score a hat trick this way, with three different projects in a year becoming platinum records. What *is* happening with greater frequency, however, is that a single hit album will sell in the multiplatinum range, anywhere from two to five million units. If you're in record production for the money, and you're able to produce artists who consistently sell in the multiplatinum range, you'll probably want to be an independent producer rather than a staff producer.

There are other, somewhat more realistic parts of the production equation to consider, however. Very few of the thousands of albums commercially released each year become multiplatinum, platinum, or gold records. Eight out of nine records released by established record companies, in fact, don't achieve break even—in such cases, the independent record producer's advance against royalties would be the only payment he received for his professional services.

Many of you will certainly feel tempted by the large figures I've used. I hope they can be attained by everyone who tries, but realistically it's not going to happen overnight. The more reasonable way to begin a production career is with some financial security behind you—in other words, a salary. As figure 2 suggests, start out as a record company gofer; work into the A&R department in the capacity of an assistant, if you can; ask the A&R executive producer to give you a shot as a demo producer; become a staff producer, and let the record company worry about getting business and making money. Only when you've established yourself as a successful hit record producer should you consider starting your own record production company.

CUSTOM LABELS

There is one other form of production entity associated with the record business, the *custom label*. Custom label owners comprise the cream of U.S. and international record producers. In essence, a custom label, which is distributed by a major label, enables the producer-owner to function somewhat independently in the areas of deciding which artists to sign; how much to pay those artists; what material to record; when to release product; and how to promote product to radio stations, record stores, and the public in general.

Because of their track records and the quality of the product they consistently tend to deliver, custom label owners are able to negotiate all-inclusive royalties (from wnich the custom label owner pays the artists and the producer, if the producer isn t the custom label owner) in the range of 12 percent to 20 percent of the retail list price of a $7.98 album. Some custom label owners go one step further: they become

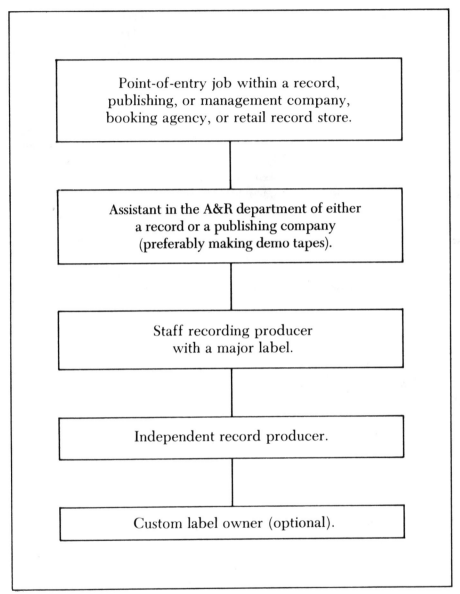

FIGURE 2. Stepwise progression of jobs taken
by most successful record producers.

fifty-fifty partners with the major label that distributes their product, meaning that after all expenses have been paid, including manufacturing, advertising, and promotion costs, as well as artist royalties, the distributing label and the custom label owner split the net profits in half.

Crossing over to custom label ownership should be weighed very carefully by any independent or staff record producer so tempted. Owning a custom label means running your own minirecord company: you're going to have to compete with every other record company, large and small, for artists, air play, and counter space. You'll be able to spend only a fraction of the time you might otherwise spend, if you remained a staff or independent producer, in the studio. You'll make more money as a custom label owner for each record you sell, but you will no longer be able to work with established artists signed to other labels.

The expense of running a custom label, which could include executive salaries for a national promotion director, operations chief, and A&R head; production costs; rent, telephone, postage, insurance, salaries, and employee benefits for secretaries and a receptionist; is staggering. You may be receiving a seven-figure advance against royalties from your distributor—you may even have one or two outstanding years back to back—but if you can't be in the money for a very long period of time, you'll be in the unenviable position of having to pay everybody else for their services while you take home the scraps (if any) from the feast.

In 1973, after having had a number of years of success with different artists, including the Four Tops and the Grassroots, my partner and I decided to get a little more deeply involved with what we did and how we did it. We made a custom label deal with Capitol Records for our company called Haven Records, which Capitol distributed in the United States and EMI, Capitol's parent company, distributed outside the United States.

Over the years, we delivered product to Capitol of the Righteous Brothers, Evie Sands, the Grassroots, and a number of new artists. Most of the talent that we had signed to us, in fact, was new, which was one of the problems we had with being a custom label. Artists feel more comfortable recording for companies whose image precedes them. Even if you're offering something extraordinary to the artist (in the case of Haven Records, it was the opportunity to work with Lambert and Potter not only as producers but also as songwriters), the new custom label owner has a tremendous number of obstacles to overcome. When you start a record company today, even one that's affiliated with a major international distributor, you're at a decided disadvantage.

Custom label ownership is a difficult undertaking. My partner and I are no longer involved in Haven Records to the extent we were during the seventies because we found the work too time-consuming and because competing with major record companies proved too difficult. As producers we felt that we had closed ourselves off from involvement with other record companies and other artists, many of whom were seeking us out to produce their records. These are some of the reasons I recommend thinking about custom label ownership as a possible, but not necessarily mandatory, final record production goal. Remaining independent, so as to play the field and stick primarily to the creative business of producing hit records, may be a more sensible career path for most producers to take.

THE RECORDING ENGINEER

The man who literally sits next to the producer in the studio control room is the *recording engineer*. He is the technical expert in charge of operating and maintaining the production equipment. The essence of his job is to help the producer achieve the sound the producer desires hearing. The majority of producers whom I know are not engineers in their own right. It takes many years of hard work and a lot of experience to become a good engineer. Engineering is a career unto itself. Some extroverted engineers do go on to become producers, but the most direct route for becoming a producer is to do just that: become a producer.

There are fewer staff engineers today than there used to be, as recording studios are finding that most artists and/or producers prefer using independent engineers with whom they've established a working rapport. Large studio complexes, however, such as United Western in Los Angeles, do maintain a resident engineering staff. Staffers earn anywhere from $200 a week, as second engineers in training, to $600 or $700 a week, as full-fledged mixers. Staff engineers also may receive bonuses based on the number of hours they spend on a particular production.

Independent engineers are hired for a particular project and paid an hourly fee of between $30 and $50. Assuming that the engineer spends the industry average of 300 to 500 hours making an individual album, and that, like the successful producer, the successful recording engineer keeps busy with at least three different projects each year, an annual income of between $27,000 and $75,000 is possible. In addition, some producers, as I do, give their engineers a share of the bottom-line profit of a hit album (some record companies and artists do this, too). This is usually not a contractual obligation, but an informal way of showing the engineer how valued his services are in making hit records.

As a rule, independent recording engineers bill record companies on a weekly basis. They are treated as independent contractors by the record company, although they do sometimes get preferential treatment: for example, a recording engineer who works with a number of artists signed to a label may be able to negotiate for up-front money in advance of his undertaking a scheduled recording project.

Most engineers are involved in all phases of recording. However, with the rise in popularity of disco product, engineers and quasi-producers have begun to specialize in mixing. A mixing specialist may be able to bill clients at higher hourly rates, but the job openings in this area at present are extremely limited. The full-service engineer, who is able to assist the producer from the inception to the completion of a studio project, is far more in demand.

THE ARRANGER

Producers rely on engineers for technical support; they rely on arrangers and possibly on songwriters for musical support if the artists they're producing aren't a self-contained group. The arranger's job is to orchestrate a song along the lines suggested by the producer. Although I do some of my own arrangements, I've enjoyed working with a number of enormously talented free-lance arrangers, including Jimmie Haskell, Artie Butler, Michael Omartian, Gene Page, and Tom Sellers. These men have been lured, from time to time, into the ranks of producers, but for the most part they return to their craft of orchestrator-arranger-conductor.

A really good arranger deserves the freedom to contribute his own spark to the music rather than be limited by a producer who might insist, for example, on three trumpets, two saxophones, and a kazoo. Arrangers can charge anywhere from $200 to $1,000 per arrangement, depending on how difficult and time-consuming the arrangement will be. Each local of the American Federation of Musicians (AFM) publishes a directory not only of arrangers but also of copyists, the people who write out the orchestral parts so that the musicians can actually read them. These directories, however, should be consulted only as a last resort: the best way to secure a talented arranger is through word of mouth.

Understanding song structure and being able to contribute to the shaping process of a song are important responsibilities of the record producer. If the producer isn't working with singer-songwriter artists and is not himself a songwriter, he must be able to obtain good songs from professional songwriters, most of whom are affiliated with major music publishers such as Chappell, Warner Brothers, and Screen Gems Music, or from the publishers directly.

Any song that has received its first commercial recording can be *covered* by a different artist on a different recording so long as recording royalties are paid by the cover artist's record company to the composer, lyricist, and publisher of the song. Most producers, even those like my partner and I, who write a lot of songs, keep a file of potential hit songs for recording situations that might arise. It's also advisable for a producer to become professionally associated with several outstanding songwriters (in our case, we usually contact writers like Barry Mann, Cynthia Weil, and Alan O'Day), among others, so that they can either submit songs for an upcoming project, or consider collaborating with the artist-songwriter featured on the recording.

THE A&R EXECUTIVE

The last VIP in record production, the A&R executive, is analogous to the editor of a publishing house or the adjudicator of a trial. His job is to say yea or nay to the producer, the artist, the manager, or whoever else solicits the participation of his company. Approaches may differ from one A&R department to another and one A&R executive to another—some do it nicely, some not so nicely—but the decision to pass on a tape, request a live audition, or sight unseen sign an unknown artist is always made by someone wearing an A&R hat.

Basically there are four ways to approach the A&R department of a record company:

1. By submitting a demonstration tape. At the most, the demo should have three or four songs on it, preferably with leader tape in between the songs so that the A&R executive can fast-forward his tape recorder from the beginning of one song to that of the next. It's also advisable to package demos with lyric sheets and the name, address, and telephone number of the producer and/or contact person for the artist.

2. By submitting a master tape. Masters look more expensive than demos (they should sound more expensive!), and they usually *are* very expensive to produce (anywhere from $2,000 to $30,000 or more, depending on the number of sides). There is absolutely no need to go to the trouble and expense of producing a master unless you've tried repeatedly and unsuccessfully to interest record companies in demo tapes and you still think you're right and the whole world is wrong. Masters somehow draw A&R people's attention more quickly, but it is risky to produce a master tape *on spec*, a risk most successful producers never have had to take.

3. By inviting someone from the A&R department to either a live performance or a rehearsal of the group. It's amazing how much money is spent by major record companies sending A&R talent scouts not just around the block but to all corners of the world to listen to artists who reportedly have what it takes. This is the least expensive way to get evaluated, although it's somewhat anxiety-producing if you're worried about the group sounding stale, flat, or nervous.

4. Through referrals. This gambit sometimes works for producers who have made a good impression on at least one previous employer who's well connected in the industry. The music business is very much a family business. Everybody knows everybody else, and it's very hard to keep a secret about talented newcomers with good production instincts. It's not even necessary, for people fitting this description, to have a demo or to be working with a group—a word-of-mouth recommendation may do the trick.

A possible fifth approach, the do-nothing approach, is unfortunately not applicable to producers. Unknown artists, if they're playing clubs that are highly visible to the industry, sometimes get discovered without really trying. Producers, on the other hand, have no choice but to be aggressive go-getters, ready to have doors slammed in their face a hundred times without giving up. One of the most essential, albeit noncreative, ingredients of success in record production is *persistence*.

THE PLAN

Here, ideally, is how the record production game should be played. First, the producer should make a commitment—then keep it—to focus his energies and pocketbook on becoming a producer, period. Some readers may consider this a given (i.e., a taken-for-granted assumption), but I'd rather not take that chance. The reason some people don't get ahead is not because they lack ability but because they haven't learned how to channel their ability: if you want to be a producer, you shouldn't try being a manager, agent, or concert promoter at the same time. Songwriting, arranging, and audio engineering courses can be justified perhaps as production related activities, but anything else, until your production star has risen in the heavens, should be verboten.

Second, which is a practical extension of step one: establish contact with the music business in some capacity and find out whether you can make a living being a record producer. This implies that you will realistically assess your ability to compete both with other aspiring and with established producers; determine the extent to which you like the business, and vice versa; and estimate the popularity quotient of the type of music you're into and its impact on your potential earnings. For instance, if you want to be a classical record producer, you can't expect to sell three million units of the Beethoven Tenth Piano Sonata or Handel's *Water Music* (unless there are three million Mark Spitzes). Lower your financial expectations for classical music, jazz, spoken voice, foreign language, and children's recordings. Also, certain esoteric kinds of rock, country, and even pop music traditionally appeal to a more limited audience than does mainstream rock, pop, R&B, and now disco and New Wave music. This preproduction learning and familiarization stage is essential for drawing a heads-up, eyes-wide-open bead on a focused, lucrative production career.

Third, if you're not one of the lucky individuals invited to become a staff producer through word-of-mouth referral, find an artist, preferably a self-contained group, to record. The group should be at a level parallel to that of your production abilities. In other words, until you know how to direct a studio session properly, and until you (or your friend turned recording engineer) have gained the upper hand over your equipment, you should not attempt to record professional ensembles. It would be better to learn from groups who, like you, have many things to learn and many mistakes (forgivable, under these circumstances) yet to make. Once the mantle of quasi-professional has been donned, however (bearing in mind that you're not a real professional until you get *paid* to be a producer), the places to discover a potentially commercial group are recording studios, clubs, instrument repair shops, local offices of the AFM, college and high school social gatherings, music business schools and conservatories, and amateur night showcases.

16

Fourth, on a personal, or gut, level, make sure there is a positive emotional response engendered between the artists and the producer. You must be able to get along with each other as human beings, as business associates, as career planners, as dreamers, but especially—assuming that the producer and the artists are both newcomers—as struggling, almost desperate contestants in the hit record sweepstakes. There will be ninety-nine parts adversity for every lucky break. If the feeling between the producer and his artists isn't as strong as the feeling between a husband and wife who love each other, the relationship is likely not to prosper.

Fifth, which is the most elusive step for beginning producers: you should try signing the artists to an exclusive record production contract. This is the producer's insurance that he will be able to participate to some extent in the event that a major label offers the group a recording contract. More about this safeguard in chapter 8.

Sixth, the first real money decision: you have to decide which way to record or showcase the group and how much money you're prepared to spend. The options available to the producer are as follows:

1. You can invite A&R personnel from various companies to hear the group perform live, either in rehearsal or in front of an audience.

2. You can record the group on an inexpensive home tape recorder. This approach, by the way, is not to be sneered at: no A&R person expects a demo tape, no matter how many production values are built into it, to do anything other than *suggest* what a finished master tape might sound like. So long as the integrity of the song and the artist come through, the sound quality of a demo, whether it's bad, good, or excellent, is of secondary importance.

3. You can record the group in a more sophisticated home recording studio. Such a studio today, including building materials and recording equipment, will cost between $10,000 and $15,000. What you get for the money is the means to produce very high quality demos, along with engineering experience. You won't have as much control over the final sound as you'd have working in a sixteen- or twenty-four-track professional studio, but if you're planning to spend a lot of time in the studio, you might actually save money (or earn money by renting the studio out for demo purposes) by producing records at home. If you're interested in learning more about this option, you may wish to consult appendixes A and B in the back of the book.

4. You can record the group in a professional studio. The preferred way to do this is without having to spend what most twenty-four-track studios are charging today: between $150 and $250 an hour. Over the years, I have listened to many tapes that were submitted to me by managers or artists who had been given studio time either at reduced cost or gratis. Studio owners understand that artists and producers somehow have to get started. The key is to find a studio that will allow you to record either when sessions are over or when there are no bookings. Some studio owners will make space available merely to help out; others will expect to be paid later on by the artist's record company or to enjoy limited participation in the artist's or producer's royalty income, or both. Getting the cooperation of a studio owner in this respect is as much a test of the producer's ability to sell himself and his product as anything else he'll encounter.

Many factors should be weighed before deciding which of these options (or the master tape option) to pursue. Chief among these factors is what can be learned from the collective experience of thousands of aspiring producers who preceded us to the A&R lion's den. The quality of the artist and his songs comes first. It's not how technically good an unsolicited tape sounds—it's whether the song and/or the artist recorded on that tape sounds unique. I don't recommend taking financial risks. My strategy, if I were a beginning producer, would be to spend as little of my own money as possible; to concentrate on developing relevant, concise material for my artist and a live presentation with punch; and to set up a live showcase for record company personnel. This plan, from a producer no less, does not even include a demo tape.

Seventh, the producer has to advertise his existence to major record companies, custom labels, studio owners, personal managers—anyone and everyone involved with the manufacturing and distribution of phonograph records and tapes. The standard record producer calling card, of course, is the demonstration tape. Other approaches can be taken using master tape recordings, word-of-mouth referrals, or invitations to a showcase performance. In sending demos out to record companies, make sure you get the name and telephone number of a contact person in A&R so that, among other things, you know whom to speak to about retrieving your tapes.

Eighth, and most important, the producer must get a response. This brings us back to the original sixty-four dollar question: how do you make your tape more important than the hundreds of other tapes, stacked one on top of the other, in the corner of the A&R department's storage closet? What do you have to do to break down the barriers of ongoing record company business, regional staff meetings and conventions held outside the office, and the incessant politicking for new jobs that has precedence over all other considerations in a record company? Those of us who are survivors of the door-slammed-shut syndrome know the answer. It's dedication—persistence—faith—ambition (a little luck never hurt anyone, either). However you do it, you must be able to get an answer. You must be able to be heard, to be seen, and to be at least tacitly regarded as an intelligent, creative young Turk.

I've tried in this general introduction to the record production business to portray in realistic, commonsense fashion the contestants, rules, and materials necessary to play the production game. It may seem odd that some people become successful producers without formal production training or even knowledge of recording technique. At the other end of the spectrum sits the aspiring producer who spends lots of money doing what is usually nonessential (such as producing an expensive master tape) rather than what costs practically nothing (such as coming up with great production ideas by listening to the radio).

Of one thing we can be confident: before you succeed, you will fail. Failing was my greatest motivation. It kept me pushing until I learned how to stop making bad records. Mine isn't an overnight success story; practically no producer's story is. We *worked* to get where we are. That process, for better or worse, is still the way most people get from A to Z in the production business: from just dreaming about becoming a producer to having a home, a swimming pool, and tennis court built on the financial rewards of gold or platinum records.

3
Getting Ready to Produce

The development of this book stems from two earlier conclusions: (1) a successful producer has majority as well as minority interests in the overall production business; and (2) there are many different ways to become a professional producer. Though record production might seem a maddeningly difficult subject to write about with any kind of order or precision, in reality it isn't (at least, it doesn't have to be). This chapter, and the one that follows, will lay the foundation for what I hope every reader gains from a perusal of these pages: a step-by-step understanding of the producer's majority area, the craft of record production, and the minority areas as well.

SELECTING MATERIAL

Regardless of how the producer chooses to expose his artist to a record company—through a live showcase, a demo, or a finished master—a rather fixed series of events should precede production. They are, in order of occurrence:

1. the selection of material to record or present;
2. the rehearsal of that material;
3. the formulation of a production budget; and
4. the selection of a recording studio or showcase venue.

The first, selection of material, is the key to unlocking doors at the record company's A&R department. "You're only as good as your last hit" is a standard industry phrase; for beginning producers, whose product may not have been released yet, it might be more appropriate to say, "You're only as good as the songs you choose to record."

It is a prerequisite for record producers to feel confident about their ability to pick good songs. If a producer feels somewhat deficient in this respect, he might be much better off working with another producer, or sometimes even two other producers, so that the all-important selection and shaping of songs is dealt with by a meeting of the minds. Some of the more successful practitioners of the team approach to record production include Kenny Gamble and Leon Huff; Jerry Wexler and Barry Beckett; Jerry Love and Michael Zager; Meco Menardo, Harold Wheeler, and Tony Bongiovi; the Bee Gees; and my partner and me.

If the producer is working with a self-contained group, he will most certainly want to listen to the artist's songs prior to rehearsal. With a self-contained group like Player, my partner and I approach song selection and shaping by holding a series of informal discussions in a relaxed social environment. We talk about what we did and did not accomplish in our last album; what our competitors' music sounds like and how it is directed; what the concept for the new album might be (but not in the sense of a self-limiting *concept album*—what we're seeking to do is establish a clear idea of what sounds or images we'd like to create on our next record); and how, in the production sense, we can make the music sound more alive.

After these friendly meetings, we spend a substantial amount of time listening to the group's songs in raw form. Hearing the words sung over a guitar or piano is all we need at this juncture. We encourage the writer-artist to play us songs that they're still working on so that we can bounce ideas around before the music and/or the lyrics are completed. Then we make copies of all the songs still in the running to be produced, take them home with us, and listen to them over and over and over again. Gradually we begin to assemble an album in our minds, to hear what kinds of effects will work in the studio, and to sense whether the overall quality of the music is good enough (with Player it always is) to go on to the next step.

Your group may not be as advanced as Player, but the principle still applies. There has to be a meeting of the minds about the songs to be selected for the record. If songs need a lot of work, the producer must be able to contribute his services as a preproduction song doctor. The producer can and should be influenced on the selection of songs by the artist and other members of the artist's team, but the final decision on which songs to produce should be the producer's. Any producer who is not looked up to by his artist as the captain or production quarterback in the studio is asking for trouble.

If the producer's artist is not self-contained, he will have to procure songs for the artist either from music publishing companies or from writers directly. As previously mentioned, most successful producers keep a file of songs that they think might become hits. These can be oldies, unrecorded new songs, foreign language hits translated to English, or songs that are presently high up on the charts somewhere in the world. Once a song has been commercially released, anyone can re-record the work provided that recording royalties are paid to the publisher of the work by the record company upon commercial release of the record. The 1976 U.S. Copyright

Law set these recording royalties at $.0275 per composition or $.005 per minute per composition, whichever amount is greater.

Here's how that works. If the producer's album includes a six-minute composition owned by XYZ Publishing Company, and if the producer's record company, after agreeing to pay statutory royalties to XYZ Publishing Company, releases the record and it sells 50,000 units, the producer's record company will be obligated to pay XYZ Publishing Company $1,500 for the use of that song on their record. If the song had been only five minutes long, XYZ Publishing Company would have received a check for $1,375 since the work was not long enough to qualify for the additional half-cent royalty. Each of the compositions used on the album would be licensed and paid for in the same way.

Again, the producer should began working with his artist on these finished songs in very raw form. After the artist has been sold on the songs, and after the producer has had several weeks in which to evaluate carefully whether the marriage of a particular song with a particular artist is a good marriage, the producer should make plans either to collaborate with the artist-musician on an arrangement of the song or to hire an outside, independent arranger.

REHEARSING

The next step in preproduction, rehearsing, is the most important step in terms of getting a group's musical act together. There is no substitute for working very hard to get the music, the lyrics, and the balance of players right. As a general rule, I like to bring artists into the studio who are overrehearsed rather than underrehearsed. I'm willing to sacrifice the chance of a good spontaneous performance, which underrehearsing sometimes gives you, for the saving of many thousands of dollars of twenty-four-track studio time, which being overrehearsed usually guarantees.

Rehearsal studios cost anywhere from $10 to $30 an hour to rent. A good rehearsal studio will have a PA system and a mixing console for the artist's equipment, as well as a stage for simulating live performance circumstances. In cases where a group is planning to rehearse extensively prior to recording or touring, it might be advisable to lease a sound-treated building on a monthly basis. Here there will be fewer distractions than in a busy rehearsal studio; there is generally less interference and concern for how loudly the band plays; and the artists can bring in their own equipment, lock it up at night, and come and go whenever they wish.

My partner and I, who are lucky enough to be working year-round, have been considering either buying or renting a rehearsal facility in Los Angeles for the exclusive use of the groups we record. There is another way to go, however, especially for beginning producers and beginning artists: use your home or school, a local church or synagogue, or the YMCA or Rotary Club in your town. You can exchange use of a facility for a free concert. Save your money wherever and whenever you can. If you rehearse five hours a day, five days a week, for eight consecutive weeks without having a recording contract, you shouldn't be running up a $2,000 bill unless there are no alternatives. Try to get a signed recording commitment from an established record company as inexpensively as possible. That is the true test of your talent and ingenuity and will establish early in your career the importance of being budget conscious.

Each producer and each artist has his own way of learning the music and of playing it for others. Some artists will want the producer around constantly; other artists will want the producer to leave them alone until they signal that they're ready. Regardless of the artist's temperament, a good producer must be actively involved in rehearsing. Material and performances must constantly be listened to, talked about, and restructured. One of the producer's most valuable contributions to a record, in fact, is the unique position he's in to say to the artist, "I think that you're wrong," or "I think this song can sound better." A ratio of three to one—three hours' rehearsal by the artist alone and then one hour of rehearsal with the producer present—is a sensible way for beginning producers to look at their role in rehearsing the artists.

FORMULATING A BUDGET

The next preproduction stage, formulating a production budget, is the one most often overlooked (usually with painful financial consequences) by the inexperienced producer. The principle underlying preparation of an expense budget is that you must *plan* what you are about to do. If you're planning to produce a master tape, you're going to incur a considerable expense. If you're planning to produce a demo, it won't cost nearly as much, but it's still going to cost something. How much you paid, whom you paid and why you paid it, when and sometimes even where you paid the money are the bottom-line questions answered, for all time, by that very valuable tool of the producer: the budget analysis sheet.

My own Recording Budget form should help introduce you to the various expenses associated with being a producer. Number 1, rehearsing, covers preproduction rehearsal sessions, including studio rental, instrument and equipment rentals, and cartage, which is the cost of transporting equipment and/or instruments to and from the studio.

Major headings under number 2, recording, are for instrumentalists and singers; the arranging and copying of music; studio time and tape cost; the engineer; instrument and equipment rentals; cartage, and the employer's contribution to taxes. This last item, letter I on the form, adds 10 percent to the cost of hiring instrumentalists, vocalists, arrangers, and copyists. It is intended to remind the ultimate bill payer (I hope the record company, not the producer!) that, in addition to the fees required under union agreements, the producer is paying money to an employee (i.e., musician, singer) although his or her work may be done in a single day. Someone has

23

RECORDING BUDGET

Date: _____ Artist: _____
Beginning Date of Recording: _____
Estimated Completion Date: _____
Producers: _____ Studio: _____
Label: _____

1) REHEARSING
  A. Studio Rental   _____
  B. Instrument and Equipment Rentals   _____
  C. Cartage   _____

2) RECORDING

A. *Instrumentalists /AFM*	# Players/Singers	$/Scale	Sub Total
Basic Tracks	_____	___	___
Sweetening	_____	___	___
Pension Welfare Fund (PWF)	(10 percent of sub total)		___
Health & Welfare (H&W)	($3.50 per man per session—separate from PWF)		___

B. Singers/AFTRA)	_____	___	___
Pension & Welfare Contribution on (7-¾ percent of sub total)			___

	# Songs	$/Scale	Sub total
C. Arrangers/AFM	_____	___	___
D. Copyists/AFM	_____	___	___
PWF (10 percent of sub total)			___
H&W ($3.50 per man per session—separate from PWF)			___

E. *Studio*	# Hours/Rolls	$Hr/Roll	Sub total
Studio Time:			
Basic Tracks	_____	___	___
Overdubs	_____	___	___
Vocals	_____	___	___
Mixing	_____	___	___
Editing	_____	___	___
Tape Duplicating	_____	___	___
Tape			
		Sub-Total	
		Tax at %	
		Studio Total	___

F. Engineer	# Hours	$/Hr	Sub total
_____	_____	___	___

G. Rentals	Description	$ per Day/ per Week	Sub total
	_____	___	___
	_____	___	___
	_____	___	___

H. Cartage   ___

I. Payroll Tax/Handling Cost
(sum of 2–A, B, C, and D @10 percent)

Estimated Total Cost
(plus 15 percent over Budget Factor)   +   ___
ESTIMATED GRAND TOTAL   ___

---

to prepare payroll forms for each session and file statements with federal, state, and city tax agencies as required by law. These tax contributions by the employer, which are not included in union scale compensation, should be treated as an additional recording expense.

It's generally understood that producers who are not yet plugged into the industry on a professional basis pay less money to instrumentalists and vocalists than do professional producers. If you're just beginning, you may be able to get artists to work for you for nothing. You may also be able to make a special arrangement with an arranger and copyist if they're impressed with you and your long-term potential. It's been many years, though, since I've had to deal with artists, arrangers, and copyists on that basis. In my case, and in the case of every other successful producer, the people we want to use sometimes insist on double and even triple scale payments and may have to be imported (flying first class, of course) at our expense.

Independent record producers can make lots of money, but only if their records sell in the hundreds of thousands of units or more. Of course, the producer needs to remember that the record company is charging him and the artist for every dollar he spends making a record. If you'd rather have your friend who lives in New York City play backup bongos on your Los Angeles session—if you can't get by with an excellent, unknown bass player but would rather have a famous bass player who knows Peter Frampton intimately and charges triple scale, on top of which he must be served Dom Perignon champagne from start to finish of the recording session—you will pay for it. Oh, will you pay for it! The difference, if you're not careful, can be many, many thousands of dollars that might otherwise be yours.

Any producer, regardless of his stature within the industry, has a responsibility to stay within a reasonable recording budget. If you're working with an unknown artist, it's unconscionable to import high-priced musicians with the thought that the record company (but ultimately the artist) will pick up the tab. In appendixes C and D, I include the most recent collective bargaining agreements between the major record companies, the AFM, and AFTRA. It may not be necessary to have more than a general understanding of these agreements, but it is very important to know what the current minimum scale rates are and how these rates are computed. When in doubt, the best thing to do is deal directly with either the record company or the local office of the union in question.

Note: Section 2–A of the Recording Budget has separate entries for basic tracks and sweetening. The *basic tracks*, which comprise the rhythm section, or foundation, of the music, are the first instruments to be recorded by the producer. These are usually the drums, bass, keyboards, and guitars. In multi-track recording terminology, everything recorded after the basic tracks is said to be an *overdub*, or *sweetening*. The sweetening line will be used for solo instruments, percussion, horns, strings, and synthesizer.

The largest single item in the Recording Budget usually is studio time. This figure has an almost chilling importance not only because it makes you aware of how enormously expensive albums are to produce (possibly more than 500 hours in the studio) but also because, next to the quality of the finished tape, the estimated studio time expense is often the standard by which a producer is judged to be acceptable or unacceptable by a record company.

Producers who bring albums in under budget that go no place are in a much better position than producers who bring albums in over budget that, in similar respect, go no place. More and more, as I indicated in the previous chapter, record companies are responding to producers who, after negotiating a production budget, demonstrate that they understand the importance of conserving speculative càpital. What you can get a company to budget for your production is one thing: what really counts, in the final analysis, is bringing the production in so that it is *below* the outside figure set by the record company. The sooner this concept is understood by beginning and intermediate level producers, the better.

The Recording Budget form is set up so that there are separate entries under studio time, in section 2–E, for the various kinds of recording done in the contemporary music business. Such a breakdown helps the producer pinpoint what his total commitment to the recording studio will be. Although it may seem difficult to estimate how much time it's going to take to record a particular artist, the producer should be able to get a feel for the artist's work habits from the rehearsal sessions. Some artists need much more time than other artists to record acceptable takes. This principle applies, as well, to record producers and recording engineers.

Assuming that the music is well rehearsed, and assuming that the producer knows what he's doing in the studio and has taken the time to gauge his artist's and his engineer's work habits, it is quite possible to come up with a refined estimate for overall studio time. On the other hand, if you don't know what you're doing in the studio, and you've never even thought about what you can do to cut hours, minutes, and seconds off your overall studio bill, I'd say you have a lot of catching up to do. That is, unless you're the son or daughter of a multimillionaire.

The cost of studio time can be influenced mightily by what hourly rate the studio owner decides to charge. Some of the more successful recording studios won't bend an inch from their normal rates; others are prepared to bend a country mile, especially if the producer books a large block of time. Somewhere in between these parameters is where most producers find themselves. If you open your mouth and you've done your homework, you should be talking with a studio owner who will give you a break.

The other items included with studio time shouldn't be ignored either. The first is the cost of two-inch master tape. Each 2,500-foot roll of this tape now costs between $130 and $160. I average ten to twenty rolls of tape per album. The second, which is the item most often overlooked by beginning producers, is state sales tax. In

California, it's presently 6 percent; in New York, it's presently 8 percent. That's 6 or 8 percent of the *total* studio expense, including, unfortunately, time.

Item 2–F applies in cases where the producer furnishes his own engineer. Staff engineers normally are figured into the cost of studio time.

Rentals, item 2–G, includes any planned use of musical instruments or *outboard equipment* (these are the electronic signal processing devices that, when patched into the recording console, create special effects) over and beyond what the recording studio comes equipped with. This should be one of the easier sections of the form to fill in.

The next to last line of the Recording Budget is in my experience the most valuable entry of all. After totaling up the estimated cost of producing a record, I add a 15 percent over budget factor as a financial cushion. For instance, if the estimated total cost of a production is $50,000, I will add another 15 percent, or $7,500, and wind up with an inflated estimated grand total of $57,500. This last figure, with its built-in fail-safe margin, is the one I'd use in negotiating a production budget with a record company.

Even if you're just starting out and you're producing demo tapes in your home, it is important to get into the habit of using a recording budget. It forces you to see the project from beginning to end. If you fill the columns in properly and you *keep receipts* for everything you purchase with respect to the production, you'll minimize the potential for disputes over how much the sessions cost and who paid for what. It's also good training for working with the A&R department of a record company since virtually every company in the world uses a recording budget form similar to the sample one we've discussed. Sooner or later (but I hope sooner) you will discover that producers who accurately estimate the cost of a production are miles ahead of producers too busy to bother.

SELECTING A RECORDING STUDIO

The final step in preproduction, the selection of a recording studio, has been covered to some extent in our discussion of finances. Producers should also be concerned with the location of the studio; the size of the studio and the sort of equipment it contains; the competencies of the studio staff and staff engineers, if the producer wishes to use one; and whether the studio has a full-time maintenance person who is *always* available to keep the equipment running smoothly (for me this is absolutely essential).

Last but not least, the producer, the independent recording engineer, and the artists should sit in the studio, try to get comfortable, and see whether they actually like the rooms. The artists must feel that they can hear each other well enough in the studio to make good music. The producer and especially the recording engineer must feel good about the recording console, the audio quality of the control room monitors, and the way the room is laid out. Over the next few weeks or months, that studio will be home to the producer, the recording engineer, and the artists. You must feel relaxed there.

If you're choosing a new studio, bring along a tape you're familiar with and listen to it in the control room. See how the room colors what you have on tape and be prepared to make adjustments. Also, it's a good idea to listen to some of the most recent master recordings made in the room (ask the owner for a list) and carefully evaluate what you hear. It would be foolish to select a recording studio without testing its acoustical characteristics in this way.

If you have any hang-ups about white acoustical tile, walnut-stained construction pine, green throw rugs, Indian tapestry panels, or black-tipped control knobs, the time to decide whether this studio is for you is *before* you make a commitment. Ideally, you will want to *block book* a studio, which means that you will be the studio's only client on a twenty-four-hour basis for the time it takes to complete the production. If you're able to guarantee the studio hundreds of hours of time, you may be able to make this arrangement at a greatly reduced cost. Otherwise, the control room, the outboard equipment, the rented instruments, and the lead singer's favorite microphone will be broken down at the conclusion of each individual session. Fortunately, setup time is usually not billed for by the recording studio.

What happens in preproduction is just as important as everything else in the sequence of recording events. If preproduction is dealt with properly, the producer will be in a strong position to go forward; if this stage is the weak link in the chain, the producer will almost certainly falter. Assuming, however, that you've gained an appreciation for the importance of having good material, being well rehearsed, knowing how much the production will cost, and selecting a recording studio, we will next introduce ourselves to the technique through which contemporary music recordings are made.

4
The Professional Recording Studio

The purpose of this chapter is to introduce professional recording practices. The focus will not be so much on *why* things work, which would get us into different subjects altogether—acoustics and electronic theory—but on *how* things work in the studio. This information is applicable to any recording situation involving multitrack recording equipment.

THE EQUIPMENT IN A RECORDING STUDIO

The word "multitrack" is at the heart of the multibillion-dollar record industry. The ability to record one track at a time, one instrument per track, along with the infinite possibilities provided by the recording console to color, blend, bring out, or conceal instruments, has enabled the producer to become, in every sense of the word, an artist.

Those producers with the talent and imagination to record individual tracks, evaluate them, and then combine them into a pleasing whole that sounds unique have a secure future in a business that constantly is looking for its own Picassos, its own creative geniuses. The producer's craft depends both on good songs and on musicians and vocalists who play and sing creatively and in tune! But the craft of production, like that of painting, can be practiced in many forms. Two-, four-, eight-, sixteen-, twenty-four-, and now thirty-two-track tape recorders each have a place within the universe of record production.

The producer will want to record at the fastest tape speed available on his machine. This serves two purposes: (1) it reduces noise and improves high-frequency response; and (2) it makes cutting the tape, or *editing*, much easier, since the recording engineer has more area in which to locate that split second when a beat hits—which is where he'll cut the tape. Unlike tape recorders designed primarily for home use, professional machines record in only one direction (obviously, if program material ran in both directions, editing would be impossible).

The more tracks, or channels, a producer has to work with, the broader his spectrum of color possibilities. Even greater possibilities can be introduced with the insertion of a recording console having as few as eight and as many as forty or more inputs. Each input can handle either a line signal or, when recording, a microphone or an instrument *taken direct*—i.e., straight into the console without having to use a microphone. These input signals can be modified, or *processed*, before they are assigned to an output channel, or *bus*, which then carries the signal to the tape recorder.

A typical input module, as shown in figure 3, might consist of (1) a *microphone/line switch* with a *microphone preamp* and *variable* or *switchable gain control*; (2) an *attenuator switch*, which reduces overloading and distortion when recording strong signals; (3) an *equalization network*, which is similar to the treble and bass controls of a home stereo receiver, though considerably more complex and sensitive; (4) *echo send/return controls*, which direct the signal to an echo chamber, or *reverb unit*; (5) a *cue system(s)*, used for channeling the signal through headphones so that the musicians can hear themselves and/or what's already been recorded while they are recording live; (6) *solo/mute buttons*, which when depressed will either mute all the remaining inputs and allow you to hear just the one input signal or mute the input that is depressed; (7) *pan pots*, a type of fader that places the input signal left, right, center, or somewhere in between the stereo image; and (8) *bus selectors*, which assign the input signal to a specific output channel.

Most consoles have *talkback* or studio monitor controls, so that the producer in the control room can communicate with the artists in the studio, and vice versa. Most consoles even have test tones built right into the system. And though no two consoles may be exactly alike, virtually every state-of-the-art board has the flexibility to serve the producer and engineer an infinite range of possibilities. In simple terms, using a recording console and a multitrack tape recorder in tandem, the producer has many more possible permutations to work with than if he were limited to recording straight into the multitrack tape machine.

Let's say that we want to record live a four-piece band consisting of drums, bass, guitar, and voice with a four-track tape recorder and possibly a recording console with eight inputs and four outputs. If we were to use only the four-track tape recorder (without benefit of the recording console), we would probably want to assign each instrument to a separate track. The drums and voice would be recorded with one microphone each; the bass and guitar could be recorded either direct or with mikes, as above. But with the aid of even a simple recording console, there would be many other possibilities:

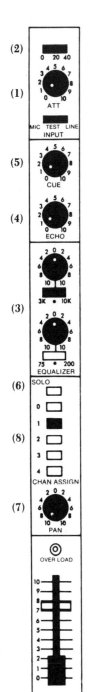

(2)

(1)

(5)

(4)

(3)

(6)

(8)

(7)

Attenuation
A 3-position switch for 0, 20 or 40 dB of padding for mic signals. The pad is located before the mic transformer and preamp to help prevent them from being overdriven, a common cause of distortion.

Trim
A rotary pot that provides from 0 to 20 dB of continuously variable gain reduction for mic, tape or line signals.

Input Selector
A 3-position switch determines the signal to be passed—mic or line. The center position on inputs 1 thru 4 is for tape reproduce from the outputs of a 4-track recorder patched into the *tape in* jacks on the back panel. The center position on inputs 5 thru 7 is off. On input 8, the center position works in conjunction with the built-in test oscillator on the master module for setting levels and general calibration.

Cue
A foldback pre EQ and fader, typically used in conjunction with tape cue (on the submaster modules) as a 12x1 independent submix for musicians' headphone feed.

Echo
A foldback post EQ and fader, before the channel assignment, typically used for echo send to an external reverberation unit.

EQ
The peak and dip equalizers provide 15 dB of boost or cut, continuously variable, at the following frequencies: 3 kHz or 10 kHz, selectable; 75 Hz or 200 Hz, selectable. The center position is off.

Channel Assignment
Solo is a momentary button which allows the operator to monitor that input signal to the exclusion of all others on the control room monitor circuit only, without disturbing the program mix.

D is a direct output post EQ and fader for that input module when it is desirable to by-pass the summing amplifiers in the submaster modules.

The color-coded, numbered channel assignment buttons allow any signal from any input module to be assigned to any or all of the four output busses.

Pan
Whenever more than one output is assigned, pan is automatically engaged. The apparent acoustic image of that signal may then be placed at its desired position within the panoramic perspective.

Overload
When the LED ignites, the first input stage is being overdriven and the attenuator/trim control(s) should be adjusted accordingly.

Straight Line Fader
Regulates the overall send level of that input module. The saddle shaped knobs make fingertip operation easy and accurate.

FIGURE 3.   Typical configuration of an input module
(Courtesy of TEAC/TASCAM.)

1. The drums could be recorded with more than one mike. This might use up two, three, or even four of the eight inputs assigned to a single output, but it would enable the producer to have more control over the recorded drum sound, which is the hardest and most important individual sound next to the vocals to record.

2. The bass and guitar could be recorded direct, each using a separate input, or they could be recorded live—i.e., with a microphone in the studio. If additional inputs were available, you could record the bass both ways (live and direct), blending the two sounds and then assigning the combined signal to one of the four channels (see figure 4). The combined sound of the bass recorded live and direct might be more pleasing than the sound of the bass recorded just live or just direct. Assuming the producer used four inputs for the drums, one input for the guitar, and one input for the bass, there would still be two inputs left for microphones to record the voices.

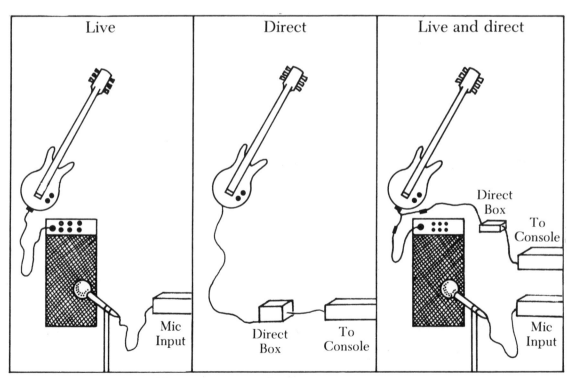

FIGURE 4.   Various ways to record an instrument.

3. As a rule, vocals should be overdubbed later. In this event, even more control of the sound is available to the producer, and additional inputs open up for the band.

In summary, with just twice as many inputs to work with as there are tracks on the tape recorder, the producer has much more of an opportunity to control the sounds of the instruments, to equalize them, to add processed coloration, and to blend the sounds as he sees fit. The only difference between this illustration using home recording equipment and what is possible in a twenty-four-track recording studio, where the recording console may have more than forty inputs, is the scale of the production.

Note: Bear in mind that the ability to overdub tends to negate the importance of a vast number of inputs. The fact that a home recording enthusiast may be working with only eight inputs should not be interpreted as a liability but as a challenge to his skill as a musician and a recordist.

The heart of a multitrack recording studio is the *multitrack tape recorder* itself. Units are available in quarter-inch-, half-inch-, one-inch-, and two-inch-tape formats. Standing alongside the multitrack tape recorder is another recorder, a two-track unit, usually called the *mix-down machine*. This unit enables the producer to transfer information stored on the larger, multitrack recorder onto a two-track format that is compatible with a typical home stereophonic system and the discs, cartridges, and cassettes plugged into that system.

The brain of the studio, the *recording console*, is where the producer and the engineer spend most of their time. For the moment, the use of the recording console is not the issue. The important thing to understand is that the console gives the producer a tremendous amount of control over the entire recording process, from the laying down of basic tracks to the final mixing and editing stages.

Note: Most recording consoles can be modified, although not easily, to take on additional inputs and outputs. This might not present a problem to an octopus turned recording engineer, but there are some limits imposed by having two rather than eight arms.

The large overhead speakers in the control room are called *monitors*. There may also be monitors in the studio itself, but these tend to be less critical and are used primarily for communication. Artists in the studio normally receive playbacks in the form of a *cue mix* sent to them through earphones. The cue system (sometimes there is more than one), which is another essential feature of the recording console, or *desk*, gives the producer the ability to send as few or as many of the tracks already recorded (or in the process of being recorded) to the earphones each artist in the studio is wearing. The cue mix can be in either stereo or mono; many artists prefer listening to only one "phone" while they're recording a live performance.

Usually there is a smaller set of speakers employed in the control room for monitoring purposes. I generally use Hemispheres and Little Davids by Visonik. Since few people have studio quality monitors in their homes or cars, the producer needs to be able to simulate the conditions in which consumers listen to records. These speakers, although they are excellent, don't reproduce high and low frequencies the way that state-of-the-art monitors do. They focus the producer's attention on the sound most people actually hear when they listen to the radio or to an inexpensive stereo system.

Next to the tape recorder, the trademarks of the recording business are the microphone and the microphone stand. The selection of microphones and their placement during recording normally are handled by the engineer. Practically all producers and engineers feel attached to at least one or two different microphones for recording a specific instrument and will use them often. Different microphones are designed to do different things, so the choice of which one to use depends greatly on the particular instrument being recorded.

For the sake of clarity, and because this subject is rarely understood, here is a producer's explanation of microphones in lay terms:

There are three basic types of microphone: dynamic, condenser, and ribbon. A *dynamic microphone* is dependable, requires no external power supply, and can take a lot of abuse with little risk of damaging it. Dynamic microphones can take bursts of power (transient peaks) and high levels of power without causing too much distortion. They are the best all-purpose microphones, especially for home recording, and are inexpensive compared to condenser and ribbon microphones. Two examples of dynamic microphones I currently use are the Shure SM 7 and the Electrovoice 666.

Condenser microphones are excellent reproducers of high frequencies They are more sensitive to dynamics than are dynamic microphones, and they require an external power supply for their low output and tend to distort more easily than do dynamic microphones. Condenser microphones are very expensive and are used primarily in professional studios. Two condenser microphones I currently use are the AKG 414 and the Neumann KM 84.

Ribbon microphones were popular years ago, but not many are made today. They are extremely sensitive and expensive. The ribbon microphones I occasionally use are the RCA 44 and the RCA 77.

Microphones are designed to pick up sound in one of three patterns. These are illustrated in figure 5. If the dynamic, condenser, or ribbon microphone picks up from all sides, it is said to be *omnidirectional*. If the microphone picks up in a heartlike pattern radiating from a central point to an arc of approximately 90 degrees, it is said to be *cardioid*, or *unidirectional*. If the microphone is designed to screen out sounds beyond a relatively narrow arc, it is said to be *highly directional*. Some microphones can be switched from omnidirectional to cardioid, and vice versa. Other microphones will provide the producer with other pickup patterns, such as a figure 8. Experience and taste dictate which microphones to use.

Another important piece of equipment, one of the more recent additions to the recording studio, is the *noise-reduction system*, which substantially improves the signal-to-noise ratio without adding significant coloration. Some producers and many engineers claim that they can hear the noise reduction system working and that they dislike the changes in sound in the high-frequency range that noise reduction creates. I believe that noise reduction systems have their good moments, but if they're not needed, the less electronics the better. I've used noise-reduction equipment on soft music and have avoided it on loud rock. I've used it on the twenty-four-track tape recorder but not on the two-track mix-down machine. The best known manufacturers of noise reduction systems are dbx and Dolby.

Several other pieces of equipment are offspring of the recording industry's quest for perfection. *Compressors* and *limiters*, which are almost always used on vocals, the bass, and the bass drum, do precisely what their names say: one compresses the dynamic response of a particular sound and creates a more constant, even level (though too much compression will create a squashed, artificial sound); the other reduces, or limits, the peaks but affects the dynamics less. A *kepex* acts as a noise

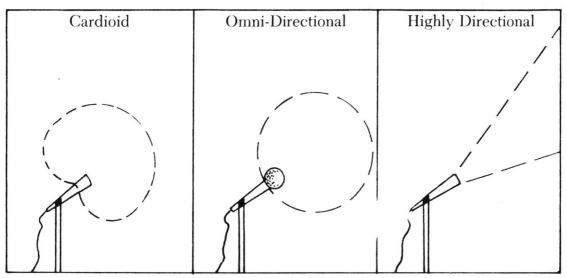

FIGURE 5. Microphone sound pickup patterns.

gate: it prevents extraneous noises below a threshold set by the recording engineer from triggering the output of the amplifier. This device eliminates noise in quiet passages but allows stronger signals to register, which masks the noise. The kepex is especially helpful in eliminating the finger and fret noises made in playing the guitar, as well as the lip noises and clicking sounds made by some singers. Please note, however, that kepexes and other noise gates can adversely affect some musical passages if the signal source is constant and resonant. The kepex is best used on the snare drum, solo tracks, and on overdubbed instruments that play only occasionally (and with long pauses or breaks) during the recording.

One of the most ingenious devices, the *harmonizer*, is able to create delay effects and change the pitch of a sound without affecting its tempo. How a harmonizer works is beyond the scope of this book, but for example the producer might use it during mixing to make a slightly out of tune performance sound better. Harmonizers can also be used to create any number of interesting processed sounds by *spreading the pitch*, using a combination of original signal and processed signal to create two slightly out of tune performances that cause a beating, or spreading, of the pitch.

Some producers, including myself, are now using computers during the mixing process. What the computer does is to remember the *fader*, or level, moves you make on the console and the relationships you've established between tracks. In the "write" and "rewrite" mode, the computer will program new information; in the "read" mode, the computer will automatically play back the tape. There are a number of problems that will have to be solved before computers become indispensable, however. First, they can't efficiently store the most important information for the producer, which is where he set the controls on the recording console for equalization, reverb, and the patches that were in the system. Second, some computers need either one or two recording tracks for memory storage: that makes a twenty-four-track tape recorder a twenty-three- or twenty-two-track machine, which isn't good. Third, they are incredibly expensive. Even so, they are helpful tools. And within two years, I'm sure that most of the computer's shortcomings in the recording studio will be eliminated.

Most of the large multitrack recording studios have a specially treated *live chamber* for the purpose of achieving echo, or *reverb*, effects: a signal is fed into a speaker positioned inside the room, the speaker is miked, and the signal returned. The producer also has at his disposal a more popular kind of a stereo echo chamber, an *EMT*, which is connected directly to the recording console. There is also a device known as a *digital delay line*, or *DDL*, which can be used for a variety of reverb and delay effects. At the low end of its performance spectrum, the DDL will enhance a sound recorded with what is seemingly a faint sound shadow, selectable in milliseconds. At the high end of its performance spectrum, the DDL will achieve the repeat effect of saying hello high in the mountains or at the lip of the Grand Canyon, with up to approximately one second of delay. This phenomenon can also be achieved mechanically, using one or more tape recorders running at varying speeds. By simply feeding the signal output back into the record head of the tape machine through the console, the multiple repeats are achieved. (DDLs can also create special effects by combining the output of the processed signal with the normal signal to simulate a phased type of sound.)

As a rule, most professional recording studios have the above equipment permanently installed. Figure 6 shows a typical installation in a control room. The portable items in a recording studio include sliding glass doors and drapes for sectioning off a part of the room; baffles, microphones, and microphone stands; *direct boxes*, which are used for routing instruments, via cable, to the recording console; musical instruments, stands, and chairs; a large assortment of connectors; and the *toys* of the production business, the less used or newer pieces of outboard processing equipment, which are discussed in chapter 6.

PROFESSIONAL RECORDING STUDIOS

Most professional recording studios consist of several rooms. Figure 7 shows the layout of a recording studio in Los Angeles with one permanent auxiliary room, to the left of the control room, and a second optional room that can be closed off from the main studio by sliding glass doors (see dotted line).

Large recording studios are designed this way in order to give the producer more flexibility. The floor and wall surfaces of an auxiliary room are often constructed of different materials from those of the main room. Likewise, the ceilings are usually higher or lower than the ceilings in the main room. The producer, in consultation with the recording engineer, will decide which rooms in a studio to use for what purposes. As a rule, though, auxiliary rooms are used to record horns and brass in a live session (if the room closes off completely), as well as strings (if they sound brighter in the auxiliary room than in the main room).

Baffles are used extensively in large rooms in order to prevent *leakage*; that is, to keep the sound of one instrument from leaking into the microphone of another instrument. For the sake of convenience, some studios also have heavy curtains positioned throughout the room to provide sound absorption. Very soon, we'll combine the studio and the equipment as we begin discussing how various instruments are actually recorded.

THE RULES OF STUDIO DECORUM

Most people seem to be experiencing their second childhood when they work in a recording studio. That's the way it should be; that's the way it can be if you follow some very simple rules of studio decorum. I think the most important thing to remember when you're recording is that no matter who you are—whether you're an engineer in training, a backup artist, or a superstar—you're participating in a team project. Within that setting, you're an equal of everyone else and they are your equal. If you're a producer, you have to learn how to get people to do things by asking them nicely. You are supposed to be loose; you are supposed to be able to take a joke, even if

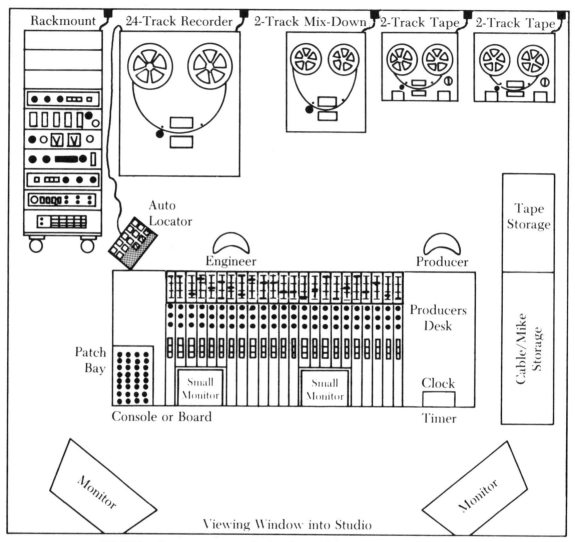

FIGURE 6.   Equipment in a professional control room.

the joke's on you. The recording studio is no place for a producer to hold a grudge, to be jealous, to be mean to an underling, or to be anything less than an intelligent, inspired leader.

No one should presume to bring guests into the studio without getting permission from the producer. The problem isn't just that extraneous people get in the way.

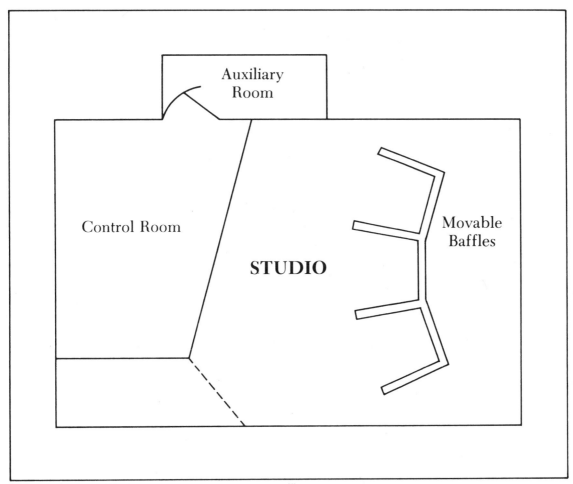

FIGURE 7.   Layout of a large recording studio.

The thing that's downright painful about having too many people in the control room is that when the producer is trying to talk to the artist in the studio over the control room microphone (which is a condenser mike with a terrific boost), conversations even thirty feet away will be sent out over the phones as an ear-splitting barrage of noise and confusion. A temporarily deafened or disoriented artist is no good to anybody; neither is an artist who's ready to scream bloody murder because an uninvited visitor invaded his professional turf. You can party *after* the production, but until then the fewer people in the studio, the better.

Similarly, artists shouldn't talk when they're not supposed to talk. Many times during overdub sessions, artists will get angry if they're not playing well and inadvertently start to speak, yell, or curse. What this does to relieve the artist's anger is beside the point: should the words be picked up by the tape recorder (usually they are), the recording engineer may lose the next perfectly good line on the tape if he's unable to *punch out* the artist's words in time. Artists should wait either for a hand cue from the recording engineer or for the tape to stop before letting off steam.

Another prescription for getting along during overdub sessions is the one I call "give a guy a break." If a lead guitarist, for example, is recording overdubs by himself in the studio with his amplifiers going full blast, he should *stop playing* before the producer or recording engineer enters the room. People have had their eardrums punctured this way. Being "blown away" by the music should never happen in the literal sense in a recording studio.

The last general words of advice on common courtesies in the studio deal with a more musical subject. It is very important for the artists to keep tuning their instruments. Nothing is more annoying than having to stop in the middle of an otherwise good take to say, "Bass guitar, you're flat again." Seasoned professionals usually aren't culpable in this respect, but I'd like to have a dollar for every time I've had to remind beginning artists to tune up.

RECORDING WORK SHEETS

I arm myself for the studio with no fewer than five different work sheets. The Track Sheet enables the producer to keep track of which instruments are being recorded on the various channels of the tape recorder. Each Track Sheet is keyed to the title of a selection, the date of recording, the name of the client, the name of the engineer, and the studio being used for recording.

The Recording Work Sheet acts like a diary. There are separate entries for the title, intro time, and total time of five different songs. Under each title, there's space for the producer to make remarks. The lower section of the Recording Work Sheet is where the producer will first begin seriously thinking about what sequence the songs should take (e.g., side A, band 1, band 2) on the finished album. This decision normally undergoes a lot of change, which is why I carry a separate Sequences Workup form.

The Credit Sheet—Individual Side is a handy device that shows which musicians, vocalists, and arranger were involved in recording a particular side or cut. The last form, the Daily Recording Cost Summary, should be used at the completion of the producer's work day. It gives the producer a running total of expenses, including instrument and equipment rentals, rehearsal and studio costs, and engineer and talent fees, making it a lot easier to come up with a final cost.

You should now be familiar with the equipment in a recording studio; the layout of the studio and the control room; the way in which to conduct oneself in the studio; and the work sheets necessary for keeping track of what goes on. In the next chapter, we'll take a much closer look at the craft of record production.

TRACK SHEET

Date_____Machine #_____

Client_____

Program_____

Engr._____Studio_____

Producer_____

DOLBY	
DBX	
LEVEL	
SPEED	
16TRK	24TRK	

SELECTION	TRACK 1	TRACK 2	TRACK 3	TRACK 4	TRACK 5	TRACK 6	TRACK 7	TRACK 8
	TRACK 9	TRACK 10	TRACK 11	TRACK 12	TRACK 13	TRACK 14	TRACK 15	TRACK 16
	TRACK 17	TRACK 18	TRACK 19	TRACK 20	TRACK 21	TRACK 22	TRACK 23	TRACK 24

SELECTION	TRACK 1	TRACK 2	TRACK 3	TRACK 4	TRACK 5	TRACK 6	TRACK 7	TRACK 8
	TRACK 9	TRACK 10	TRACK 11	TRACK 12	TRACK 13	TRACK 14	TRACK 15	TRACK 16
	TRACK 17	TRACK 18	TRACK 19	TRACK 20	TRACK 21	TRACK 22	TRACK 23	TRACK 24

RECORDING WORK SHEET

Artist: _____   Tentative LP Title: _____

	Title	Intro Time	Total Time

1. _____

Remarks   _____
_____
_____

2. _____

Remarks   _____
_____
_____

3. _____

Remarks   _____
_____
_____

4. _____

Remarks   _____
_____
_____

5. _____

Remarks   _____
_____
_____

Working Sequences

Side I	Time	Side II	Time
_____	_____	_____	_____
_____	_____	_____	_____
_____	_____	_____	_____
_____	_____	_____	_____
_____	_____	_____	_____
Total:	_____	Total:	_____

Sequences Work-up

Artist: _____   Tentative LP Title: _____

Side One   Time   Side Two   Time

_____ _____   _____ _____

_____ _____   _____ _____

_____ _____   _____ _____

_____ _____   _____ _____

_____ _____   _____ _____

_____ _____   _____ _____

Side One   Time   Side Two   Time

_____ _____   _____ _____

_____ _____   _____ _____

_____ _____   _____ _____

_____ _____   _____ _____

_____ _____   _____ _____

_____ _____   _____ _____

FINAL SEQUENCE

Side One   Time   Side Two   Time

_____ _____   _____ _____

_____ _____   _____ _____

_____ _____   _____ _____

_____ _____   _____ _____

_____ _____   _____ _____

Final LP Title: _____

Daily Recording Cost Summary

Date	Rehearsal	Rental	Studio	Engineer	Talent	Daily Total

Credit Sheet—Individual Side

LP _____

Title _____

Piano _____ Electric Piano _____

Clavinet _____ ARP _____ Synthesizer _____

Bass _____ Drums _____ Percussion _____

Guitar _____

Horns _____

Concertmaster _____

Solos _____

Background Vocals _____

Arranger _____

Special Instrumentation _____

5
Getting a Good Sound

Good sound, for me, is *transparent sound*. That's a term engineers often use: it means to be able to "hear" through the record; to have the low-, middle-, and high-frequency ranges pleasantly balanced; and to have each of the instruments distinguishable from each other.

Getting a good sound is achieved in part by the acoustics of the recording studio. There is also a technique for producing contemporary music records called *separation recording*, or *layering*, which has been used with great success. I am now going to take you through a hypothetical recording production so that I can explain what I do and why I do it. The situation I'll be describing, that of recording a rock and roll group, will be germane to most of you. If it's not, these recording techniques can, with confidence, be applied in a general sense to multitrack recording projects involving classical, country, pop, disco, jazz, or any other music.

Beginning now, reference will be made to the plastic record included in this book. The purpose of this record, which I narrate, is to demonstrate aurally what is being discussed in the text. The record was produced in stereo and was specially put together for this book from an actual number one hit single, "Baby Come Back." The instrumentalists and vocalists performing on the record are members of Player, a five-piece band that recorded two albums for RSO Records, which my partner and I produced. Their participation in this project is gratefully acknowledged.

In all candor, there is absolutely no substitute for learning how to record by going into a studio, setting up the microphones and tape recorder, and doing it. Nevertheless, I hope in this and the next chapter to present a clear picture of how a professional producer goes about his job in the studio so that you can at least gain a professional orientation.

47

Note: The presumption in this discussion is that a rock and roll group is working in a twenty-four-track recording studio with state-of-the-art equipment. But there is also a discussion in appendix B with reference to recording demonstration tapes in a home studio. Read chapters 5 and 6 first, then appendix B.

THE PLAN

The plan, as previously stated, is to obtain a good sound. The way most producers go about achieving this goal is to record a selection in layers, starting with the rhythm tracks, then adding instrumental overdubs, vocals, and special effects. Layering enables the producer to isolate each musical element in a performance so that it can be listened to, worked on, polished, and recorded with 100 percent attention to detail. Within each layer, the producer will be sifting, blending, and minimixing. When the layers of the recorded "cake" are ready to be placed on top of each other, they should fit perfectly. The "icing" on the cake —i.e., the final mix—should be like a sunrise warming an already idyllic setting.

Figure 8, the track sheet for "An Imaginary Song," offers a graphic illustration of the layering concept. I've included strings and horns, though these instruments are not often integral components of rock and roll records, for the benefit of discussing all forms of overdubs. The mating of tracks to instruments has little to do with technical considerations—it's mainly what makes the producer (and more often the engineer) feel most comfortable. The outside tracks do tend to wear more readily, however, which causes a slight loss in the high frequencies of instruments such as the drum cymbals and tambourines. Needless to say, if it's a twenty-four-track machine, the producer should not assign either of these instruments to track 1 or track 24.

I've always felt that step number one belongs on track 1, step number two belongs on track 2, etc. There may be a slight variation between the planned track assignments and the actual tracks recorded, owing entirely to the producer's revised conception of what the music should sound like and what tracks are left open. Still, there is a basic pattern for assigning tracks to a four-piece rock and roll group. In my case, they are as follows:

- Track 1 is for the bass;
- Tracks 2 through 5 are for the drum kit;
- Tracks 6 through 8 cover the rhythm keyboards;
- Tracks 9 through 11 are for the rhythm guitars with an echo effect;
- Tracks 12 through 18 are for instrumental overdubs;
- Tracks 19 and 20 are either for the two alternate performances or a doubled performance of the lead vocal;
- Tracks 21 and 22 are for background vocals;
- Tracks 23 and 24 are for computer storage (see chapter 4).

Ours is the era of *close-miking*. Most instruments will be miked about six inches

Date_____Machine #_____

Client_____

Program_____

Engr._____Studio_____

Producer_____

DOLBY	
DBX	
LEVEL	
SPEED	
16TRK	24TRK

SELECTION	TRACK 1	TRACK 2	TRACK 3	TRACK 4	TRACK 5	TRACK 6	TRACK 7	TRACK 8
"An Imaginary Song"	Bass Guitar	Kick Drum	Drums— Overhead Left	Drums— Overhead Right	Snare Drum	Keyboard— Wurlitzer	Keyboard— Fender Rhodes STEREO	
	TRACK 9	TRACK 10	TRACK 11	TRACK 12	TRACK 13	TRACK 14	TRACK 15	TRACK 16
	Rhythm Guitars		Guitar Echo Effect	Clavinet	Instrumental Overdubs			
					Horns	Guitar Solo	Percussion STEREO	
	TRACK 17	TRACK 18	TRACK 19	TRACK 20	TRACK 21	TRACK 22	TRACK 23	TRACK 24
	Instrumental Overdubs Strings STEREO		Lead Vocal	Lead Vocal	Background Vocals		Computer Tracks	
SELECTION	TRACK 1	TRACK 2	TRACK 3	TRACK 4	TRACK 5	TRACK 6	TRACK 7	TRACK 8
	TRACK 9	TRACK 10	TRACK 11	TRACK 12	TRACK 13	TRACK 14	TRACK 15	TRACK 16
	TRACK 17	TRACK 18	TRACK 19	TRACK 20	TRACK 21	TRACK 22	TRACK 23	TRACK 24

FIGURE 8.   Track sheet for "An Imaginary Song."

to a foot away from the sound source. However, if the studio has a good live sound, the producer often will install an omnidirectional overhead room microphone so that he can add that dimension to his track-by-track minimixes. Usually when cutting the rhythm section, the room microphone will be assigned a separate track. But on overdubs it's generally introduced as a blend with the microphone recording the guitar or the keyboard amplifier. This blend, if it enhances the sound, will then be combined onto a single track.

Let us, for the sake of clarity, examine this situation further. A producer is recording an electric guitar by itself. The guitar signal, which will be routed to its own track, can be fed into the recording console in three ways: (1) directly into the console, which will produce a sound with no amplifier coloration; (2) with a microphone about a foot away from the guitar amplifier, which will produce an entirely different sound (i.e., distortion, feedback, and effects such as tremolo); and/or (3) with an overhead room microphone, which in a live room will give the sound added reverberation characteristics. The producer, if he so elects, can record the guitar using these three techniques simultaneously. He can also record the guitar using a two-way mix or a one-and-a-half-way mix (e.g., one part close mike, a half part room mike). Other possibilities are to record just direct or just close-miked. What sounds best to the producer after reviewing these possible combinations ultimately will be recorded as a take on the master. *Listen to sides 1 and 2 of the demonstration record* for guitar recording techniques. The freedom to pick and choose among many different ways to record an instrument is available to the producer, with few exceptions, on every musical track. And since the premix establishes the relationship with a single track, there is usually no need to assign the room microphone to its own separate channel (except when cutting the basic rhythm tracks).

Regardless of which numerical tracks are assigned to the particular instruments, the order in which performances take place in the studio is usually the same:

The basic rhythm tracks are recorded first. After carefully evaluating the performances alone and as a minimix, the producer will probably proceed with one or more of the musicians to repair the basic rhythm parts (e.g., one bar of bass contains a *clam*, or mistake; one section of guitar doesn't *swing*, or feel good).

A *reference vocal*, which is a temporary track used in recording overdubs, is recorded. Most instrumentalists will want to hear this reference vocal during recording so that they know where they are in the song (otherwise, they will hear a cacophony of drum beats, cymbal crashes, and guitar choruses). As previously stated, the cue mix can be fine-tuned by the producer or the recording engineer for each artist's personal needs.

50

One by one, although the order may vary, the producer records the following overdubs: keyboards; solo guitar; strings; horns; percussion; and synthesizer.

The reference vocal is replaced by the final lead vocal and backup vocals. Sometimes the lead vocal is *doubled*, or assigned two tracks and recorded twice. A doubled performance can be (1) two different performances of the vocal blended together, or *double tracked*; (2) parts of the two vocals combined into a single performance and then premixed, or *ping-ponged*, onto another track; or (3) the same performance recorded using several different microphones and microphone placements.

Consulting the *VU meters*, or *LEDs*, on the input module in use, the recording engineer will monitor the sound level of each of the instruments being recorded. Each input module on the console and each track on the tape machine has its own VU meter, depicted in figure 9. For alignment purposes, the meters are generally adjusted to zero VU. A comfortable recording level registers between −10 and −3, depending on the sound source. Instruments with strong *transients* (peaks and dips), such as the tambourine, would be best recorded conservatively; electronic instruments with a constant signal level (such as the synthesizer) can be carried *hotter*. Occasional peaks in the +3 range are not generally undesirable, but persistently high VU levels will cause overloading, distortion, and a loss of transparency (in recording jargon, this is referred to as *packing the tape*).

It might seem very important for the recording engineer or the producer to keep a log of microphone placements, cable connections, and recording console calibrations, but it really isn't. With the twist of a control knob, the slight movement left or right of a baffle or microphone, a good recording engineer will be able to duplicate the sounds from a previous session or create new ones that are even better.

What does require a lot of careful planning is what I call the thinking through of the tracks. A good twenty-four-track tape recording is supposed to be the sum of its parts. If you use up too many tracks, you will be forced to combine performances and/or effects that *cannot* be changed. This defeats the purpose of the layering technique, which is intended to give the producer maximum control over the recorded material prior to the most critical stage of production, the mixing of the master tape. Ping-ponging may be necessary if you have a limited number of tracks to work with, but it's bad form to combine performances in a twenty-four-track studio simply because you've run out of channels. From beginning to end, the producer should know where he is in the production, what he's planning to add, and why his particular recording plan is sensible.

The last piece of the overall plan involves communication. It is vital for the producer to be able to articulate precisely what he wants done. The cardinal sin is for the producer to sound vague: this attitude is picked up instantly, causing a lot of wasted time in the studio. I can't overemphasize the importance of having everyone understand what the producer is saying.

Microphones used in Figure 10.

1. Bass (guitar)   Direct
2. Bass (guitar)   Electro Voice RE-20
3. Kick drum   Shure SM-7
4. Snare drum (top)   AKG 451-E (10 db. pad)
5. Snare drum (bottom)   AKG 451-E (10 db. pad)
6. Hi hat   Neumann KM-84
7. Overhead (drums)   AKG 451-E (10 db. pad)
8. Overhead (drums)   AKG 451-E (10 db. pad)
9. Tom tom (drums)   AKG 451-E
10. Tom tom (drums)   AKG 451-E
11. Tom tom (drums)   Neumann KM-86
12. Guitar (electric)   Sennheiser MD 441 U
13. Guitar (electric)   Sennheiser MD 441 U
14. Fender Rhodes (piano)   Direct
15. Fender Rhodes (piano)   Direct
16. Wurlitzer (piano)   Direct
17. Hammond B-3 (organ)   Shure SM-57
18. Hammond B-3 (organ)   Shure SM-57
19. Vocal   AKG 414-EB   Neumann U-47   Neumann U-87
    Beyer M-500   Sennheiser 441
20. Room microphone   Neumann U-87

*Vocals can be recorded in the booth during the session if the singer(s) are not involved in laying down the instrumental tracks.

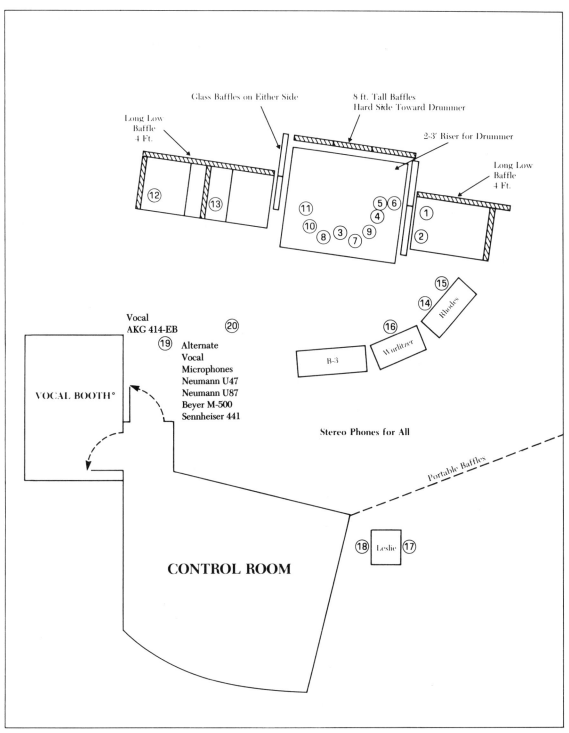

Glass Baffles on Either Side

8 ft. Tall Baffles
Hard Side Toward Drummer

Long Low
Baffle
4 Ft.

2-3' Riser for Drummer

Long Low
Baffle
4 Ft.

⑫   ⑬   ⑪   ⑤⑥ ①
      ⑩   ④
       ⑧ ③ ⑨ ②
           ⑦

⑮

⑭   Rhodes

⑯

Vocal
AKG 414-EB

⑳

⑲ Alternate
Vocal
Microphones
Neumann U47
Neumann U87
Beyer M-500
Sennheiser 441

Wurlitzer

B-3

Stereo Phones for All

VOCAL BOOTH°

Portable Baffles

⑱ Leslie ⑰

CONTROL ROOM

FIGURE 10. Overall recording studio setup for a
rock and roll band.

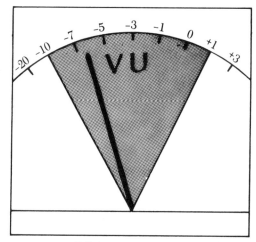

FIGURE 9.   VU meter.

The jargon of producers, recording engineers, and artists is highly descriptive. Drums are supposed to sound *punchy*. A full sound becomes a *fat* sound. A good overall live sound is a *crispy* sound. If you want more energy in a performance, you want more *juice*. Admittedly, this talk is sometimes difficult to be understood, but if the general vibe is good the sessions usually flow smoothly. See the glossary in the back of this book for a larger sampling of record production slang and technical terms.

Most recording sessions begin with run-throughs to loosen everybody up. This gives the recording engineer an opportunity to adjust the microphones, see that the cables are properly connected, and get the kinks out of the recording console. I usually begin by doing the basic tracks of one song plus whatever overdubs are needed to replace an unacceptable performance. We then go on to the next song and do that basic track, and so on for at least three or four songs or perhaps the entire album, assuming that everything feels good.

Then we return to the first song and do a little more work on it so that we don't lose track (no pun intended) of what we're aiming for. Gradually, step by step, we get around to every song this way, taking it always to the next highest level of completion.

Figure 10 shows the overall recording studio setup we use for a rock and roll band. You'll probably want to refer to this diagram as we discuss how the individual instruments in the band (as well as the optional sweeteners) are recorded.

RECORDING THE DRUM KIT

It is essential for the producer to have maximum control over the most fundamental recording sound, the drums. Since the drums are usually recorded on the same session with the bass, rhythm guitar, and rhythm keyboards, I prefer to isolate the drums somewhat from the other instruments by placing them on a riser and screening them on three sides with baffles. This semi-enclosure allows the musicians to have visual contact with each other but cuts down tremendously on leakage from the other rhythm instruments into the miked sound of the drums.

In a twenty-four-track studio, the drum kit is practically always recorded live and as a unit, as opposed to recording the kick drum, snare drum, tom-toms, cymbals, and high hats separately. See figure 11. I like to use as few microphones on the drums as possible. Minimally, that means there will be one mike for the kick drum; one mike for the snare drum; and two overhead mikes for picking up the cymbals, tom-toms, high hat, and the overall sound of the drum kit. If four mikes don't seem to be cutting it, I may try as many as four more mikes: three for the tom-toms and high hat (if the kit is large) and one to record the snare drum from the bottom, which is where the snares are. This technique produces a "snarier" sound than does miking only the top. The more microphones you use to record the drums, the greater the risk of *phase cancellation*, which in lay terms is a primary loss of low-frequency response followed by a high-frequency loss as the signal deteriorates. This unpleasant effect is caused by the interaction of too many microphones picking up the same sound source at slightly different times. To illustrate the basic principle, I know of an artist (he shall go unnamed) who brought a stereo tape to a radio station to broadcast during an interview. The tape was played over the air on an AM mono station and because the left and right channels were 180 degrees out of phase, all the center information— i.e., vocals, kick drum, and bass—was gone! Had someone not been monitoring the broadcast carefully, the listeners would have had three-and-a-half-minutes of meaningless guitar strumming. If you're seeking to record a good drum sound, phase cancellation must be avoided at all costs.

Most drummers know that they should place a piece of foam, a pillow, or a blanket inside the kick drum in order to get a really punchy sound during recording. As figure 12 shows, this is accomplished by removing the skin facing away from the drummer, then stuffing the foam into the drum so that it rests against the inside surface of the skin hit by the mallet. The microphone used to record a kick drum (often a dynamic mike like a Shure SM 7 or an Electrovoice 666) will point directly toward the muffled side of the skin and be only inches away from the casing of the drum. Care should be taken that the pillow or blanket doesn't create a loud poofing sound as the air around it is dispersed. If the poofing sound can't be eliminated entirely at its source, it is usually dealt with by deflecting the kick drum microphone away from the drum itself.

Some musicians don't particularly like the sound of a stripped down kick drum. Graham Lear, for example, who is Santana's drummer, uses a kick drum with a six-inch hole cut in the center of the skin that would normally be removed. This drum did create a nice sound on *Inner Secrets*, Santana's album, but we kept getting a strange poofing noise that required much more deflection of the

FIGURE 11. Setup and microphone placements for a drum kit.

kick drum mike than usual. The recording engineering should attend to
eliminating these extraneous sounds before the tape recorder is turned on.

Again, in order to maximize control over the sound of the drum kit, the producer will assign more than one track to the drums. I always assign the kick drum to one track; the snare drum to one track (with a blend of the top and bottom snare mikes if I'm recording that way); the overhead left microphone to one track; and the overhead right microphone to one track. Any additional mikes used for the tom-toms would be balanced and assigned to the left and right overhead tracks, respectively. Recording the overheads and tom-toms on two separate tracks gives the producer more flexibility in assigning the drums to the left, center, or right of the stereo panorama in the mixed-down two-track master tape, as we'll see in chapter 6.

The choice of microphones to record the drums should be based on experimentation and personal taste. Currently I use AKG 451 Es for the overheads; Neumann KM 84s or U 87s and AKG 414 EBs for the tom-toms and high hat; and a Shure SM 57 or an AKG 451 for the snare. As mentioned previously, a dynamic mike like a Shure SM 7 or an Electrovoice 666 would be used on the kick drum. I wouldn't hestitate, however, to replace any of these mikes with another mike if I obtained a better sound as a result.

Strangely enough, when you listen to the individual components in the drum kit by themselves, they don't tend to sound particularly good. The snare drum especially sounds bad by itself. And yet, when you open up the whole kit, the blend can be

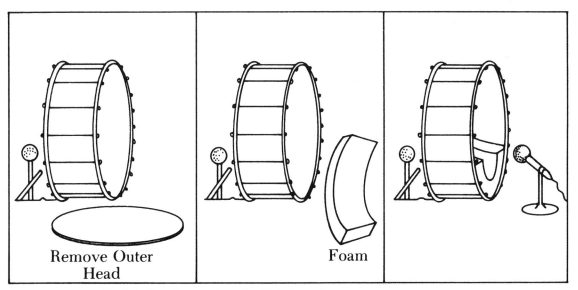

Remove Outer
Head

Foam

FIGURE 12.   Preparation of a kick drum for recording purposes.

marvelous. *Listen to side 1 on the demonstration record for further insight into recording the drum kit.*

RECORDING THE BASS AND RHYTHM GUITARS

As shown in figure 10, the electric guitars used in recording rhythm tracks are also usually screened with baffles. The bass, as a rule, stands close to the drum kit so that the musicians can both see and hear each other and literally feel the vibrations put out by these very loud instruments.

The bass is almost always simultaneously recorded direct and live, but the direct sound inevitably wins out. The ambient quality of the room has to be considered, however, in choosing the right amplifiers to use for recording purposes. Sometimes less is more, in the sense that groups seeking a big, wide, stadium sound would be served more appropriately by small amplifiers that sound better in the studio. During the recording of their debut album, *RockRose*, Frank Demme, the base

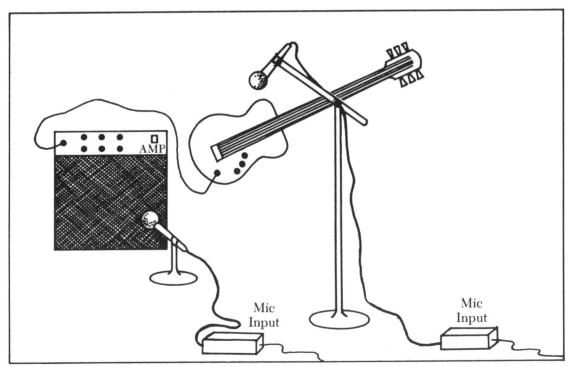

FIGURE 13.   Overdubbing a guitar performance
with room ambiance.

player, used a Mitchell amplifier with a Gauss speaker. This equipment is in the mid-to large-sized range, but we were dealing with new artists who didn't have the luxury of being able to choose from a multitude of different kinds of amps. Although the Mitchell amp sounded fine, the direct track was ultimately used.

The guitar used for the RockRose rhythm sessions was a Gibson–Les Paul special. It was played through a Boogey amp with a Sun Coliseum top. We recorded this guitar by close-miking the amplifier and adding a little of the overhead room sound to the overall rhythm ensemble. In some cases, we're shooting primarily for a *drum* room sound. At other times, we're shooting for an overall roominess. This is where the placement of microphones and their pattern of sound pickup bear heavily on getting a good sound. See figure 13.

Occasionally an electric guitar other than the bass is recorded direct. This technique produces a completely different sound, uninfluenced by an amplifier, and is usually associated with a cleaner, softer, more mellow music than rock (although it has been used discriminatingly on hard rock records, too). *Listen to side 1 on the demonstration record for further insight into recording the bass and rhythm guitars.*

In the event that an acoustic, or nonelectric, guitar were included on a rhythm section, it would probably be isolated in a separate room in order to prevent leakage. The musicians would be fed the acoustic guitar signal through the cue mix in their earphones. If, however, the producer wanted to record the acoustic guitar with an electric pickup, he would treat it like any other amplified instrument and record it in the main studio, live or most often direct.

RECORDING THE KEYBOARDS

The selection of keyboards is primarily the artist's decision, though again, as in the case of the electric guitars, the producer may want to experiment with different instruments and amplifiers in order to find the right sound for a particular song. The primary keyboards used on the Player albums, *Player* and *Danger Zone*, were a Wurlitzer and a Fender Rhodes electric piano. On one song, the Wurlitzer and the Fender Rhodes went through a Boss Chorus, which is a stereo phasing device, and they were recorded direct. Occasionally, I like the Fender Rhodes going through a Leslie speaker with a Variac, a device that can speed up or slow down the vibrato of the Leslie, and the Fender Rhodes recorded live in stereo (i.e., in the classic XY position, using two microphones and two tracks of the twenty-four-track recorder). On the RockRose LP, numerous outboard devices were used on different songs, including *phase shifters* and an *echoplex*, to enhance the keyboard sounds.

I would include an acoustic piano on a rhythm session if the piano were playing primarily chords in a rhythmic pattern. But if the piano were asked, in the jargon of the recording studio, to *step out*, or play a solo, I would probably record it later as a separate overdub. *Listen to side 1 on the demonstration record for further insight into recording the rhythm keyboards.*

RECORDING THE PERCUSSION

Of the many percussion instruments used in contemporary music, the only ones that from time to time are recorded as part of the basic rhythm tracks are bongos and congas. All other percussion instruments are usually overdubbed later, when the record has begun to take more shape. As a rule, if the percussion is recorded live, a dynamic mike would tend to deliver more of the *meat*, or fundamental sound, of the instrument. A condenser mike on overdubs would provide a wider response, especially in the high frequencies.

EVALUATING THE BASIC RHYTHM TRACKS

After the basic rhythm tracks have been recorded, it's a good idea to do a rough mix, take a copy of the mixed-down version home, and listen to it carefully. At this stage, I prefer evaluating the rhythm tracks without the reference vocal, which may already have been recorded. The main thing the producer should be listening for, other than the overall quality of the individual performances, is how much music there is on the tape. Remember that this is just the beginning. Too many notes and too much stepping out on the rhythm tracks won't leave enough space for the solo instruments and vocals that follow. There will be plenty of time to add material, but as time goes on it gets awfully hard to subtract material—especially if that material is part of the bedrock of the song.

It is quite common for a producer, after listening very carefully to the overall quality of the different *takes*, of performance run-throughs, to decide that performances on several different takes should be edited or cut together to achieve an optimum studio performance. If, for example, the first ninety seconds of the drum kit on take number three were a superlative performance, and if the next ninety seconds on take number four were superior to that same performance on take number three, the producer might ask the recording engineer to splice the two sections together. This procedure is perfectly acceptable and is done quite often, but only if there is no tempo fluctuation at the point where the edit takes place. These combined takes should be evaluated carefully by all concerned before a commitment is made to go with the edited rhythm tracks.

Any performances of other instruments that don't jibe exactly at the point of editing will have to be re-recorded, or *punched in*, as overdubs. The normal way this is handled is for the instrumentalist to listen to his performance in the studio with earphones; play along with the music; and have the recording engineer electronically punch in the musical bridge linking the two previously recorded performances. When punching in, it is not necessary for the entire performance to be re-recorded, provided there is a momentary pause, or *hole*, in the music that the engineer can use for punching in and out. These are the critical junctures at which the musician, in order to facilitate clean "ins" and "outs," should refrain from speaking, muttering, or cursing until the tape recorder has stopped. *Listen to side 1 on the demonstration record for further insight into recording a satisfactory rhythm section.*

PRELIMINARY INSTRUMENTAL OVERDUBS

Many artists, after hearing the rhythm tracks the producer has decided to go with, will ask for another chance to re-record their parts. Although they're technically overdubs, these performances are actually replacement performances and should be dealt with prior to adding new material.

GUITAR OVERDUBS

In many respects, the electric guitar has become the center stage star of pop music and especially of rock and roll bands. One of the most common techniques used to bring out the sound of a particular guitar is to record the same performance twice and to feature both performances on the finished master. Doubling a performance should be no strain on the artist if he knows his part well and is listening to his performance with earphones while recording the second, almost identical performance. Parts that are doubled are recorded on a separate track just in case the producer decides later that he doesn't want to use the second performance.

In reality, the guitar solo is doubled much less often than one might think. The operative word here is "solo," which implies an individual performance of movement and technical excitement. Great solo performances are hard to duplicate. They are especially hard to double if the performer is a creative artist who practically never plays the same phrase in exactly the same way. Doubling can work for heavier, mechanical guitar performances, but it is ill-suited to someone like Carlos Santana, for example, who is an electric guitar virtuoso.

Most guitar amplifiers have bass, treble, and mid-range adjustments that can vary the color of the sound to an almost infinite extent. In addition, a host of processing devices—phasers, *blue boxes, octave dividers*, echoplexes, *graphic equalizers*, DDLs, *wah-wah pedals*, and *flangers*—can be used either by the guitarist or by the control room to create some absolutely amazing sound effects. Processed guitar sound can be recorded live and/or direct during an actual performance, or it can be added during the mixing of the album simply by patching the desired processor(s) into the recording console. *Listen to sides 1 and 2 on the demonstration record for further insight into processed solo guitar recording.*

If the producer wants to record a large stadium sound, he should install one or more amplifiers in the main room and experiment until the right blend of room and close-miked amp sound is achieved. If, at the opposite end of the tonal spectrum, the producer wishes to have the guitars speak very clearly on the record, smaller amplifiers and less reverberant room sound should be factored into the equation for getting a good sound.

The procedure for recording guitar solos is for the artist to render several different interpretations of the solo, with each interpretation assigned to a separate track. Later on, the producer, recording engineer, and the artist will evaluate the different versions of the solo to select which performance, or sections of different performances, to use as a finished take. I like to avoid bouncing pieces of solos together. I think the best way to deal with this potential problem is to make the guitar soloist feel very comfortable in the studio and to offer him a lot of constructive oral feedback. A confident artist almost always does a superb job from beginning to end of the solo.

Again, the general rule for doing overdubs is for the artist to play along with the music previously recorded up to the beginning as well as through the conclusion of the solo. This helps the recording engineer, who is trying to make the punching in of new music an absolutely silent, unnoticeable process. Of course, playing along with previously recorded music is made possible through the use of earphones.

KEYBOARD OVERDUBS

Keyboards tend to speak more consistently than do electric guitars and are somewhat easier to record. Most of the time, the electric keyboards are recorded direct. The color of their sound can be affected in three ways: (1) by using the instrument's bass, treble, vibrato, and tremolo controls; (2) by connecting one or more outboard processors to the instrument; or (3) by adjusting the sound at the recording console. Many of the processors used for recording electric guitars can also be used for recording electric keyboards. *Listen to side 1 on the demonstration record for further insight into keyboard recording.*

In addition to the acoustic piano, which is the fundamental keyboard instrument, the keyboards I've used most often in the studio are the Wurlitzer electric piano, the Fender Rhodes electric piano, the Hohner electric piano, the Hohner clavinet, the Hammond organ, and the Yamaha electric grand piano. Sometimes it is necessary to double a keyboard line. At other times, the producer may feel that the sound would be enhanced by recording the keyboard live as opposed to direct. Whenever possible. keyboards should be recorded in stereo using two of the twenty-four tracks. This will enable the producer to isolate more of the keyboard's octave spread on either side of the stereo *image*.

FIGURE 14. Microphone placements for lead
vocalist and backup vocalists.

VOCAL OVERDUBS

Vocals are the most important part of a record. Few instruments are more difficult to record technically than is the human voice, and no instrument carries as much emotional weight.

Coaching the singer and adequate song rehearsal are the keys to getting a good vocal performance. The time to begin rehearsing is weeks before the recording session. The way singers rehearse varies greatly, although I like to give singers cassette copies of the basic rhythm tracks for sing-along purposes at home. Periodically the producer should check with the lead vocalist to see how he's feeling, how his voice feels, and when to schedule the vocals, as well as to answer any questions the singer might have about interpretation. Often in the midst of recording instrumental tracks day after day, there is a tendency to forget that the vocals sooner or later must be done.

On the day of the vocal session, I ask the singer to get to the studio early and warm up. Indeed, the vocalist should start warming up at home, singing a lot so that his voice gets opened up and feeling comfortable.

In terms of recording technique, the most important thing the producer has to do is create a relaxed studio environment. For most singers, this means that there should be as few people around as possible. A quartet composed of the singer, the producer, and the recording engineer, with a member of the vocalist's group providing moral as well as technical support, almost always does the job. If he feels it would

63

help his singing, the singer may request a somewhat larger audience. I'll indulge a professional singer that way, but if the request were made by a beginning vocalist, I'd probably wait to see what happened in the quartet situation first.

The lead singer can be placed either in a separate vocal booth or in an area of the main room in line with the control room. (I tend to prefer the latter setup so that I can communicate with the singer by eye as well as through the cue system.) Though one microphone usually is sufficient, every voice has a unique timbre and every singer projects differently; as a result several different mikes and microphone placements will have to be tried to achieve the best sound. Most vocals I do sound great with an AKG 414, a Neumann U 47 FET, or a Neumann U 87—all condenser mikes. If the artist is accustomed to performing live on stage, a dynamic mike such as a Shure 545 or SM 7 might work better to achieve a good vocal sound.

If the vocalist is a foot-thumper, the producer will want to install padding underneath the singer to cushion the thumps. Singers also have a tendency to close their eyes when singing, which means that they may unintentionally move off mike while recording. It's a good habit for the producer to remind the vocalist periodically to remain as stationary as possible, about a foot or two from the mike. When everything is ready, the tape starts rolling.

Recording vocals is a very exacting business, particularly because so much material has to be punched in (or edited out, if you prefer) by the recording engineer. Accordingly, everyone in the control room should have a copy of the lyrics to consult as needed.

The worst thing that can happen to a song is for the singer, the producer, and the recording engineer to rely too much on the remedial capabilities of the equipment. It's the performance that counts. This is where some producers really begin to shine. If they know how to work with singers, this talent will come across loud and clear on a record.

Having been a lead singer in my youth, I feel that I'm a good producer of vocals. I know how to put the artist at ease. The artist is aware of my own ability to understand phrasing and the importance of good intonation. He knows that I know whether a performance is on the money and whether it's believable. Pitch and phrasing, for me, are less important than are emotion and sincerity. If I have to make a choice, I'll pick the emotional rendering much sooner than I'll pick the well-pitched, well-phrased performance that lacks feeling.

There is only one standard to apply to recording vocals: perfection. The performance has to be consistently strong. The edited final take (assuming that the recording engineer had to punch in replacement portions of the song) has to sound like a single strand of vocal expression. It can be done, and it *is* done every day by seasoned producers who coax, tease, frighten, or otherwise extract superlative performances from vocalists. Producers who are just beginning will learn this art as they go along.

Backup vocals are usually recorded after the lead vocal has blazed the trail and completed the solo track. Some producers, including myself, even sing backup. (Incidentally, this is an extra source of income for the producer since the record company must pay at least the minimum AFTRA scale to each singer involved in the recording.)

Normally, one microphone is used for up to three backup singers; the pickup pattern is usually cardioid or a figure 8. With groups of more than three, an omnidirectional pattern (360 degree arc) usually works best, enabling the singers to take positions around the microphone. See figure 14. Each singer will hear the lead vocal and rhythm tracks through earphones. They may also be conducted by a member of the group in the studio to help achieve tight, well-phrased cutoffs.

Backup vocals usually take much less time to record than lead vocals, but sometimes the reverse is true. You can never predict what will move along briskly or slow down to a crawl, which is one of the fascinating, changeable aspects of recording that I enjoy.

As he does with other solo instruments, the producer has the choice of either doubling the lead vocal by recording it twice on two separate tracks or recording it on a single channel. Rock artists tend to double their lead vocals, or at least part of the lead, for effect. I don't think the doubling technique would be advantageous, however, for singers like Beverly Sills, Barbra Streisand, or Johnny Mathis. As a rule, the decision to treat vocals with electronic processing equipment is made during the mixing stage, as I discuss in the next chapter.

Listen to side 1 on the demonstration record for further insight into recording vocal overdubs.

HORN OVERDUBS

Many producers working with either self-contained rock groups or singer-songwriters around whom the rhythm tracks are built feel that a song would be better served through sweetening. In that case, the producer will schedule a preliminary meeting with an arranger to discuss the musical concept of the album and the direction the sweetening *charts* should take.

I usually have a definite idea about the types of *licks*, or musical lines, I want added to a performance. Often the artist and/or songwriter contributes constructive ideas in this area as well. The best way to convey these ideas is to sing them to the arranger over the basic tracks. Remember, however, that these are only ideas and that the arranger should be given enough room to create his own feeling for what the music should ultimately sound like.

If the producer is concerned with keeping the cost of overdub sessions down, he may want to produce the sweetening session in one live three- to five-hour sitting. The preferred way, of course, is to schedule a separate recording session for each of the orchestral sections: horns, strings, and percussion. (The word "horns" is used idiomatically by record producers for winds as well as for brass instruments.)

Figure 15 shows how the horns are normally set up in the main room of the recording studio. If the horn section is small—from two to six players—the producer will ask the musicians to play in a straight line. If it's a larger section—from seven to ten players—the producer will put the trumpets and trombones on one line, the saxophones on another line approximately ten to fifteen feet away from the brass. As a general rule, each instrument is close-miked separately and then blended onto a single channel of the twenty-four-track machine. Less conventional approaches may occasionally be tried, often with good results.

There is not much call in contemporary pop music for the more exotic brass or woodwind instruments, although my partner and I have sometimes used bassoon, oboe, English horn, and French horn. The French horn is somewhat difficult to record since the bell of the instrument faces down and away from the microphone. The technique we've used most often is to install a sound reflector, such as a

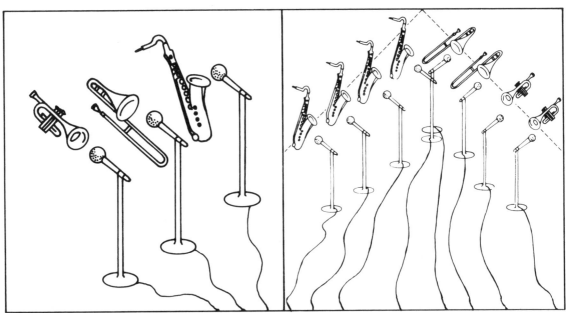

FIGURE 15. Microphone placements for a three-piece and an eight-piece horn section.

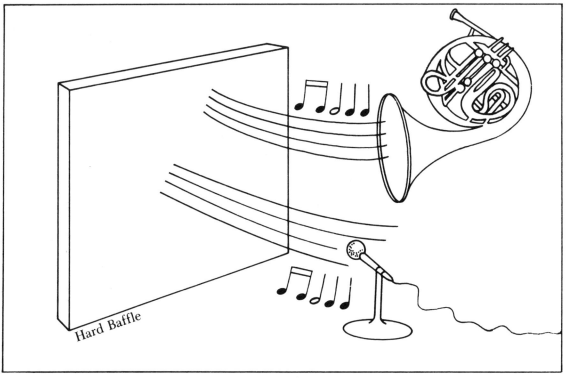

FIGURE 16.   Setup and microphone placement
for a French horn.

hard-surfaced baffle, approximately three to six feet behind the French horn player; stand a microphone two to four feet from the baffle; and record the reflected sound of the instrument. See figure 16. If leakage is a problem, close miking or overdubbing may be necessary.

Horn players are usually a crazy bunch of guys. They are the most fun to be with during the recording process, and they work particularly well with the producer and arranger in regard to last-second changes in their parts. Characteristically, they almost never ask to hear the vocals in their cue mix, as vocals tend to cover the rhythm, which makes tight phrasing difficult.

This is as good a time as any to point out that the placements of microphones, baffles, and instrumentalists as described in these pages are only possible solutions to getting a good sound. There is no right way to do things when you are attempting to create fresh, exciting music. Sometimes one microphone will work better than two mikes. Sometimes I experiment with an overhead mike directly opposite the players to record a small horn section. Since every recording studio presents the producer with a different set of acoustical parameters, the producer must realize that any suggestions are nothing but suggestions. You should apply this information and be guided by it, but you should allow yourself the freedom to experiment. You'll often surprise yourself with the results.

STRING OVERDUBS

The role of strings in contemporary music has changed a lot since they first began to be used in the late fifties. When I began my production career in 1965, if I used a string section at all it would have contained four violins, two violas, a cello, and some mirrors (the last is an old studio joke). Currently I am using eight to twelve violins, four to six violas, and two to four cellos on most projects that require strings and a somewhat larger section if the strings have a dominant role on the record. See the setup and microphone placement shown in figure 17.

Many producers believe a string section should contain as many as twenty violins, twelve violas, four cellos, and two bass violins. However, close-miking techniques should make a four-piece violin section sound very full to most people. But generally speaking, strings should not be close-miked: the room sound better enhances the overall tonality of strings and creates a richer, smoother sound.

(Nevertheless, in small sections the cellos usually are close-miked for the sake of overall balance and clarity. But where a good blend can be achieved with either two overhead mikes or a stereo mike like an AKG C 24 and some spot miking, so much the better.)

Strings are recorded in stereo and then assigned to two of the twenty-four tracks. During the mixing of the record, the strings will be panned to some degree left and right in the stereo image to create a full-bodied, three-dimensional sound. Any strings that are close-miked, such as the cellos or a solo violin (which probably would be treated as a separate overdub), may pick up a lot of bowing sound. This is a generic trait of the string family and not much can be done to change it other than to deflect the microphone slightly away from the bow or to request the use of more rosin. The latter approach is usually the more effective solution to reducing bow noise.

String players often require special handling by the producer. Since they are steeped in classical training, it is essential either to have a basic understanding of musical notation or to have a competent translator at the producer's side, such as the arranger. The speed with which string players go through the arranger's road map of the arrangement and work up their parts is amazing. String players will give the producer a 100 percent effort. But of all the musicians the producer will encounter in the studio, they are the ones most likely to expect a reciprocal 100 percent effort from the producer and his staff since quite often they are deciphering notes and pressed for time.

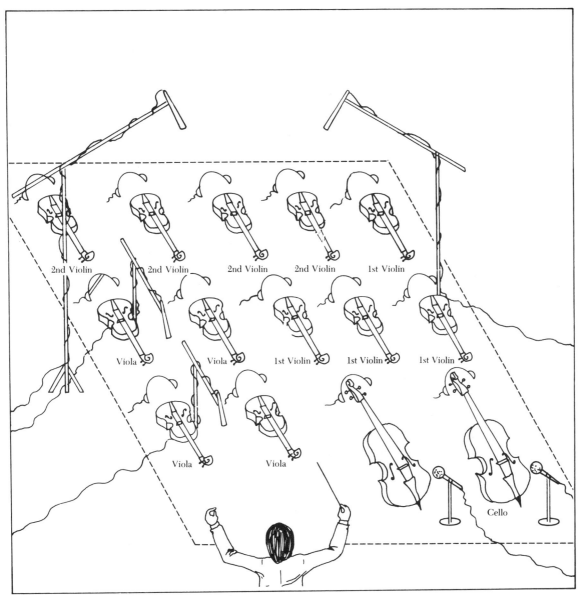

FIGURE 17. Setup and microphone placements for a fourteen-piece string
section (eight violins, four violas,
and two cellos).

Occasionally, as a producer, you sense that the arrangement you ordered is not exactly what you had in mind. If the licks you intended aren't being stated properly, or if it seems that there's too much playing, the best thing to do is call for an immediate powwow with the arranger, who in most cases will be conducting the session. Arrangers, as a rule, are very capable of making changes on the spot. Having had a great deal of experience with the players on the session, the arranger is also very good at communicating these changes to the rest of the orchestra. What might otherwise take days will be revised, rehearsed, re-recorded, or punched into the master tape in a matter of hours or even minutes when you're working with a highly professional group of musicians. String sections have a concertmaster, or leader, who directs the group with reference to the intonation, phrasing, and overall interpretation of the arrangement. The concertmaster is the arranger-conductor's liaison with the section at large. Sid Sharp, a Los Angeles-based musician, has been concertmaster on practically every session I've done, and his ability to interpret what is written and convey that feeling to the rest of the section is unequaled.

PERCUSSION OVERDUBS

Though they can be recorded as basic rhythm tracks, most percussion instruments are overdubbed toward the completion of the record. This gives the producer and the percussionist a better opportunity to gauge what kinds of hits, slaps, beats, knocks, and bops will work in the production and where they should be added. The people playing percussion may be members of the band; the producer, if, as in my case and my partner's case, he has a very good sense of rhythm and a reasonably good technique; or free-lance percussion specialists, who carry their own percussion kits.

Involving a free-lance percussion specialist in a recording production is an extraordinary experience. In Los Angeles, my partner and I have been using Gary Coleman, Victor Feldman, and Steve Forman of late, and they are all complete musicians. Rather than work from charts, these percussionists sit down with the producer, evaluate the tracks already completed, and recommend an approach based on instinct. Many times their rhythmic and sound inventions, as recorded in the studio after a few minutes of rehearsal, are the highlights of the finished track.

Percussion instruments are invariably close-miked. They are recorded either in the vocal booth on a live session or in the main room with baffles. Even for Santana, which with its three full-time percussion players was a percussion experience to record, my partner and I opted for the methodical layering technique rather than record the group live. This was perhaps a little awkward for the percussion players at first, but in the end they were delighted with the separation and precision we were able to get by recording the percussion in stages. (This group, incidentally, has some of the finest bongo and conga drum players and equipment I have ever heard. Excellent musicianship, excellent gear.)

70

Stacking, another recording technique, is used, for example, to make two pairs of hands sound like a whole army. The live hand-clappers (let's say there are two people) are recorded in the studio. The tape recorder will play back and re-record, play back and re-record this performance on a number of different tracks until the combined performance, which will eventually be assigned to one track, sounds like four, eight, sixteen, thirty-two, or sixty-four people, etc.

SYNTHESIZER OVERDUBS

Probably the most difficult instrument to record is the synthesizer. It's not that the instrument itself, which is almost always taken direct, is hard to record; what's difficult is getting a sound you like—one that blends with the texture and mood of the nearly completed twenty-four-track tape.

My partner and I have been working with a synthesizer player and programmer named Mike Boddicker whose equipment during recording takes up practically the entire control room. (Since the synthesizer is taken direct, it really doesn't matter where it's recorded. We use the control room so that we can communicate without having to use earphones or the talkback system.) Mike is particularly adept at listening to the music, getting a general idea of what kind of sound we want, and then coming up with something that is really close to the ideal. From there, it's just a question of refining the sound, adjusting levels, and turning on the tape recorder.

In a sense, it's a bargain to use someone like Mike Boddicker. He does charge a reasonable equipment rental (his gear must be worth $100,000), and he receives the appropriate union scale payment, as well he should, along with a cartage reimbursement from the record company. But it would be far more expensive (not to mention far more difficult) for the producer and the engineer to rent individual pieces of synthesizer equipment and then patch them together. Furthermore, it might not be possible to get as good a sound from rented equipment. Using specialists may appear to be an unwarranted luxury, but sometimes they can save the artist and the producer money (remember that both artist and producer ultimately pay for recording sessions out of royalties).

Listen to side 2 on the demonstration record for examples of synthesizer sweetening used on the Player single, "Baby Come Back."

This completes our discussion of the layering technique insofar as the recording studio is concerned. Most, if not all, of the twenty-four tracks should be filled with sound information at this time. The musicians should be able to go home, rest up, and perhaps ready themselves for their next concert tour or their next session, as the case may be. For the producer and the recording engineer, however, it's a different story. Their work on the album is far from over.

71

6
Mixing, Remixing, and Editing

The art of record production is difficult to describe. You have to be there to understand how the producer and the recording engineer work their magic in the studio and in the control room.

This is especially true for mixing, which is an art form itself. To write about mixing, and later about editing, will take only a few pages. But the arts of mixing and editing cannot be learned from a book. They have to be studied in the studio, working with the equipment, twisting the knobs on the recording console, and developing an aesthetic sense of what's right.

WHAT IS MIXING?

When the producer has finished recording all the instruments for a particular album, he will have a two-inch tape that contains twenty-four tracks of musical information. This is not, in any sense of the word, a finished product. It has not yet been balanced, blended, and polished, nor is it in a format that consumers of records and tapes could purchase at a retail store.

The performances are finished, but the production is still raw. In order to make these performances sound like a finished record, and in order for the tape to be formatted for the consumer's home stereo system, the producer must do the following:

1. He must establish relationships among all the tracks on the album so that the instruments have a clear, distinct, transparent sound. This is accomplished through the use of EQ, reverb and the fine-tuning of balance controls.

72

2. He must limit unwanted sounds on the tape by using various pieces of noise-reduction equipment.
3. He must add whatever processed sound he feels is necessary.
4. He must assign each track to its proper place in the stereo image, or panorama, of the record.

The above steps constitute mixing. If the producer doesn't like the sound of the mix, then he will continue to make adjustments. It is not uncommon to make fifty passes before the producer and engineer feel ready to "try one on," as we say. Eventually the producer will be satisfied with a rehearsal and wish to record it on the two-track mix-down tape recorder. This two-track tape, after it has been edited, is the finished master tape recording that will be delivered to the record company.

THE CHRONOLOGY OF MIXING

Mixing a serious performance is itself serious business. And like many other creative processes, it is best done quietly behind closed doors. The people in the driver's seat in the control room are the producer and the engineer, working in tandem. All others are nonessential to the mixing process.

Preparation for the session begins with a careful cleaning of the tape heads; alignment of the tape recorders, recording console, and noise-reduction equipment; and the patching in of processing equipment likely to be used. These preliminaries can take two or three hours.

Once mixing begins, a song is brought up on the monitors one track at a time. The drums are listened to first, followed by the rhythm section, the solo instruments, and the vocals. Work is usually done "on the fly," which means that the tracks are added as the song continues from beginning to end. Even so, it can take an experienced producer and engineer as along as one hour just to position the drums and the bass on a single song. Here's why:

Each of the individual drum tracks (with Player we used four) must be listened to alone and then in conjunction with the other drum sounds. The recording engineer will experiment with EQ so that each track has the *brightness, bottom,* clarity, and resolution desired. At the same time, the producer must decide where he wants the drums to sound on the finished record relative to the other instruments. As additional tracks are brought in, levels are fine-tuned. The kick drum is always placed dead center in the record; the left and right overhead tracks, since they contain a lot of the fundamental drum sound, usually will be spread to the extreme left and the extreme right of the stereo panorama. Generally, the snare drum is placed in the center, which creates an even balance for the overall kit. The assignment of these tracks to their place in the stereo imaging of the record is controlled by a *pan pot,* a type of fader on the recording console that acts in similar manner to the balance control on a home stereo amplifier.

73

By feeding an equal amount of signal to the left and right channels, the signal appears to be coming from the phantom center. But when more signal is channeled to one side than to the other, the position of the sound moves accordingly. The producer will sit back, listen to the mixed version of the drum tracks, and decide whether the drum balance (so far) is good. If the producer wants a dry (no reverb added), present sound, nothing more may be needed. But if the producer wants either a little or a lot more coloration or transparency on the snare drum and the overheads, he might add some reverb. After any of a half dozen different settings have been tried—after the recording engineer has double-checked and triple-checked the relationships he's established with the four drum tracks—the song will be taken to the next higher stage of completion. *Listen to side 1 on the demonstration record for further insight into balancing and equalizing the drums.*

What may seem like too much reverb on an instrument when it's soloed may actually be too little reverb in context. When monitoring at loud levels, reverb tends to be obvious, but when listening on small speakers at a modest level the effect sometimes disappears. I usually put a little reverb on the snare drum and the two overhead tracks. I prefer leaving the kick drum dry, although I always have the option of adding or subtracting reverb as the record takes shape.

I also use a limiter on the kick drum to create a more even dynamic response so that the bottom end of the record stays solid. The kickdrum, along with the bass, is the very foundation of a track and should be as consistent as possible. On the snare drum, a kepex is frequently used to cut off noise and rattle and to tighten up the overall sound of the kit.

Next, the rhythm guitars and keyboards are added. In a rock recording, the placement of these instruments in the stereo panorama usually correlates with the stage positions a group takes during a concert. See figure 18. If, for example, the keyboards face the audience on the right, the producer normally will place the keyboards so that they are heard through the right speaker of a home stereo system. Likewise, since the vocalist performs in the center of the stage, he will have a center position in the record. Although there is no general rule regarding the placement of the musical components of a group, I believe that it's best wherever possible to simulate a live feeling. Panning effects can be interesting, but I try to avoid gimmicks in favor of a solid, well-constructed stereo balance.

Bear in mind, however, that two guitars—one on either side of the drums—don't have to be placed to the extreme left and right on the finished master. They can be placed to sound as though they were either both on the left or both on the right. I will move an instrument, for purposes of mixing, if the record would otherwise sound left-heavy or right-heavy.

The producer also might want an instrument to sound as though it were

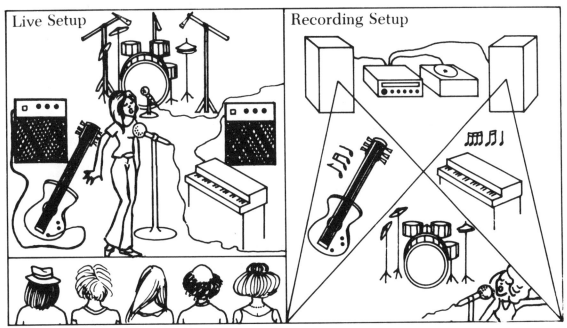

FIGURE 18. Parallel imaging (live performance
to assignment in the stereo panorama).

being played on one side with the echo spilling out onto the other side of the
stereo panorama. To create such an echo effect would require instrumental
placements that the artists would not normally assume during a concert. I am
usually very cooperative with groups, such as Santana, who want their albums to
sound live. But if a production value is more important than simulation of a live
performance, I'll lean toward improving the record.

Solo instruments that are doubled are usually assigned left and right placements
in the stereo imaging, although lead vocals and guitar solos are more often in the
center. Any instruments such as strings or percussion that were recorded in stereo
will be assigned parallel left and right placements in the master recording. The bass is
almost always placed in a center position in a mix relationship with the kick drum.
*Listen to sides 1 and 2 on the demonstration record for further insight into mixing
rhythm and solo instrumental tracks.*
Next to the art of recording a good vocal, the mixing of vocals may seem to be
child's play. Here, as an example, is how I mixed the lead vocal in "Rhinestone
Cowboy," sung by Glen Campbell:
1. After listening to the vocal track, which was recorded close to *flat*, I felt
that Glen Campbell's voice sounded a little too husky in the low end. I compen-

sated by having the recording engineer, Joe Sidore, *roll off* a little of the bottom in the vocal frequency range. This produced a slightly smaller, narrower sound, but it fit into the track as a whole much better.

2. We used an EMT chamber for reverb and adjusted it for what we felt was the right *decay* time for the performance.

3. We added a little limiting to minimize the dynamics, create a smoother performance, and eliminate having constantly to *ride the vocal*, or work the fader up and down.

4. Both tracks of Glen's voice were panned to the center of the stereo image.

5. We satisfied ourselves that the relationship between the lead vocal tracks and the tracks already mixed was technically and aesthetically acceptable. Then we proceeded to bring up the remaining few tracks so that we could record the two-track finished master.

This methodical process may strike some readers as being rather perfunctory. But in reality, mixing is very much like performing. It is an intense emotional experience that requires the producer and engineer to be ever vigilant and inspired. Successful producers very rarely keep notes. We feel a record in our blood, and if we go home at night with work unfinished, we know in our hearts that the next day, starting from scratch, we can mix the same record better. We won't *zero the console*, which is returning all controls to off, unless we have to. This can save lots of time the next day.

As I noted previously, the star of the record, the lead vocal, receives center placement in the stereo panorama. Depending on the concept you're after, the backup vocals are also usually placed in the center. However, if the backup vocals are double-tracked, it's quite common for them to be placed either to the extreme left and right or to left of center and right of center if the producer wants a less dispersed sound. *Listen to sides 1 and 2 on the demonstration record for further insight into mixing lead and backup vocals.*

It's important to have the song pretty well laid out before deciding where to place the percussion and synthesizer tracks. If the percussion is rhythm oriented (e.g., involving tambourine, bongos, and congas), I'll usually deal with it earlier. But if the percussion is melodically oriented (e.g., involving vibraphone, bells, or chimes), I find that it's one of the last things I factor into the finished tape.

Similarly, synthesizers are introduced into the mix in keeping with their function. Solos might be listened to, equalized, and balanced early. Stringlike synthesizer passages might be saved for evaluation nearer the end of the mix. Having recorded each track during the layering process, you become quite familiar with what's on tape. Then it's simply a question of what works best for you during mixing, as opposed to what some other producer might do. Again, there are no hard-and-fast rules applicable to mixing.

If instead of a rock and roll album I were mixing a disco record, I would shoot for a very dry, super-punchy rhythm sound. This can be achieved by using little or no reverb on the drums and by using either a compressor or limiter on the bass and kick drum. Percussion would also be featured, but here I might use some reverb and delay effects. I would also boost a lot of extreme high and low frequencies to make this characteristic disco sound very pronounced. This mixing technique was used with great success in one of the earlier disco hits, "It Only Takes a Minute," which my partner and I wrote and produced for Tavares.

There are times during mixing and recording when the *variable speed oscillator* (*VSO*) and the preset running speeds, such as fifteen, thirty, and sixty inches per second (ips), can be used to create a special effect. During the recording of "Rhinestone Cowboy," for example, we felt that an unusual drumlike sound was needed to strengthen the tom-tom fills. We scheduled a percussion overdub session in order to record a set of timbales—not at 30 ips, which is our normal recording speed, but at 60 ips. When the overdub was completed, we played the tape back at 30 ips and the timbales sounded like the deepest tom-toms you ever heard. This created a very imposing sound, which was exactly what we wanted. (Of course, the musician had to play at double speed, which can get a little tricky. But if you plan in advance, any such special procedure usually works out fine.)

The opposite side of this coin is for an instrument to be recorded at half speed and then played back at normal speed during the mixing of the master tape. We used this technique quite effectively on Santana's album *Inner Secrets* to create a tinkling effect at what appeared to be breakneck speed during a performance of rolling arpeggios. If a performance sounds impossible to play, it probably is: with selectable speed control, the producer can create the impression that chipmunks are singing or that instruments from outer space have landed.

The variable speed control on a tape machine also comes in handy when a lead singer wants to raise or lower a key slightly when he overdubs a performance. The secret here is to monitor carefully how the vocal sounds played back at normal speed. If the sound of the voice is too severely affected, use less pitch change. I don't normally go beyond a quarter tone for the voice. The VSO also enables you to "tune" the tape machine to a particular instrument that is slightly out of tune.

REMIXING

After many hours in the control room, the producer will achieve what he thinks is a satisfying mix of the songs on an album. What should happen next is precisely what did happen on my recording sessions with Santana. Several copies of each song were forwarded to Devadip Carlos Santana so that he could listen to the material and solicit opinions concerning the tapes from other key Santana personnel. About a week later, I received a very well thought out critique of the overall production, with specific suggestions on which songs needed more work.

Then, as a gesture of friendship as well as a demonstration of his concern for the album, Devadip Carlos Santana came to Los Angeles to be with us during the last few days of mixing. My partner and I and our engineer, Matt Hyde, continued to work by ourselves in the control room, but we analyzed each new mix with Devadip at night. The final remixed tapes (actually, there were very few revisions) met with everybody's complete acceptance.

Just as writing is essentially rewriting, the essence of mixing is remixing. There is nothing wrong with having to do a mix over again if either the producer or the artist feels it can be done better. I think it's extremely important for the producer to live with the tapes for several days at home: to relax with them, to evaluate them, to be critical of them, and perhaps most crucial, to be moved by them. Sometimes what you think is right is wrong. At other times, what you felt was wrong turned out to be right. An example follows:

All through the mixing of "Baby Come Back," the hit single from Player's debut album included as a demonstration in this book, Jay Lewis, our engineer, my partner, and I were bothered by the feeling that we weren't giving the record a big enough sound. This feeling was confirmed when we took the tapes home and lived with them for several days. But when we went back into the studio and remixed the song, giving it a much *wetter* sound than it previously had, we were amazed to find that the original mix was far better. It had the punch and the clarity we wanted, with none of the negative side effects that too much reverb (which tends to take the up-frontness away from the sound of an instrument) sometimes creates. We wouldn't have known that the first mix was right, though, if we hadn't gone to the trouble of remixing "Baby Come Back."

The final step in mixing, after the two-track master tape has been recorded for each song, is for the producer and engineer to assemble the songs in a sequence that will become the finished album. Occasionally this requires transferring the separate song reels onto an oversized, twelve- or fourteen-inch reel, which will become one complete side of a long-playing record. Assembling is actually a form of editing, but I recommend going through the assembly stage before undertaking additional editing.

The spacing between *cuts*, or individual performances, can be created by using either white paper leader tape or blank tape. I have always preferred blank tape because it doesn't put a bump (or noise) on the tape the way leader usually does. The bump is insignificant in level, however, and the paper leader makes for easy identification of each song on the reel. Again, it's a matter of individual preference whether to use white leader tape or to have your transitions from song to song be totally silent.

EDITING

The ultimate phase of record production, editing, involves two seemingly contradictory processes. The first is one of excising fat from the song, such as unnecessary opening or closing passages and development or bridge sections that are too long. As a rule, a separate singles version is required for each song on the album intended for the singles (45 rpm) market if in the opinion of the producer the singles version should be shorter. Note, however, that with the growing popularity of disco singles, there is now a reason to edit cuts so that they are *longer* than normal!

The second aspect of editing, like mixing, is to combine material, though in this case it's not tracks that will be combined—it's the songs themselves. I make this point because just as in mixing there is remixing, so in the assembly, or sequencing, of an album there is resequencing. After living with the tapes for a few days, the producer undoubtedly will make changes in the order of songs. It's a good idea to present your best work up front (side 1, first three bands) since radio programmers and industry opinion makers are deluged with new product and often listen to only a few cuts on side 1 before going on to the next LP. At the same time, the producer must remember that the public is going to want a fluid, entertaining show for their record dollars. Mood, tempo, key signature, and song duration should always have a bearing on how you ultimately decide to sequence your album.

Listen to side 2 on the demonstration record to hear excerpts of the final edited version of "Baby Come Back," by Player. Remember that the excising of material is strictly a matter of aesthetic preference. After several days of listening to the completed two-track album tape, and after several days of evaluating the edited two-track singles versions, the producer should be able to call the record company and say, "My work on this production is finished."

I have attempted in this chapter to show what typically goes on during the mixing, remixing, and editing stages of record production. I have deliberately avoided being too technical since every production requires its own careful analysis by the engineer and the producer and there is no such thing as a uniform EQ setting, reverb level, or mixing chronology. As with any art form, it's easy to rap about mixing but very difficult to say, "This is precisely how you do it." Becoming expert at mixing and editing takes years of hands-on and ears-open recording experience.

7
Presenting the Product
to a Record Company

Before a record company can consider either a master tape or a demo for eventual release, the producer must deliver to the company other materials relating to the production. This chapter discusses what those materials might be in each of three categories: producers already signed to a contract; producers submitting master tapes on spec; and beginning producers presenting demonstration tapes for review.

FIRST CATEGORY—PRODUCERS ALREADY SIGNED TO A CONTRACT

As discussed in chapter 6, the taped materials needed to satisfy most record contracts are one two-track stereo master tape, formatted for sides 1 and 2 of a single long-playing album; and edited versions (usually shorter in length, unless they are disco singles) of the performances on that album deemed to be potential hit singles. Most independent record producers and practically all custom label owners will be required to submit the following items in addition to these taped materials:

- letters of consent (i.e., written authorizations) that will allow the record company to feature the names and/or photographs of artists under contract to other labels on the album jacket and/or inner sleeve;
- a technical credit sheet;
- a copy of the lyrics of each song recorded on the two-track master tape; and
- any photographs, logos, or line drawings the artist or producer wishes to include on the album and/or inner sleeve (subject to record company approval).

80

Technical Credit Sheet

Artist _____

LP _____

Single _____

Produced by _____

Arranged and conducted by° _____

Engineered by _____

      Recording _____

      Remix _____

Recorded at _____

Mastered at _____

      By _____

Production coordinator _____

Personal management _____

Exclusive booking agency _____

Special thanks to _____

_____

_____

Miscellaneous remarks _____

_____

_____

_____

_____

°See individual tunes if more than one (1) arranger.

This shopping list of materials is the record company's insurance that the product they release won't get it or anyone else into trouble. Authorizations to use the names and/or photographs of artists will prevent the record company from being sued subsequently either for violating a person's right to privacy or for infringing upon another company's exclusive rights in a recording artist. The technical credits are a nice way to say thanks on the album to the people responsible for both the success of the artist and the sound quality of the record. The lyric sheets will be reviewed to see whether there is a need to print them on the inner sleeve. Usually the record company will agree to include a lyric sheet with the album if the artist or producer so requests.

At about the same time the record company will begin laying out an album cover, which includes selecting photographs, designing graphics, setting type, writing copy perhaps, and assembling credits for the label and jacket. The producer will receive company authorization to begin a process called *mastering*. Not too many years ago this was considered a routine record company function. But today, in an effort to follow through from the rehearsal of an album to the hanging of a platinum record award on his wall, the producer is well advised to play an active supervisory role in the mastering of the record.

The mastering procedure involves two steps: (1) equalizing the two-track tape to maximize the impact of the material; and (2) transferring the material from the two-track tape to disc form.

In step 1, the finished two-track master tape is brought up through a console and evaluated by the producer and the mastering engineer. Since the acoustical environment of the mastering room is well known to the engineer, he can immediately detect any deficiencies or exaggerations in particular frequency ranges that need boosting or attenuating. Overall levels are adjusted, and further fine-tuning takes place. On the Glen Campbell album, *Rhinestone Cowboy,* for example, each band of the LP was played and adjustments were noted on a master sheet with specific reference to EQ, limiting, levels, etc. On one song we boosted the extreme low frequency to add a fuller bottom; we boosted the mid-range to brighten the vocals and make them seem to *pop* a little better; and we attenuated (or lowered) the high frequencies to help pull back some overbright cymbals on the drums. After step 1 was completed for each song, we moved on to step 2.

In step 2, a reference disc, or *acetate*, is cut. The acetate is made of a vinyl substance not unlike the material used in the records we play at home. All of the refinements to the sound are incorporated in this disc, which the producer then takes home to evaluate on his stereo system. When the producer gives his approval, the record company will order the cutting of finished masters, or *lacquers*, which will be shipped to the various record pressing facilities so that mass quantities of product can be made.

It is customary in the record business for the manufacturer to pay for the mastering, plating, and stamping of test and finished records. Some companies, however, may charge the cost of producing lacquers and acetates to the artist's and producer's royalty accounts. Although the costs represented by mastering time and the making of lacquers and acetates may seem to be nominal compared to studio recording and mixing expenses, I think it is appropriate for the record company to absorb the former 100 percent. This is a small but nevertheless important point to discuss during the negotiation of a production contract with a major record company.

The ultimate quality control juncture in the manufacturing stage of record production is when the records are actually being pressed. I have been involved with records that would have been stamped out dirty—with an excessive amount of dust and debris on the metal plates—if I hadn't gone to the trouble of carefully evaluating test pressings from each plant. This dirt will become the ticks, pops, and other extraneous noises you fought so hard during recording to eliminate. It's *your* sound, after all, that's going to be released to the public, so it is in 'the best interests of the producer to see that the quality of the sound, from beginning to end of the production process, is all that it should be.

Another postrecording concern of the producer or the custom label owner is the delivery date of the product. Although most recording contracts will not pin the producer and the artist to a specific delivery date, there is usually some understanding that the materials necessary to release an album will be delivered to the record company within a certain period of time: maybe three months from the commencement of the recording project; ninety days prior to the end of a calendar year; or sixty days prior to the album's scheduled commercial release.

Nothing causes more consternation at a record company than an eagerly awaited project that is delivered weeks, months, or sometimes even years behind schedule. The reasons for late delivery are diverse: the artist may have become ill; the artist may have gotten involved in a motion picture or in a television series; a force majeure, such as an act of God or a civil disturbance, may have interrupted the recording sessions; the original group may have broken up and new members may have had to be found; or some of the songs scheduled for the album may not have been approved by the producer or the record company's A&R department. In many situations, however, the producer or the group itself contributes to delaying the delivery of an album.

Certainly the album must be satisfactory to the producer before it is submitted. But some producers spend much more time (and money) during the mixing and remixing phase of production than is necessary. This is to remind you that producers are not judged *solely* on the merits of the finished tape. If they can't deliver a complete package of edited tapes and accompanying materials, and if they can't deliver the product within a reasonable period of time, their prospects for a continued association with a particular record company are not good.

SECOND CATEGORY—PRODUCERS SUBMITTING MASTER TAPES ON SPEC

Although I don't recommend this approach unless all else has failed, I would suggest presenting this package of materials along with the two-track master tape:

- several edited singles if the master tape is for an album;
- a technical credit sheet;
- a reel-to-reel and two cassette copies of the master tape so that the A&R executives have the option of listening to the production either in the office or on the road; and
- a photograph of the artist.

It is not necessary to present the company with master discs, acetates, or *parts*. Also, it is not necessary at the outset to furnish the company with a copy of the exclusive production agreement (though there should be one) between the producer and the artist. What counts at the beginning is for the A&R executives to like the tape.

It is true, to a certain extent, that A&R executives take master tapes ·more seriously than they do demos. For the most part, masters are a badge of professionalism. They can facilitate live exchanges among the producer, the artist, and the A&R executive. I would be reluctant, therefore, just to drop off a master tape at a record company. Something would be very wrong if the producer, who has gone to the considerable expense of producing a master, couldn't use that device to schedule a meeting with an A&R person and have the tape evaluated—preferably during the meeting. Bear in mind, however, that most A&R personnel will want to do their serious listening on their own time and in their own inimitable fashion. They may agree to meet with you as a courtesy, but until they've lived with the tape for up to a week, it would be unfair to castigate A&R representatives for failing to give you an answer.

It does happen sometimes that an A&R executive, after listening to a master tape, will want to sign the producer and the artist. What happens with far less frequency is that the A&R executive evaluates the tape and concludes, "This is truly a finished master tape. I wouldn't change a note, nor would I change a production value. We'll manufacture it as is."

If the record company is impressed with the producer and the artist but wants a new master tape produced from scratch, the producer may have to eat his out-of-pocket costs for producing the unusable master. Very few record companies are willing to pay for the expense of an unusable master (especially if it cost between $5,000 and $10,000 to produce), over and above what the company will offer the producer for each side or single performance he produces under contract. I repeat: only the very wealthy or the very desperate should take this gamble for getting a production deal with a record manufacturer.

THIRD CATEGORY—BEGINNING PRODUCERS
PRESENTING DEMONSTRATION TAPES FOR REVIEW

Unless the producer has access to multitrack professional or home recording equipment (see appendix B), the demo should feature the song and lead vocal, with little attention paid to production values. It should be packaged as follows:

- Include a copy of the lyrics for each song on the demo.
- There should be no more than four songs on the demo.
- The demo should be submitted in two formats: reel-to-reel, for the office, and cassette, for listening at home and/or in the car.
- Use leader tape on the reel-to-reel demo so that the A&R executive can fast-forward the tape to the beginning of each new song.
- The demo should be labeled (both the package and the reel or cassette itself) with the name of the artist; the name, address, and telephone number of the producer; and the titles and timings of each song.
- The lyrics should be pasted to the reel-to-reel tape box so that they're not misplaced. If there are a lot of lyrics, the lyric sheets should be reduced at a photocopying center prior to attaching them to the inside front and back of the tape box.
- A photograph and biography of the artist, along with pertinent press clippings, adds a nice finishing touch to the demo package.

There are several ways to present demo tapes to A&R executives. The worst way is to send them through the mail as unsolicited material. If no one at the other end is aware that a tape is being mailed to them, the tapes will be considered junk mail at most leading record companies and will be either thrown out or returned unopened.

The more sensible approach to take with demos is for the producer to call his shots. This means that the producer should contact a record company's A&R department; find out whether the company is interested in listening to new artists and new producers (most companies are); and to whom the demo tape should be addressed. If I were the producer, and I had just been furnished with the name and telephone number of the A&R executive in charge of evaluating demos, I would ask to be connected immediately with that person's office to alert people there that I would be sending my tape shortly. Then I'd wait a week to ten days and telephone the A&R executive to see whether my tape had been evaluated.

Persistence and courtesy eventually will be rewarded with serious evaluations of the producer's demos. If you are nice, and you come back again and again to a particular company (each time, I hope, with a better piece of product), your ambition and your love for music will make a positive impression. If the A&R executive doesn't like a particular demo, the producer shouldn't get upset. Instead, he should ask the A&R executive why he didn't like the tape. These can be valuable learning experiences provided you understand how to take constructive criticism and put things in perspective. It is a plus, for instance, even to be in the same room with an A&R executive; the fact that he passed may be unfortunate, but the fact that you made a connection—not just today but for the future—should be viewed as an important achievement.

One more comment on submitting material to record companies. Much to my surprise, it took almost six months to find a home for Player, a group whose first album sold 750,000 units and contained a number one single and a top ten single. Just because a person is in A&R doesn't mean that he or she can consistently identify potential hit songs or artists. Even for major league producers, it is a constant struggle to get new artists placed. But if you really believe you've got a hit, somehow or other you will find a way.

8
Understanding
Production Deals

The crystallization in writing of any business arrangement is generally referred to as a contract. Although it's a mistake in most cases for a producer to negotiate his own contract, it is extremely important for the producer to have a real grasp of contract terminology and the framework for making a deal. In this chapter, I'll offer some general advice on how to cope with, frame, and negotiate various forms of production deals.

MUSIC BUSINESS LAWYERS ARE INDISPENSABLE

In my experience—and I've had an excellent relationship with my own attorney for more than ten years—the need for a lawyer to represent the producer is great. Besides being a master of the technical language of contracts, a good music business lawyer can be a valuable advisor and friend to the producer. Lawyers are aware of new developments in the business and are constantly speaking to other lawyers whose clients may be interested in what the producer is doing. I have found that music business lawyers can be extremely effective business finders for producers, especially if the lawyer has a flair for music and matchmaking.

Finding the attorney who's right for you may take time, but it's important to make the right decision. If you don't know any music business lawyers, ask professional people in the industry for references. Meet with different lawyers, if you can, and base your selection on the attitude of the lawyer; how busy he is with other clients; how interested he is in helping develop your career; and whether he is willing to play ball with you with reference to legal fees. Believe it or not, many qualified music business attorneys won't charge the producer for legal services until they know the producer is able to afford them.

The value of the lawyer is inestimable during a difficult contract negotiation. If there is going to be any unpleasantness, the lawyer, not the producer, can yell at the record company. Experienced lawyers are experts at negotiating contracts, just as the producer is an expert in the recording studio. The sooner the producer realizes that there are limitations on what he can do extremely well, and that his interests would more likely be advanced through expert legal counsel, the better his chances will be for surviving and eventually for thriving in the business.

BASIC PRODUCTION AGREEMENTS

Producers who are just beginning to make waves in the record industry need to understand four basic types of production agreements:

1. *Artist signed to producer.* This preliminary agreement, if you can get it, has the artist or group of artists signed exclusively to the producer before a deal is made with a record company. It is the producer's best insurance for being able to participate in everything that subsequently happens. If the only way the record company can obtain the artist is through you, that's not a bad situation.

2. *Independent production contract.* This agreement is used when an independent record producer agrees to produce master recordings for an artist signed directly to a major record company. Currently this is the most common form of production deal. A similar contract (an exclusive production agreement) might be entered into between the record company and a staff producer employed by the company if this were the company's normal operating procedure.

3. *"All-in," or overall, production contract.* An *all-in* contract is used either when an established artist is producing himself or supplying a producer or when an established producer with an artist signed to him exclusively is able to negotiate the payment of advances and royalties encompassing both the producer and the artist under one agreement. These deals usually involve heftier royalty percentages and advances than are realized by producers and artists signed directly with the company. In some cases where the artist and the producer in an all-in agreement are not the same person, the producer's royalty may end up being quite a bit higher than it would normally be. This is because the artist is signed to the producer exclusively, and if it's a beginning artist the producer may have the leverage to make his own deal with the artist (whom the record company does not directly control) so that in the end the producer can receive, for example, somewhere in the neighborhood of 5 percent of an *overall* royalty of 12 percent of retail. Keep in mind that taking advantage of a new artist will come back to haunt you, if you're not careful, so above all be fair.

4. *Master purchase agreement.* This contract will facilitate the purchase by a record company of a master tape produced on spec by an independent record

producer. The record company would purchase the product and all rights to it and subsequently release it commercially. Usually at the company's option, they can continue with the artist and the producer, releasing other records for which royalties are paid and other obligations fulfilled. In short, the agreement says, "If things work out, we all go forward. If they don't, we go our separate ways."

For reference purposes, appendix E contains a blank form of an independent production contract and appendix F contains a blank form of a letter of intent between an artist and a producer, which although it's not a full-blown thirty-page contract will bind the artist exclusively to the producer during the search for a record company. I am now going to review the most important general articles relating to these contracts, but I do want to stress that this information is only general and that it is intended to establish merely the parameters of what is commonly negotiated among artists, producers, and record companies.

Each contract you receive poses a different set of facts and a different combination of words. The agreement should be read in its entirety not just by the producer but also by a highly qualified music business attorney. Nevertheless, there are many areas of similarity in the various forms of production contracts, as we'll see in a moment.

CONTRACT DURATION

The term, or length, of the agreement between the record company and the independent record producer really depends on whether an artist is locked into the deal or whether the producer is an established producer. If it's an overall artist-producer contract, the standard practice over the last fifteen years of my experience has been for the company to sign the artist and producer to a minimum term of one year, with either three or four consecutive one-year options that can be exercised by some form of notice (or lack of notice, depending on the contract) in writing.

The reason for the fairly long-term relationship has to do with economics. Today a major record company will spend on the average as much as $250,000 just to produce an artist's first album, manufacture the product, and promote it in the marketplace. With that kind of money involved, and with the often slow public response to new artists and their first few releases, it's no surprise that the record company wants to retain the services of the artist and the producer for a sufficiently long period of time to recoup its major up-front investment. Of course, if the producer's albums aren't selling, the company may decide not to exercise a renewal option, leaving the artist and the producer free to sign with another company.

Similarly, if the producer has a good track record the company may wish to offer a contract for perhaps two or three albums (or an equivalent number of sides) to be recorded in a one-year period by different artists, with options to extend the relationship with the producer. As a rule, the artists to be recorded would be mutually selected by the company and the producer. On the other hand, if it's an unknown producer or an unknown artist-producer combination, the company may want to limit its initial commitment to a single piece of product—let's say one or two 45 rpm singles or a long-playing album—that may already have been produced and build in to the deal subsequent options on the company's part to continue if sales warrant such a decision.

The initial term of a letter of intent between a producer and an artist signed exclusively to him is usually six months to one year. If during this time the producer does not cause a record company to extend a recording contract to the artist, it is customary for the producer to release the artist from his contract unless there are extenuating circumstances. But if the producer succeeds in obtaining a contract, the producer should have the right to exercise one-year renewal options for as many as three, four, or five years. The longest term I have ever seen binding artists to producers or producers to record companies was for a total of seven years.

MINIMUM RECORDING COMMITMENT

Every form of production agreement speaks about what the parties agree is the *minimum* number of sides or performances of individual songs that will be recorded under the contract. If you read very carefully, you will discover that the term of the contract can be extended or suspended if the producer and/or artist doesn't fulfill his minimum recording commitment on schedule. Years ago, managers and attorneys bargained for the maximum amount of product a record company would take from the artist (usually two albums per year). It was a feather in the cap of any lawyer if he got that kind of commitment. Today the trend is "less is better." Artistic careers are better served by less product on the market, protecting against saturation, and by owing less product to the record company on terms agreed upon when the artist was untested. Most contracts still include a clause or sentence that gives the record company the right to demand an additional album in each year of the agreement. Probably the best solution is for each party to compromise and to negotiate for the delivery of a number of sides that averages out to fewer than two albums per year but more than one (such as two albums over eighteen months or three albums over two years). I would also strongly recommend the producer put in for a *guaranteed release* clause, which would obligate the company to distribute the product commercially or risk losing its right to the services of both artist and producer.

RECORDING COSTS

Production contracts with major record companies state that the company will pay all arranging, copying, talent, studio, and engineering costs in the form of advances against the artist's and the producer's royalties. If, for example, the cost of a recording session is $100,000, the first $100,000 in artist and producer royalties will be retained by the record company to pay back the session costs.

As producers and artists advance in stature (and *sales*), there is a tendency for the company to be less concerned about holding them to a fixed budget, and to pay whatever it costs to get a good finished master recording, since the likelihood of recouping costs is great. Ideally, the producer should negotiate for an all-in production grant so that if he spends only three-quarters of the money allocated for the production, he and the artist can pocket the rest as an additional advance. This concept works to everyone's advantage since it gives the producer and the artist an incentive to record intelligently and it enables the company to project fairly accurately what its overall recording expenses will be by limiting its financial exposure to an agreed amount of recording costs.

ADVANCES

The record company, besides advancing recording costs, will usually agree to advance the producer (and in an exclusive artist production deal the producer will usually agree to advance the artist) an amount of money based on the producer's (or the artist's) track record. Superstar producers may receive advances against royalties in excess of $40,000 or $50,000 per album, and established artists with tremendous sales histories often are guaranteed as much as $500,000 per album and more! No one, of course, starts out at these figures. They are earned and negotiated on the basis of consistent sales in the upper stratosphere.

Today, with everyone so concerned about the skyrocketing cost of vinyl (which is made from oil) and the rather somber inflationary scenario, the record company's bargaining position with the producer is, "Show us what you can do first; then we'll discuss a big advance." Generally speaking, you will find that every reputable company will offer you the same ballpark advance, especially if you're an unknown, beginning producer. I would advise you not to be greedy about advances the first few times around. If a company offers you $5,000 or $500 a side, it might be all right to request another $1,000 overall, but it would be a mistake to ask the company to double or triple the advance. Getting some quality projects under your belt, no matter the size of the advance, should be your number one priority. Gradually, one record at a time, you can prove that it's in the company's interest to give you VIP treatment.

ROYALTIES

Royalties are based on either the wholesale or the retail price of phonograph records and tapes, less container charges. Regardless of how the royalties are computed, a beginning artist can expect to make between $.35 and $.45 an album today; a beginning independent producer can expect to make about $.15 or $.20 an album. Note that if the royalty is based on wholesale price (which is about one-half retail price), in order for it to come out to the same amount of money it will have to be *double* a royalty based on retail price. This gives merely the appearance of a higher royalty, so you really have to know whether the royalty is based on the wholesale

91

price (presently for an unknown producer it is 4 to 6 percent) or on the retail price (again presently for an unknown producer it is 2 to 3 percent) before you can begin to evaluate whether you're getting a good deal.

It is common today to negotiate higher royalties when sales of a record exceed certain levels. An overall artist-producer royalty, for example, might begin at 18 percent of the wholesale price, or 9 percent of the retail price, less container charges in both instances. The royalty might escalate to 20 percent wholesale or 10 percent retail on unit sales above 250,000 and to 22 percent wholesale or 11 percent retail on unit sales above 500,000. It is very important to point out here that the record business is a quasi-consignment business (i.e., dealers have a 20 to 100 percent return privilege on albums, singles, cartridges, and cassettes, and that product is not technically sold until it has been purchased by a consumer, as opposed to a dealer or a wholesaler, and until the record company has received payment for the product. Since the company may not be able to compute how many records shipped were actually sold for many months, the customary practice in the industry is for the company to pay the artist and the producer only a portion of their eventual royalties during the first accounting period. (The other records will be credited to the artist's and the producer's reserve accounts, which are used for *crediting* product eventually sold and *debiting* returned goods.)

It would be highly advantageous either for the producer to negotiate for the liquidation of the reserve account within a reasonable period of time or for the company to agree to a fixed percentage for reserves; in that way if the figure for reserves, for example, was 25 percent, the producer could anticipate being paid on 75 percent of the product that was actually shipped by the record company to wholesalers and dealers, less free goods to stimulate sales. In any event, it's a good idea prior to signing to familiarize yourself with the record company's general reserve policy as stated in the contract.

There are quite a few special categories of sales for which a record company may not pay the artist and the producer a full royalty. Budget record sales, for example, usually pay only one-half the normal royalty rate. Reissues, or oldies, usually pay only one-half. Product sold through record clubs usually pays only one-half, although there is a trend now for established producers and artists to negotiate 75 percent of their regular royalty rates from such sales. *Cutouts*, which are products deleted from the record company catalog and sold at salvage value, usually don't pay anything. Until recently, it was also customary for many record companies to pay royalties on the basis of 90 rather than 100 percent of records sold. This practice arose during the heyday of 78 rpm records, when breakage was a significant cost factor. Most companies will agree today to pay on 100 percent of records sold if you ask for this arrangement.

Tape sales have risen dramatically in recent years, and most companies are willing to pay the artist and the producer the full royalty rate (after deducting a somewhat higher container charge than is deducted for records) on 100 percent of tape sales. Where the U.S. record company owns or controls foreign record companies, it is often willing to pay the full 100 percent royalty; otherwise, if the product is licensed overseas, the artist and the producer can expect to receive anywhere from 50 to 75 percent of their normal royalty rates.

No royalties are paid on free goods to stimulate retail sales or on records used for promotional purposes. But in cases where a single side is licensed to a company like K-tel Records for direct consumer sales through television and key advertising outlets, the artist and the producer usually receive one-half of what the record company receives in their respective pro rata shares. For example, if the record company receives $1,000 for allowing XYZ Company to include one of your productions on its special album, the record company would keep $500 and distribute the remaining $500 to the artist and the producer in the following shares: if the artist's royalty is 7 percent of retail and the producer's is 3 percent, seven-tenths of $500, or $350, to the artist; three-tenths, or $150, to the producer. Obviously, there are special and rather complicated sections of the contract. It should be studied, evaluated, and negotiated by a qualified expert who has a very good idea of what the company will be willing to concede and what the company will consider an outrageous request by the producer and/or the artist.

PUBLISHING LICENSES

If the producer writes songs or is the publisher of the artist's music he will be entitled to receive mechanical or publishing royalties (based on sales), as stated in U.S. copyright law. Most major record companies will agree to license songs at the statutory rate of $.0275 per composition or $.005 per minute per composition, whichever amount is greater. Usually, however, companies attempt to (1) limit the total amount of royalties on one album to ten times the cost of one song (if you record twelve songs, for instance, the company will pay you for ten); (2) pay only on records sold, holding large numbers of reserves; (3) pay nothing on free goods; (4) pay one-half the otherwise applicable royalty on budget sales; and (5) pay one-half the otherwise applicable royalty on record club sales. All of these arrangements are subject to negotiation, but in light of the fact that the producer or the artist is a captive publisher, it may be difficult to bend the record company.

Producers who are just getting started may be asked to assign their songs or publishing to the record company's publishing affiliate for administration and/or co-publishing. If you grant such participation, which will require a separate publishing agreement, make sure that the dollars earned under the publishing contract can't be used to recoup session costs and advances under the recording agreement. This is known as *cross-collateralization*, and it is the bane of recording contracts in general. If you happen to be a good songwriter or publisher, you are entitled to your publishing income. It would be unfair if a company had the right to take away your publishing income in order to pay back the cost of recording an album. This is a risky

93

business, but certain risks (and the lion's share of the profits, if any are made) must be taken by the record company.

ROYALTY ACCOUNTING

The company will specify to the producer (and if the artist is signed to the producer, the producer will specify to the artist) when royalties will be paid. Record royalties are usually paid semi-annually, within ninety days after completion of the accounting periods ending June 30 and December 31. Publishing royalties are usually paid quarterly, within forty-five days after completion of each calendar quarter (March 31, June 30, etc.). The producer and the artist should have the right to audit royalty statements during normal business hours at least once for each accounting period within a reasonable time after statements have been issued. This is a very important right because even the best of companies make mistakes.

These are the main areas for contract negotiation among artists, producers, and record companies. There may be many more articles in the contract dealing with warranties, representations, indemnities, notices, definitions, assignments, and restrictions, but they are not meat and potatoes issues. They may never even be invoked if things go smoothly among the company, the producer, and the artist.

But the parties to the agreement will have a continuing need to evaluate their performance with reference to expenses and profits. As new areas for exploitation are created—posters, T-shirts, and other marketable products featuring the producer's artist or "sight and sound" videodisc or videotape recordings—they should be incorporated into the overall agreement. But the evaluation of how good a contract is should be based on the actual circumstances of an ongoing relationship, not on what you read in the trades or in textbooks or on what someone else tells you they're getting.

Too many producers today are totally unfamiliar with contracts. They should be understood by producers, but they should almost never be negotiated by producers. Generally speaking, if a company is interested in signing you, a beginning producer, to a deal, you should be very grateful for the opportunity (at *any* reasonable price) to show the world what you're capable of doing. It is so easy and so common to upgrade a deal to reflect sales performance. But it's painful to realize that many talented producers are hurting themselves because they are so ill-equipped to grasp the principles that shape contracts and to perform under them efficiently.

9
Financing a Production Deal

It is common in the record industry (though not necessarily recommended) for enterprising producers to involve private investors in financing master tapes on spec, or without a firm commitment from a record company to release the master recordings. I've had occasion to involve private investors only once, at the beginning of my career, but I am familiar with the theme and variations used for raising investment capital to produce master tapes. Here, then, are some comments and suggestions that will help you plan a successful deal with a private investor.

GENERAL CONCEPT

Speculative recording productions should be sold on the basis of their return-on-investment profit potential. Recently enacted changes in the Internal Revenue Code provide that they can no longer be sold to investors as tax shelters. The basis for the appeal to a potential investor is that the master recordings, if properly produced and released by the right record company or on a record label started for this venture, can make a fortune for everyone who owns a piece of the action, or a percentage of the master tapes. This return-on-investment concept should be the producer's guiding light in seeking investment capital.

Any person, partnership, or corporation with capital reserves and an affinity for contemporary music might invest in a master recording if the right deal came along. There are three basic elements in such a deal: (1) the artist featured in the recording; (2) the producer-entrepreneur who is going to record the artist; and (3) the deal itself. By far the most important single element is the artist. If it's not a great artist, you should forget about seeking investors until such time as you find a great artist. As is often the case, investors rarely know the state of the market; their assessment of talent will be based primarily on their lifestyle. Often you must convince the money people of the marketability of your artist (e.g., how many middle-aged business people evaluating a potential recording investment would have recognized the talents of Boston or the Cars?). Salesmanship is an important tool to use at this stage of securing an investor. If the producer has ever recorded and released product for a major label, he may encounter far less difficulty securing funds, as practical experience and a record under your belt are equated with credibility.

VARIATIONS IN DEAL FORMATION

There are many different ways that production deals can be packaged. Depending upon what kinds and how many exclusive contracts the artist or artist-composer enters into with the producer (more on this later), the following types of deals could be offered to a potential investor or syndicate of investors:

Standard Production Deal

The investor will receive a portion of the producer's earnings (advances and royalties) on the signing and release of the master recordings by a record company.

Overall Artist-Producer Production Deal

The investor will receive a portion of the producer's earnings (advances and royalties), which are based on a slightly higher or graduated royalty, since the record company is paying artist as well as production royalties to the producer, and the producer's royalty will usually be one or two percentage points higher than normal.

Overall Artist-Producer Production Deal Coupled with Music Publishing

If the producer is the publisher of the artist's songs the investor, in addition to receiving a portion of the overall artist-producer royalties, will receive a portion of the producer's portion of the artist-composer's publishing income and/or copyrights.

Overall Artist-Producer Production Deal Coupled with Music Publishing Coupled with Personal Management

If the producer is also acting as the artist's personal manager the investor, in addition to receiving a portion of the overall artist-producer royalties and a portion of publishing income, will receive a portion of the producer's management commission.

Each of these permutations (and there are many variations on these four principal themes) is based on the ability of the producer to secure various rights from the artist. It is not uncommon, however, for enterprising producers to sign unknown artist-composers to exclusive publishing contracts at the same time that the artist is signed to an exclusive production contract. It is also not uncommon, though it happens with less frequency, for producers to sign artist-composers, if they so elect, to exclusive personal management agreements. As we'll see in a moment, the greater the producer's overall participation in his artist's career, the greater his ability to present a potential investor with an attractive deal.

THE PROFESSIONAL FUND-RAISING PROCESS

The same logical progression of fund-raising steps presented here applies to all producers and to all production situations.

Step 1 is securing an exciting, marketable artist. This is easier said than done, but it needs no further explanation.

Step 2 is for the producer to sign the artist to an exclusive production contract. This can be either a letter of intent or a more formal document, but it is essential for the producer to be able to say to a potential investor, "Only I [the producer] have the right to record this artist." See appendix F for a sample letter of intent.

Step 3 is researching which investors (either individuals or a syndicate) are in the market presently to invest in master recordings. These can be wealthy friends of the producer; business executives; attorneys and accountants, acting either for themselves or on behalf of clients; successful entrepreneurs; doctors; and general music lovers. Sometimes the artist himself (or a backer he has secured) is prepared to invest in his future. But banks, credit unions, and government lending institutions will almost never agree to invest in speculative master tapes since in their view the probability of a huge return on investment is not very great. They will also claim (rightly so) to be largely ignorant of the music business. The companies and/or people you need must be very wealthy music aficionados who are able to withstand a complete loss of their speculative investment if the project goes bust.

Step 4 is designing a prospectus, or offering. This should be done on a customized basis, as each potential investor has his own set of idiosyncrasies and deal-structuring preferences. Every prospectus, however, should include a business plan, a budget, and a projection of earnings broken down into low, medium, and high ranges. For example, you will want to show the investor how much money will be made if 100,000 albums are sold; if 300,000 albums are sold; and if 500,000 albums are sold. Using the Recording Budget in chapter 3, you will be able to show how much money the master tape will cost to produce. With a little practical experience, you'll become a master at formulating concise, complete summaries of proposed ventures that can be grasped quickly by a person with a business mentality (i.e., the potential investor).

Step 5, which can take either a few hours or many months, depending on how good the artist is, is the actual selling of the prospectus to potential investors. Demo copies, as well as photographs and a biography of the artist, will have to be circulated, or live auditions will have to be held. The producer will have to spend hours each day on the telephone trying to get through to potential investors; once contact is made, and if the potential investor wishes to pursue the matter, these telephone calls must be followed up by an endless series of person-to-person meetings between the producer and the potential investor.

Step 6 is the formalization and signing of an agreement between the producer and the investor with reference to how much equity in the master recordings the investor will be entitled to and whether the investment will be treated as either an interest- or a non-interest-bearing loan. Once the agreement is signed between the investor and the producer, the producer should be able to go into the studio, produce a finished multitrack master recording, and pay the recording costs out of the investment.

Regardless of the deal, the producer should always strive to limit his personal liability under the agreement and to receive some form of immediate compensation (as opposed to waiting for a record company advance) for producing the master tapes. The most expedient way to limit personal liability is to say just that in the agreement with the investor. Alternatively, you can form a regular corporation that will technically own the rights in the master tapes. The corporation, rather than the producer, will then be responsible for repaying the investment. With reference to advanced payment for the producer, although it is true that nothing may happen with the master recording it is also true that the producer will have contributed many hundreds of hours toward the project. Any money the producer receives up front can be deducted from the first royalties the producer and the investor receive if the master recording is released and becomes a hit. It is very important for the producer to negotiate a professional fee, even if it's just a few hundred dollars, for administering the venture and producing the master tape.

The best way to present a deal is to be yourself. It's not necessary to affect a Cambridge accent or to shave every day if that's not the real you. What impresses potential investors is your personal experience, your honesty, and your understanding of the music business and recording practices. You are going to have to sound legitimate in order to get through, but it's certainly not necessary in the music business to wear Brooks Brothers suits when you're looking for money.

Instead of hyping the project, sound calm and collected. Although it's important to show the potential investor that you have confidence in yourself and your product, the proof should be "in the grooves," or in the rough demonstration tape or audition you present as exhibit A. Before you do more than simply outline the deal, give the potential investor an opportunity to evaluate the performer through a live audition or a demo tape. If the investor decides to pass, you shouldn't become hysterical. It's better to be polite, thank him for his time, and solicit constructive criticism. Some of the potential investors you go to will be very shrewd men and women. They may be able to pinpoint a flaw in your concept, businesswise or even musicwise. This is valuable information that might make the difference the next time you go to bat—

perhaps with the same person or company you once said good-bye to on a friendly basis.

STRUCTURING A DEAL

Generally speaking, the deal between a producer and an investor should be based on what each party is contributing to the venture. The producer, who is responsible for making the master, should always have at least a 50 percent interest in the royalty income. The investor's royalty participation should be keyed to both the amount of the investment and the amount of work and/or services contributed to the venture by the investor. If the investor is putting up a lot of money, he would certainly be entitled to receive anywhere from 25 to 49 percent of the royalty income. (I think it is a mistake for a producer to get involved with an investor on a fifty-fifty partnership basis unless the control remains vested in the producer.) If the investor is putting up only part of the money or a smaller amount of money and wishes to be a silent partner, his equity position might be considerably lower—perhaps between 5 and 25 percent. But in either case, most deals with outside investors stipulate that until the investment has been recouped 100 percent, the first monies received as income will be used to pay back the investor's capital outlay, including interest payments. Whether the investor will also be reimbursed for the producer's professional fee, as previously discussed, is a matter for negotiation.

Deals can be influenced by how much participation the producer is willing to give up in other areas. For example, if the producer has the right not only to produce the artist but also to publish the artist's songs and to manage the artist's career, the investor might be willing to accept a lower profit percentage on a deal involving production income as well as publishing or management income. These are referred to as "package deals." They are one of the most effective ways to stimulate investor interest and actually to clinch a deal, as the following hypothetical case illustrates:

Doug Producer, an aggressive entrepreneur-producer, signs John Q. Artist to three separate contracts: an exclusive production agreement; a publishing agreement, whereby Doug Producer receives the standard publisher's share of income, or 50 percent of the overall copyright income; and a personal management agreement. Doug Producer contacts Anthony Moneylender to see whether Moneylender would be willing to venture $55,000 to produce a master long-playing album featuring nine of John Q. Artist's songs. Anthony Moneylender listens to the tapes, sees the artist perform live, likes the music and the performance, and invites Doug Producer to make him an offer.

The first offer Doug Producer makes is for Anthony Moneylender to receive 100 percent of the production royalties earned on John Q. Artist's first long-playing album from zero to $60,000 (this will reimburse Moneylender for his initial investment plus interest) and 25 percent of the album royalties thereafter. Working on the assumption that Doug Producer will receive an independent

99

production royalty of 3 percent of the retail list price of a $7.98 LP less container charges, or approximately $.21 an album, Doug Producer projects the following results:

- If 100,000 units are sold, Anthony Moneylender will lose $39,000.
- If 300,000 units are sold, Anthony Moneylender will earn $750, besides recovering his original investment.
- If 500,000 units are sold, Anthony Moneylender will earn $11,250, besides recovering his original investment.

This arrangement is unsatisfactory to Anthony Moneylender. Doug Producer then asks whether Moneylender would invest if Doug Producer obtained an overall production deal from the record company whereby his royalty would climb, at various levels of sales, to 5 percent of the retail list price of a $7.98 LP less container charges, or approximately $.30 an album averaged. This changes the results to read:

- If 100,000 units are sold, Anthony Moneylender will lose $25,000.
- If 300,000 units are sold, Anthony Moneylender will earn $8,750, besides recovering his original investment.
- If 500,000 units are sold, Anthony Moneylender will earn $23,750, besides recovering his original investment.

Moneylender feels more comfortable with this arrangement but is still unwilling to risk $55,000. Doug Producer then asks whether Anthony Moneylender would invest if a percentage of publishing income from the nine songs recorded by John Q. Artist on the album were added to the deal. Doug Producer explains that by being the publisher of the music he is entitled to receive one-half of $.0275 as the publisher's share on each song ($.0137), or $.12 (rounded off) for the nine songs on the album. (The other $.12 goes to the songwriter, John Q. Artist.) *Because he is including publishing income, however, Doug Producer wants to reduce Anthony Moneylender's participation from 25 percent to 20 percent.* With the adjustments for publishing income and the lowering of Anthony Moneylender's percentage, this changes the results to read:

- If 100,000 units are sold, Anthony Moneylender will lose $13,000.
- If 300,000 units are sold, Anthony Moneylender will earn $14,200, besides recovering his original investment.
- If 500,000 units are sold, Anthony Moneylender will earn $31,000, besides recovering his original investment.

This arrangement is satisfactory to Anthony Moneylender, and he agrees to advance Doug Producer the money.

In this hypothetical situation, Anthony Moneylender was perfectly willing to commit for 20 percent rather than for 25 percent when the publishing income was added. Doug Producer could also have cut a deal for an even smaller overall percentage if the projected income for personal management commissions were included. But Anthony Moneylender was satisfied with the overall production deal coupled with music publishing. Doug Producer was doubly satisfied: first because Moneylender agreed to put up the money and second because he was able to lower Moneylender's profit participation by 5 percent.

This is no more than a bird's-eye look at the wheeler-dealer actions taken by ambitious producers and by investers desiring to get into the business, but it should give you a clearer understanding of how deals are parleyed and why it is so important to have as many rights in an artist as possible. Let me hasten to add that wheeling and dealing over production agreements can become very complicated. If you don't know what you're doing, you can be taken very easily. Again, get yourself a highly qualified music business lawyer to go over your plans, make suggestions, and participate in the contract negotiation from beginning to end.

Raising money to produce a master tape on spec can be a real adventure. If you've tried everything else and you still haven't been able to get through, you may have no other choice but to seek an investor. Most investors today, however, will be highly skeptical of enterprising young people seeking money for master tapes. The leading questions an intelligent investor will ask are, "Why are you coming to us with this project?" and "Why haven't you been able to get this artist recorded by a major record company?" These may be painful issues for the producer to face, but with so many record companies aggressively seeking to sign the best new artists and the best new producers they are fair questions to ask.

10
Conclusion

I have attempted in this book to give you a greater understanding of the ingredients that go into making hit records. Together we have looked at the procedure for rehearsing, budgeting, and scheduling a recording session. We've analyzed a number of helpful work sheets. We've actually produced, on paper, a finished master recording and have heard illustrations of recording technique on the enclosed demonstration record. We have defined dozens of important terms, emphasized do's and don'ts, and delivered product to the record company. We've also discussed production contracts, letters of intent, contract negotiation, financing production deals, and the role of the A&R department at a record company. In truth, we have covered a lot of territory in a short space of time. I hope I haven't gone too fast and that you've retained most of this practical information.

As long as there is a recording industry, there will be a market for gifted recording producers. Aspiring, talented producers will be in the forefront of creative changes in music. They may actually do the thinking for the artists they record. In many cases, they will do the songwriting and the arranging. They will be totally into whatever music causes them to go into a studio and put their time and energy (and sometimes their money!) on the line, on the slight chance that they'll become successful. This is how it is; this is how it's always been; and in the United States, at least, this is how it's going to be for many years to come.

I myself don't know where music is going in the next decade. By 1980, disco may have crested. By 1985, rock and roll may be only a faded memory—then again, it may have a resurgence and once more reign supreme. Whether the dominant music of the 1980s will be jazz, rhythm and blues, country, new wave, or an altogether different kind of sound is anyone's guess. Your guess may be as good as or even better than mine. But even if you guess right—and you're going to have to if you want to become a successful producer—you should be aware by now that it's going to take more than having good ears to make it. You're going to have to learn how to get along with other people. You're going to have to be patient. You're going to have to tolerate the system. The record business is a multibillion-dollar industry, and it's not going to change—certainly not for an unknown producer.

What is most intriguing about all this is the word "guess." Basically that's why record companies are willing to be so generous with successful record producers—because the producer has the ability to guess right more often than not. The problem with guessing, from the standpoint of being an author, is that you really can't teach a person how to guess. Everybody does it differently. But learning to guess right is the bedrock of becoming successful as a record producer. And in my experience, the best way to improve your odds for success is not to read voluminous treatises about guessing but to go out, work very hard, and *do* what your instincts tell you is right.

Overview information, such as contained in this book, is essential. So is hands-on recording experience, which can be obtained either for free (if you're lucky and hang around enough) or in any number of vocational engineering courses around the country. But after that, it's you, your ability, and your desire to succeed that will make the difference. You can end up being more talented than another person perhaps, but it's not going to happen if your plans are formulated solely in an armchair. So get out on the street, apply yourself as never before, be guided by the information in this book and others like it, but above all live the experience of being a record producer. Doing it that way, you just might make it.

Some readers with a leaning toward audio engineering and/or a hobbyist's interest in constructing things for the home may wish to build their own private recording studio. This appendix presents overview information on designing and equipping a home recording studio with either four- or eight-track recording equipment. Following these directions, the home studio owner should be able to record demonstration tapes and even masters of a very high, almost professional, caliber.

The whole purpose of a recording studio is to create a controlled environment wherein sound, which left to its own physical nature is basically uncontrollable, can be *predicted* to do certain things that the producer requests of it. Some studios tame sound more than others do. A *live* recording studio is one wherein sound, though controlled, is allowed to exhibit many untamed characteristics. A *dead* recording studio, which has more sound absorption than a live room, takes out much of the natural reverberation, allowing more control in the blending of individual sounds. In return, it enables each sound to have its own separate clarity and, in a sense, its own space within the room.

When close-miking techniques are used (see chapter 5), it becomes relatively easy in a dead room to isolate each instrument in a small band so that the instruments can be assigned to their own separate recording tracks. This technique, which gives the producer maximum control over how the sounds recorded will be processed, mixed, and edited, is precisely why recording studios have their special role in the music business. As producers gain experience in the studio, they tend to introduce more and more untamed, live sound characteristics into the recording environment. But for beginning producers, the preferred studio environment is one whose characteristics register somewhere in between moderately dead and very dead.

In order for a recording studio to be effective, it must be completely isolated from any extraneous sound disturbances. Here are the steps that will normally be taken to fabricate a soundproofed room-within-a-room recording studio:

    1. It is essential to find out what structural components were used in making the

producer's home and in particular the house frame. Once you know where to anchor the floor, walls, and ceiling of the studio and have carefully estimated how expensive this undertaking will be, you're ready for step 2.

2. The ideal recording studio has a hard-surface floor, no parallel walls, and a ceiling that's higher than the walls are wide. The dimensions of the room, of course, will dictate what you can and cannot do, but assuming that you have the space to build an ideal studio, it will look something like figure 19.

Studios can also be three-, five-, or seven-sided affairs if there is enough space to move several of the studio walls in from the already existing walls. The purist's reason for not having a four-walled recording environment is that it virtually eliminates any possibility that the walls facing each other will act as sound reflectors. It is much better either to deflect unwanted sound, using nonparallel surfaces, or to add more insulation to the walls, ceiling, and floor of the studio. The way this problem is gotten around by professional recording studios is through careful microphone placement and the use of portable sound-treated walls called *baffles*. This approach can be used, as well, by the home recording enthusiast.

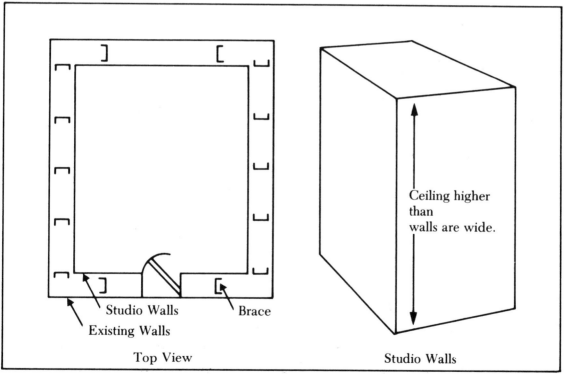

Studio Walls

Existing Walls

Brace

Top View

Ceiling higher than walls are wide.

Studio Walls

FIGURE 19. Model of a four-walled room-within-a-room recording studio.

105

3. Once the dimensions of the recording studio are known, the next step is to assemble building materials. You will need two-by-fours made of number 2 construction pine for the studio frame and half-inch-wide number 2 construction pine for the walls; sheetrock to close off the outside of the studio frame, or the side between the existing wall and the finished wall of the studio; fiberglass insulation; burlap to seal off the insulation so that it doesn't get into your eyes, nose, and throat; acoustical tile for the ceiling and/or walls of the studio, if you'd prefer using tile rather than wood; two doors—one for entering and leaving the studio and the other for the control room, which, although it's part of the studio, needs to be soundproofed from the room where the musicians play; a pane of glass, preferably thermopane, for the window of the control room; three-quarter-inch plywood for the floor of the studio; weatherstripping, caulk, and putty to seal off the room completely; stain or shellac to protect the wood (but not varnish—this would seal the pores of the wood rather than keep them open to absorb and actually to enhance the sound in the room); and a large assortment of staples, nails, anchors, bits, etc.

4. Begin building the studio by anchoring the two-by-fours in the already existing house frame. Your studio frame will be spaced at intervals of twelve, sixteen, or twenty-four inches, depending upon how your home was constructed. Staple the fiberglass insulation, which is available in matching widths, in between the two-by-fours, then install the plywood floor. There is no need to use burlap for the floor. (The reason you need burlap for the walls is that the insulation should face *into* the studio. It will be stapled to the outside of the frame, so from the inside it needs to be closed off with burlap, wood, or a combination of the two.)

Nail the wall frames into the two-by-fours anchored to the house frame, then the ceiling frame into the wall frames. At least one wall plus the ceiling should be firmly anchored to the house frame. If there is not enough room between the existing walls and the walls and ceiling of the studio for you to insulate as you go along, then you will have to use prefabrication techniques. The frame will be closed off from the outside with plaster-board. Prior to that step, you should be stapling insulation between the frames so that it faces into the studio.

5. After being anchored, the walls and/or ceiling will be finished with burlap, wood, or acoustical tile. The studio walls, in profile, should resemble figure 20. At this time, it's absolutely essential to caulk any air holes where sound might escape from the enclosed room. Use weatherstripping so that the door of the studio closes tightly. The ideal way to test whether a recording studio has been 100 percent soundproofed would be to drop it in the ocean; if it floated without leaking, you'd be in business.

6. The same building principles apply to the room-within-the-room-within-the-room; the studio control room. The dimensions of this room should be based primarily on how wide and deep the recording console, or control board, is. Frame out a ceiling-to-floor partition; insulate the partition as discussed earlier; then cut a door in the partition so that you can enter and leave the control room at will and a window so that you can see the musicians in the studio. Either side of the partition should receive a piece of thermopane rather than regular glass. The door to the control room should also be weatherstripped.

Needless to say, if at any point in this exercise you feel the services of an experienced carpenter might prove beneficial, I would strongly recommend your contacting that person!

After the studio is completed, I'd advise the producer to make several baffles and a

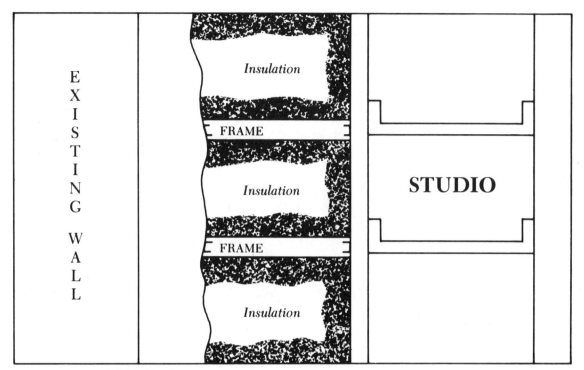

FIGURE 20. Side view of sound-treated recording studio wall.

portable platform in anticipation of actual recording situations. If everything comes out all right, you'll have a recording environment wherein, no matter what you record, you can predict what will happen when the tape recorder is running.

Now for the equipment. You can spend a relatively small amount of money on studio equipment, or you can spend a fortune. Even if price were no object, there are so many personal considerations involved in choosing equipment—such as whether the equipment is available in your area, how reliable it is, how much power it needs to be driven, how easily it can be repaired, how much it weighs, and how the controls are laid out—that it would be foolish for me to do anything other than suggest what I would put into my home recording studio if I built one.

Much of the equipment listed here is explained in detail in chapter 4. I am under no compulsion to recommend one brand of equipment over another brand. I'm merely presenting this information (prices subject to change) to indicate what I would be shopping for if I had to equip my own demo recording studio.

Mixing Console and Submixer
(1) Sound Workshop Model 1280-B Mixing Board
   (12 inputs, 8 outputs, known as 12×8) $3,000.00
(1) Teac TASCAM Model I Submixer (8×2)   148.50

Tape Machines
(1) Teac TASCAM Model 80-8, ½″ 8 Track Tape Machine   3,307.50
(1) dbx DX-8 Noise Reduction (designed for use with Teac 80-8)   1,190.00
(1) Teac Model 3300SX2T, Stereo ¼″ ½ Track Tape Machine   917.00
(1) Teac Model 2300SX, Stereo ¼″ ¼ Track Tape Machine   660.00

Signal Processing Equipment
(2) dbx 161, Compressor/Limiter with Rack Ears (at $305 each)   610.00
(1) Orban Parasound Model 111B, Reverb Unit   749.00

Microphones
(1) Shure SM 56   138.00
(1) Shure SM 57   100.00
(1) Shure SM 58   138.00
(1) Sennheiser Model ME 20, Omnidirectional Head   64.00
(3) SesCom Model SMIA, Direct Box (at $48.75 each)   146.25

Amplifier and Speakers
(1) BGW 250-D, to power the Monitors   659.00
(1) BGW 100-B, to power the Cue System   439.00
(2) JBL 4313 Studio Monitors (at $340 each)   680.00
(2) Hemispheres (loudspeakers)   400.00

Miscellaneous Cabinets and Cords
(1) Soundolier Model 400-24, Equipment Rack   81.00
(1) Cable Harness (price includes labor and installation)   100.00
(4) Beyer Model St210/2, Microphone Stands and Booms   216.00
(6) 25′ Microphone Cables (at $12 each)   72.00

TOTAL $13,615.25

APPENDIX B:
Demo Recording Techniques

An entire book could easily be devoted to recording techniques recommended for semiprofessional home studios. But a careful study of the twenty-four-track recording procedures that are outlined in chapters 4 and 5 will be of great value to you when working in demo studios.

The only significant differences are in the limitations of some of the equipment, and these can be satisfactorily gotten around if you carefully plan what you are going to do and how you can best achieve high quality tapes.

A somewhat typical home recording studio was laid out in appendix A. With that equipment at your fingertips, talent and imagination can have a field day. Most home studios are built with the one-man band concept. That is to say, the majority of the recording will be done one instrument at a time. Where this approach is followed, the size of the studio can be substantially smaller and the need for microphones, mike stands, cables, etc., is greatly reduced. One or two of each at most would suffice.

Also, the control room and the studio itself become one and the same. This setup enables the solo producer-musician-engineer to function efficiently with all the gear right there in front of him. If your intention is to record an entire band simultaneously, you would be well advised to construct a more elaborate studio that includes a separate control room (as described in appendix A) and equip it for that purpose.

There is no substitute for hands-on experience in the home demo studio. Functioning as musician, producer, and engineer, you cannot help but learn every time you attempt to make a new recording. Unlike twenty-four-track state-of-the-art studios, home studios demand more of your ingenuity by virtue of the equipment's humbler characteristics. Building tracks to a record's ultimate completion is more difficult when there are only four or eight tracks to work with, and getting good sounds from microphones that cost $100 (not $800) are some of the challenges you must face and overcome.

109

In this chapter, I will attempt to clarify what can and should be done when working with semiprofessional equipment to get good sounds without spending $150 to $250 per hour in a downtown recording studio.

PRIOR TO RECORDING

A good habit to get into after doing work in a studio is to zero all the equipment: undo the patch bay assignments, return all knobs on the console to the off position, realign the pan controls, etc. You'll appreciate this the next time you come to use the equipment, as will your fellow engineer if you share the studio. Cleaning the tape recorders should also be an automatic procedure. Even the tiniest speck of dirt or oxide on the heads can cause considerable sound dropout and loss of frequency response. Checking on the alignment of the tape machines, make the necessary adjustments. If you record at one speed all the time (I recommend 15 ips), you'll probably find that nothing has changed from your last session. Once the above steps are completed, you are ready to roll.

SIMPLE SINGLE INSTRUMENT DEMOS

If you're making a demonstration tape of a vocalist-musician, it might be unnecessary to record the piano track, the guitar track, and/or the vocal track separately. There is often a certain blending or feeling that an artist gets when he plays and sings at the same time. In the case of a piano and vocal demo, a baffle separating the sounding board where the microphones are placed from the singer's microphone would be helpful. Although it's difficult to eliminate all leakage, controlling this problem as best you can will improve your recording.

Close-miking an acoustic guitar and getting a good strong signal on tape without creating distortion will also enable you to record the voice without too many serious leakage problems. As you will come to find out with experience, leakage can work to enhance the overall sound of a recording by introducing a liveness not present when each track is recorded separately. Simultaneously recording the vocal requires a little extra careful monitoring, and it may take several rehearsals before you learn the moves of the singer—i.e., where the dynamics of a performance need some help from you at the fader controls. Of course, limiting helps solve the problem of inconsistent levels, but not if the singer has little concept of microphone technique. Quite often, new artists who lack studio experience must be positioned and guided as to how to work the mike for best results.

As a general rule, the less you have to concentrate on and record at once, the better the result will be. Where possible, record the guitar or piano track first, then the vocal.

MULTITRACK OPTIONS

Before you begin recording the first note of music, you must plan—and I stress *plan carefully*—how you are going to use the available eight tracks (if there are only four, you've got your work cut out). Even with twenty-four tracks at my disposal, I seem to be forever running out of room. I suppose in this era of separation recording, we're conditioned to do things in a certain fashion—to achieve the ultimate option of isolation every step of the way. With a very limited number of channels, this is just not possible, but good sound is by all means achievable. There are bound to be several musical relationships that must be locked in and combinations that must be arrived at early on, but in the end, it's all going to two tracks anyway!

With the exception of the guitar, all electric instruments should be recorded direct. The sound tends to be clean, unaffected by amplifier distortion of any kind. The electric guitar and its amplifier have taken on an ever increasing importance in contemporary music, and as a result the sound is often the coloration that the amp achieves. When this is the case, I recommend an overdub of the guitar. On some recordings, it will be possible to record the guitar with the rest of the band if the levels are kept within reason and baffles are used to help isolate the sound source.

Acoustic instruments (piano, drums, guitar, the voice, etc.) will of course have to be recorded via microphone. As discussed earlier, different microphones have distinct advantages and disadvantages. When we talk about microphones, we frequently hear "to each his own." I couldn't agree more. I have found my own taste constantly changing as I experiment with different mikes in similar applications. I believe what sounds good is good. If you try a particular mike and you like what you hear, use it.

TRACK ASSIGNMENT

Let's assume that we are going to do a demo session that requires the following instruments:
1. drums
2. electric bass
3. electric guitar
4. piano (acoustic)
5. electric piano

Say that we also plan to add a lead singer and some background vocals. What appears to be a simple matter of arithmetic (five instruments, one lead singer, one background group = seven tracks) presents in actuality some rather difficult problems to solve. It is true that we have eight tracks to work with and seem to need only seven; however, we are no longer living in a *mono* world, and it would be infinitely better to record some of the instruments in stereo. Another possibility to consider is the doubling (or double tracking) of certain other parts, which may seem almost essential. Assuming, then, that we will record the drums and the acoustic piano in stereo and double-track the background vocal parts, we are suddenly facing the need for three additional tracks, or a total of ten. Since we have only eight available, we must work out ways to open up extra tracks.

If the session began with the recording of the drums (two tracks), bass (one track), and acoustic piano (two tracks), we would have used a total of five tracks. By combining, or ping-ponging, the drums and piano to two different tracks in a stereo balance (left and right), we would once again have five unused tracks available. Of course, the tracks that the piano and drums were originally recorded on would be erased and recorded over. Alternatively, we could record the drums (two tracks), bass (one track), electric piano (one track), and electric guitar (one track) and ping-pong as follows: the piano and guitar could be combined on one track and the bass and drums could likewise be combined, after critical balancing, to two new tracks.

Once again, there are no firm rules other than careful planning and good execution. Should you ping-pong two musical elements together and realize upon playback that the relationships could be better, you are free to try again—and again—until you are pleased with the sound. You become locked in only when you have erased the original performances and

111

sent them on to magnetic heaven. I should stress that it is very important to do several rehearsals before you combine, and once ping-ponging is accomplished you should check the results, monitoring at soft levels. Balances tend to be more critical when listened to at low volume.

Although I recommend it less, you can also consider combining a live performance with an already existing one by going to a *new* track and assigning the one already on tape to it. This maneuver often is tricky and should be avoided where possible.

A few additional tips:

1. Avoid recording instruments with a lot of high frequency information on the outside tracks (1 and 8).

2. Never ping-pong to an adjacent track (e.g., don't ping-pong track 1 and track 3 to track 2 or track 4).

3. Avoid combining vocals with instruments.

4. Never erase original performances (after ping-ponging) until you have to.

NOISE REDUCTION

If it can be afforded, noise reduction is a tremendous tool to have in a home studio. The amount of tape hiss increases with the number of tracks you have, and the inevitable combining, or ping-ponging, that takes place creates even more noise as second generation material is introduced. If any third generation tracks are unavoidably created (usually because of too much overdubbing), noise reduction is absolutely necessary. Fortunately, there are units available at a somewhat modest price from both Dolby and dbx that can greatly improve the quality of home tapes. The technical theory on which these systems function is, at best, extremely complicated, and the circuitry they contain is highly sensitive and exacting. Suffice it to say that if you can afford noise reduction, get it.

SETUPS AND MIKE PLACEMENT

As mentioned earlier, when recording a band, leakage can be best controlled by recording the applicable electric instruments direct. The cue system on the console can provide all the musicians with a headphone mix, doing away with the need, for example, of a bass amp in the room.

Care should be taken in setting up a session adequately to baffle and isolate instruments like drums and acoustic piano. Drums, although loud by nature, usually require several microphones to be properly recorded; consequently, more signal in the room finds its way to these microphones, translating to leakage. This can contribute to a mushy drum sound. Intelligent use of baffles and careful placement of the kit in the room can greatly control this potential problem. Acoustic piano is often played softly, and some drum leakage will almost always occur. The piano could have a thick blanket draped over the open lid (facing away from the drums or live guitar), or the lid could be closed, taking care properly to position and cushion the microphones inside. However, I recommend that the piano be overdubbed to avoid leakage.

Electric guitar, once again, would be best overdubbed on account of its loud amplification. If this instrument is going on the session live, a small amp positioned away from the drums and acoustic piano and baffled on both sides will help keep leakage to a minimum.

Miking close to the speaker (six inches) and using a directional pattern is standard operating procedure to keep things as clean as possible.

Vocals should be overdubbed, plain and simple, but if there is a need for a reference vocal during tracking, locate the singer in another room (assuming you don't have an isolation booth). In-the-room singing should be as soft as possible and directed squarely into the microphone set up for that purpose.

PRIOR TO MIXING

It may have become apparent along the way that keeping track of what you do (and undo) is very important. Nothing is more disconcerting than to see signals appear on the VU meters for which you have no notations on the track sheet. Professional studios usually custom print their own track sheets; you can easily design a master form and photocopy as many sheets as you will likely need. Remember, *write it* when you *do it*.

Before you approach mixing from a creative point of view, get the drab and boring details of materials preparation out of the way. Keep handy a supply of tape (one-quarter inch), masking tape (to label each track on the console), marking pens, grease pencils, etc., so that once you are into the consuming process of evaluating and carefully focusing your creative energy, you aren't searching all over the place for these little things.

When you are ready, make sure that the board is zeroed—everything switched off or brought back to flat—and check to see that the mode selectors on the tape machines are properly set. Be prepared to spend a considerable amount of time analyzing and absorbing the musical elements that are on tape. You cannot rush through this final phase of production. I have often heard it said that the record is made in the mix. Track by track, introduce the musical components, making adjustments to the EQ to correct or enhance a particular frequency range. Experiment with reverb in an attempt to create natural depth and a sense of transparency on instruments like the drums and on vocals. Monitor both soft and loud to check your reaction to any changes you've made and to reevaluate critical relationships like that between bass and drums.

Gradually, you should make progress and develop a sense of confidence and well-being. As you already know, or will soon enough learn, mixing is the total blending of all the musical elements on a tape in order to produce a finished record that sounds of a piece. Of course, there are numerous trade-offs. In other words, you can't have your cake and eat it, too! When one instrument comes up, be it through the use of EQ or through overall gain, something else *apparently* has to come down. Simply to hear more of one thing, you must hear less of something else.

With careful and creative use of EQ, reverb, and stereo placement, good mixing should come easily. The sooner you begin to flow with the arrangement, the better the moves you will make, capturing that special feeling of cohesiveness you strive for in the final mix.

Remember: Mixing is the sum of a lot of little things you do that together give the product that extra edge—the snap, the final dose of sound excitement. Whether it's helping the dynamics of a vocal, muting tracks to keep the noise level down, eliminating singers' or instrumentalists' noises that occur while they are not performing, these kinds of procedures and countless others add up to a cleaner, tighter, more professional sounding tape. Prepare to concentrate—and I mean *concentrate*—and you will consistently produce satisfying, often inspired, final mixes.

113

Appendix C
Phonograph Record
Labor Agreement *

November, 1975

Dated: New York, N. Y.

American Federation of Musicians of the
   United States and Canada
1500 Broadway
New York, N. Y. 10036

Gentlemen:

    In consideration of the mutual covenants herein contained, of the promise of the under-signed company (herein called the "Company") fully and faithfully to perform each and every term, condition, and covenant on its part to be performed pursuant to the Phonograph Record Trust Agreement (November, 1975) and to the Phonograph Record Manufacturers' Special Payments Fund Agreement (November, 1975), both of which the Company is executing and delivering simultaneously herewith, and of other good and valuable considerations, the American Federation of Musicians of the United States and Canada (herein called the "Federation") has entered into this agreement with the Company setting forth the terms and conditions, including those set forth in Exhibits A, B, and C hereto attached, pursuant to which persons covered by this agreement may be employed by the Company in the recording of phonograph records.

    1. This agreement shall cover and relate to members of the Federation wherever they shall perform, as employees, services for the Company as instrumental musicians or as leaders,

°See pp. 149-50 for phono-recording scales effective Nov. 1, 1979 to Oct. 31, 1980.

contractors, copyists, orchestrators or arrangers of instrumental music (all of whom are collectively referred to as "musicians") in the recording of phonograph records, and to any other person employed as a musician in the recording of phonograph records within the United States or Canada or a present territory or possession of either (herein called "Domestic Area"). This agreement shall also cover and relate to any resident of the Domestic Area engaged within the Domestic Area to perform such services outside the Domestic Area. It is further agreed that if a resident of the Domestic Area is engaged outside the Domestic Area to perform such services for the Company outside the Domestic Area, he shall, as a condition of employment, be and remain a member in good standing of the Federation. The Federation shall exercise full authority in order that its locals and members engaged in such activities shall do nothing in derogation of the terms and intent of this agreement.

2. The Company shall not require, request, induce, or in any manner attempt to influence any person covered by this agreement to play, or perform for recordings, or render services pertaining thereto, except as permitted by this agreement.

3. For the services rendered by the persons covered by this agreement in the making of recordings, the Company shall pay at least Federation scale as provided in Exhibit "A". The Company shall fully and faithfully perform the terms and conditions of its individual agreements with such persons. In addition, the persons covered by this agreement in the making of recordings shall be entitled to their respective portions of the musicians' share of the Fund under Exhibit "C" hereto.

4. Following the execution of this agreement, the Company shall promptly furnish to the Federation, upon request, a copy of all of the Company's record catalogs, and a schedule of its manufacturer's suggested retail prices for each record in its catalogs, and thereafter from time to time, a schedule listing all amendments and additions thereto, as and when established.

5. At the end of each month the Company shall advise the Federation of all recordings made by the Company during such month, of the serial or other number thereof, and of any additional information in connection with any such recording which the Federation may reasonably require. Upon request by the Federation, the Company shall promptly furnish to it a copy of any such recording. The Company shall respond promptly to reasonable requests by the Federation for information relating to the Company's performance of the terms and conditions of this agreement and of any and all individual agreements with persons covered by this agreement.

If the Company shall sell, assign, lease, license or otherwise transfer title to any other person, any master record (as defined in Addendum A to the Phonograph Record Manufacturers' Special Payments Fund Agreement) produced under this agreement (or its predecessors if such transaction occurs after November 1, 1975) for the purpose of allowing such other person to manufacture phonograph records for sale, the Company shall report to the Federation the name and address of each such purchaser, assignee, lessee, licensee, or transferee and shall identify the record involved. The Company shall report all such transactions monthly.

6. Except as otherwise specifically provided in Exhibit A hereto and without regard to the duration of this agreement, the Company shall not dub, re-record, or re-transcribe (herein called

"dub") any recordings containing performances by persons covered by any Phonograph Record Labor Agreement with the Federation since January 1954 and rendered during the term of any such agreements, provided that during the term of this agreement the Company may dub if it shall first give notice of its intention so to do to the Office of the President of the Federation. In the event of such dubbing the Company shall pay to all persons covered by this agreement as additional compensation for the rendition of such original performances an amount equal to the scale for such new use and shall also make any and all additional payments applicable to such new use. For the purposes of this agreement, the term "dub" shall not include the use of all of the contents of any master, matrix, mother, stamper, or similar device from which records can be produced (herein called "master record") for the production of new phonograph records (1) which in their entirety only contain the identical content of the records originally produced from such master records, and (2) which are intended to be used for the same purposes to which the records originally produced from such master record were principally devoted.

7. Persons covered by this agreement shall not make or be required to make phonograph records containing commercial advertisements, or any phonograph records to be used by or for performers as accompaniment for or in connection with their live performances. The Company shall not furnish orchestra tracks without vocals to artists or any other person.

8. The Company shall not make recordings of instrumental music, or permit the use of its facilities or otherwise give aid and asistance in recording instrumental music, for or on account of any other person, firm or corporation unless authorized in writing by the Federation, which authorization shall not unreasonably be withheld.

9. The Company agrees not to make recordings of any radio or television programs, containing the services of persons covered by Phonograph Record Labor Agreement (November, 1975), off-the-line or off-the-air, without first obtaining written permission from the Office of the President of the Federation, except that no such permission shall be necessary in instances where such recordings are (a) for reference or file purposes, or (b) for the purpose of making delayed broadcast transcriptions which have been authorized in writing by the Federation.

The Federation agrees that in all cases it will not unreasonably withhold permission to make such off-the-air or off-the-line recordings, and that in such other instances where granted, permission shall be given on payment of the phonograph record scale, and of any and all additional payments applicable to such new use. This agreement shall not in any way modify any obligation independent of this agreement which the Company may be under to obtain other individual approvals as may be necessary in connection with such off-the-line or off-the-air recordings.

10. The Company hereby recognizes the Federation as the exclusive bargaining representative of persons covered by paragraph "1" of this agreement.

11. The following provisions contained in this paragraph "11" shall apply only to recording services to be rendered hereunder in Canada where not prohibited by applicable law.

Appendix C: Phonograph Record Labor Agreement

(a) Only the services of members in good standing of the American Federation of Musicians of the United States and Canada shall be used for the performance of all instrumental music, and in the copying, orchestrating or arranging of such music, in recording phonograph records, and, in the employment of persons who are eligible for membership in the Federation, only such persons as shall be members thereof in good standing shall be so employed.

(b) As the musicians referred to or engaged under the stipulations of this contract are members of the American Federation of Musicians of the United States and Canada, nothing in this contract shall ever be construed so as to interfere with any obligation which they may owe to the American Federation of Musicians of the United States and Canada as members thereof.

(c) Any members of the American Federation of Musicians of the United States and Canada who are parties to or are affected by this contract, whose services thereunder or covered thereby, are prevented, suspended or stopped by reason of any strike, ban, unfair list, order or requirement of the Federation against any employer, shall be free to accept and engage in other employment of the same or similar character, or otherwise, for other employers or persons without any restraint, hindrance, penalty, obligation or liability whatever, any other provisions of this contract to the contrary notwithstanding.

12. The following provisions of this paragraph "12" shall apply to recording services rendered in the United States, its territories and possessions.

(a) It shall be a condition of employment that all employees of the employer covered by this labor agreement who are members of the union in good standing on the execution date of this union security agreement shall remain members in good standing and those who are not members on the execution date of this union security agreement shall on the 30th day following said execution date become and remain members in good standing in the union. It shall also be a condition of employment that all employees covered by this labor agreement and hired on or after said execution date shall on the 30th day following the beginning of such employment become and remain members in good standing in the Federation.

(b) As to the musicians referred to or engaged under the stipulations of this contract who are members of the American Federation of Musicians of the United States and Canada, and to the extent to which the inclusion and enforcement of this paragraph is not prohibited by any presently existing and valid law, nothing in this contract shall ever be construed so as to interfere with any obligation which they may owe to the American Federation of Musicians of the United States and Canada as members thereof.

(c) Any member or members of the American Federation of Musicians of the United States and Canada who are parties to or are affected by this contract, whose services thereunder or covered thereby, are prevented, suspended or stopped by reason of any lawful strike, ban, unfair list, order or requirement of the Federation against any employer, shall be free to accept and engage in other employment of the same or similar

117

character, or otherwise, for other employers or persons without any restraint, hindrance, penalty, obligation or liability whatever, any other provisions of this contract to the contrary notwithstanding.

13. (a) All present provisions of the Federation's Constitution and By-Laws are made part of this agreement to the extent to which their inclusion and enforcement are not prohibited by any applicable law. No changes therein made during the term of this agreement shall be effective to contravene any of the provisions hereof.

(b) The following provision shall be included in, and whether or not so included, shall be deemed part of all contracts calling for recording services between the Company and persons covered by this agreement:

"This contract shall not become effective unless and until it shall be approved by the International Executive Board of the American Federation of Musicians of the United States and Canada or by a duly authorized agent thereof."

14. The duly authorized representatives of the Federation and also of the local (affiliated with the Federation), upon presentation of proper identification to the Company, shall each be granted access to the studio or other place where services are being performed hereunder. Each shall be permitted to visit that place during working hours for the proper conduct of the business of the Federation or such local, respectively.

15. (a) The Company agrees that it shall furnish to the Federation, simultaneously with its delivery thereof to the Trustee and to the Administrator named in the Special Payments Fund Agreement (November, 1975) copies of any and all statements submitted to the Trustee and to the Administrator.

(b) The Company agrees that the Federation shall have the right from time to time, without limitation to the duration of this agreement, and at all reasonable times during business hours, to have the Federation's duly authorized agents examine and audit the Company's records and accounts concerning all transactions involving the Company's sale of phonograph records which it shall keep pursuant to said Trust Agreements and to said Special Payments Fund Agreements and such other records and accounts as may be necessary; such examination and audit to be made for the purpose of the Federation's verifying any statements made by the Company pursuant to said agreements, during a period not exceeding four (4) years preceding such examination, and of determining the amount of payments due by it thereunder. It is agreed that the four (4) year period provided herein shall not effect the operation of the applicable statute of limitations. The Company agrees to afford all necessary facilities to such authorized agents to make such examination and audit and to make extracts and excerpts from said records and accounts as may be necessary or proper according to approved and recognized accounting practices. Examinations and audits made pursuant hereto shall be coordinated, to the extent practicable, with examinations and audits made under the aforesaid Trust Agreements and Special Payments Fund Agreements so that inconvenience to the Company may be minimized.

16. If during the term hereof, the Federation shall enter into an agreement with any phonograph record company upon terms more favorable than or different from those contained in this agreement, the Company shall have the right at its option to cause this agreement to be conformed therewith, provided, however, that no such right shall come into being by reason of the compromise of any claim against any recording company by reason of the insolvency, bankruptcy or other financial difficulty of such company.

17. Any contract in existence at the termination of this contract (whether such termination is caused by expiration, breach or otherwise), made and entered into by the Company with local unions, persons covered by this agreement, booking agents, personal managers, recording companies, symphony associations or others, for the employment of and rendition of services by persons covered by this agreement, shall not impose any obligation to render further musical services for the Company unless this contract is renewed or a new one entered into permitting the same; in the event this contract is not renewed or a new one is not entered into, such persons covered by this agreement may, at their option, render services to any others without obligation or liability to the Company.

18. The Company shall not produce any phonograph record from recorded music acquired or taken from or licensed by any other person, firm or corporation, in the making of which there was utilized instrumental music recorded within the Domestic Area or by a person who, at the time of the recording, resided within the Domestic Area unless the music was recorded under a Phonograph Record Labor Agreement with the Federation (and the scale wages set forth therein were paid) or the musicians in the bargaining unit (including instrumentalists, leaders, contractors, copyists, orchestrators and arrangers) have been paid for such phonograph record use not less than the scale wages required under this agreement and the contribution required in Exhibit B has been made, provided however, that if such music was recorded outside the Domestic Area, no payment need be made pursuant to this paragraph if the music was acquired, taken or licensed before January 1, 1964. The Company may satisfy its obligation under this paragraph by incorporating in an agreement under which it acquires the right to use recorded music, a representation and warranty by the seller or licensor (which the Company shall guarantee if the seller or licensor was not a party to a Phonograph Record Labor Agreement with the Federation when the recording was made) that such recorded music does not come within the terms of this paragraph or that the requirements of this paragraph have been satisfied and a statement that such representation and warranty was included for the benefit of the Federation (among others) and may be enforced by the Federation or by such person or persons as it may designate. Upon request, a signed copy of such agreement shall be furnished to the Federation. No rights or privileges existing or accrued between January 1, 1959 and October 31, 1975, shall be deemed waived by reason of the provisions of this paragraph. (Numbered "17" in some prior agreements.)

19. Except as specifically provided in paragraphs 6, 8, 9 and 18, nothing contained in this agreement is intended to or shall be deemed to relate to the rendition of services or to dubbing in connection with the production of devices other than phonograph records as such devices are presently known.

20. This agreement shall be personal to the Company and shall not be transferable or assignable, by operation of law or otherwise, without written consent of the Federation.

Without such consent, the Company shall not transfer or assign any individual contract (or part thereof) for the performance of services by any person covered by this agreement or give anyone else control over such contract or such services. Nevertheless, if the foregoing is violated and services are thereafter performed by such person, the obligations and duties imposed by this agreement shall be binding upon the transferee or assignee. The obligations imposed by this agreement upon the Company, shall be binding upon the Company and upon such of it subsidiaries as are engaged in the production of phonograph records in the Domestic Area. The Federation, at its option, may terminate this agreement at any time after a transfer of any controlling interest in the Company.

21. The Company will simultaneously herewith execute and deliver the Phonograph Record Manufacturers' Special Payments Fund Agreement in the form attached hereto as Exhibit C, or in such other form or forms, with such other terms and conditions, as the Company and the Federation may hereafter and from time to time agree on, and such agreement when so modified or changed by the Company and the Federation shall be binding upon the Administrator under said Special Payments Fund Agreement and he shall execute a counterpart of such changed or modified Special Payments Fund Agreement.

22. The parties reaffirm their long established and prevailing policy and practice that every person shall have an opportunity to obtain employment without discrimination because of race, creed, color, sex, or national origin. In furtherance of such policy and practice the parties agree that in the hiring of employees for the performance of work under this Agreement neither the Company nor the Federation shall discriminate by reason of race, creed, color, sex, national origin or union or non-union membership against any person who is qualified and available to perform the work to which the employment relates.

23. This Agreement shall be effective for the period from November 1, 1975 to and including October 31, 1977.

Your signature in the space provided below will constitute this a binding agreement between you and us.

Very truly yours,

_____

Exact Legal Full Name of Company

By: _____

Signature of Company's Authorized Officer or Agent

_____

Print Name and Title of Company's Officer or Agent

_____

Company's Address

EXHIBIT A

I

MINIMUM WAGES AND OTHER WORKING CONDITIONS

INSTRUMENTALISTS, LEADERS, CONTRACTORS

Instrumentalists, leaders and contractors shall be paid not less than the rates set forth below and the conditions set forth shall apply:

A. *In the case of phonograph records other than those recorded by symphonic orchestras:*

(1) There shall be a minimum call Basic Regular Session of three hours during which there may be recorded not more than 15 minutes of recorded music; provided, however, that in a session where sweetening (i.e., instrumental performances added to music recorded at a previous session) is performed not more than 4 single record sides or 4 segments of long play or extended play records may be sweetened. Subsequent continuous regular sessions may be arranged if the musicians have been notified and consented thereto before the end of the preceding session and if there is a 30 minute rest period between the two sessions.

(2) There shall be a minimum call Special Session of 1½ hours during which there may be recorded not more than two sides containing not more than 7½ minutes of recorded music. Unless the musicians are notified when they are engaged that the call is for a Special Session, it shall be deemed to be a Regular Session. In a Special Session there may be no sweetening. The maximum overtime in a Special Session shall be ½ hour, paid for in quarter hour units, which can only be used to complete the one or two sides of the original Special Session.

(3) Overtime for Regular Sessions shall be paid for in units of one-half hour or final fraction thereof. During the one unit of overtime for a Regular Session there may be recorded or completed not more than five minutes of recorded music; provided however, that in a unit where sweetening is performed, not more than one single record side or one segment of a long play or extended play record may be sweetened.

Notwithstanding the above, overtime may be paid for in quarter hour units if such time is used only to complete the music recorded within the permissible limits of the foregoing provisions.

(4) There shall be two 10 minute rest periods during each basic Regular Session and one 10 minute rest period during each Basic Special Session. No rest period shall commence sooner than 30 minutes following the beginning of any session call provided that all musicians who are scheduled to participate in the call are present at the commencement of the call. In addition, there shall be one 5 minute rest period during each hour of overtime, it being understood that such a rest period need not be called during the first half-hour of overtime.

(5) The minimum pay, per sideman, shall be as follows:

	Basic Rate	Overtime Rate ½ Hour Unit	Overtime Rate ¼ Hour Unit
Regular Session	$110.00	$36.67	$18.34
Special Session	72.60	24.20	12.10

Note: See A (2) and (3) for overtime restrictions.

(6) *Health and Welfare Fund Contributions*
(Non-Symphonic):

The Company will contribute to any existing lawful Health and Welfare Fund of any Federation Local and commencing thirty days after notice in writing to any such lawful Fund as may be established hereafter by any other Federation Local, the sum of $3.25 for each original service on non-symphonic records performed within the jurisdiction of such Federation Local by each musician covered by this agreement.

With respect to any such original service performed within the jurisdiction of a Federation Local where no such Fund is established, the Company shall pay to each such musician said sum of $3.25.

No such Health and Welfare Fund contribution whether paid to any Fund or paid directly to a musician shall be the basis for computing the applicable AFM-EPW contribution or any other payments under this agreement such as doubling, overtime, premium time pay, etc.

(7) *Premium Rates* (Non-Symphonic):

(a) One and one-half (1½) times the basic session and overtime rates shall be paid for all hours of recording, (i) between midnight and 8:00 A. M., (ii) after 1:00 P. M. on Saturdays and (iii) on Sundays.

(b) Two times the basic session and overtime rates shall be paid for all hours of recording on any of the following holidays:

In the United States

New Year's Day	Labor Day
Washington's Birthday	Thanksgiving
Memorial Day	Christmas
Independence Day	

In Canada

New Year's Day	Dominion Day
Good Friday	Labour Day

Appendix C: Phonograph Record Labor Agreement

Easter Monday	Thanksgiving
Victoria Day	Christmas

Each of these holidays shall be observed on the day on which it is observed by employees of the United States Government or of the Government of Canada.

(c) The premium rates provided for in this paragraph numbered 7 shall not apply to show album recordings on Saturdays and Sundays nor to location recordings made on location during public performance, nor to Royalty Artists as defined in Paragraph K (f) (i) (Page 21) unless such an artist is performing in a session scheduled at the express request of the Company.

B. *In the case of phonograph records recorded by symphonic orchestras:*

(1) There shall be a minimum call Basic Session of 3 hours or 4 hours, determined in accordance with sub-paragraph (3) below, during which the playing time shall not exceed an average of 40 minutes for each hour with an average rest period of 20 minutes for each hour. The intermission shall be divided by the contractor so as not to interrupt proper recording of symphonic works subject to (4) below. The wages and working conditions for symphonic recordings are predicated upon the fact that the orchestra will have had rehearsed numbers in its repertoire and therefore will need no rehearsals for recordings.

(2) Overtime shall be paid for in units of one-half hour or final fraction thereof. During one unit of overtime, the playing time shall not exceed 20 minutes.

(3) The basic session shall be three hours unless the company by notice prior to any session elects a four-hour basic session, provided that no more than one such four-hour session may be called for any day. Unless such notice is given the session shall be deemed to be a three-hour session. No more than an average of seven and one-half minutes of finished recorded music may be made from each one-half hour segment of a recording session (including all overtime periods), and for this purpose multiple sessions devoted to the same composition shall be considered one session, so that the seven and one-half minutes of finished recorded music may be averaged out of each such session.

(4) No musician shall be required to work for more than 60 consecutive minutes without a rest period of at least 10 minutes.

(5) All members of the symphony orchestra, whether called to the engagement or not, shall be paid for at least the first two (2) hours of the basic session call $77.74 and shall not be called or required to attend if they are not scheduled to perform.

(6) The minimum pay, per sideman, for a basic session (Column A or B), for a unit of regular overtime before the completion of six (6) hours of work in any day (Column C—1½ time) and for a unit of premium overtime after the completion of six (6) hours of work in any day (Column D—double time), shall be as follows:

A	B	C	D
		½-Hour	½-Hour
"Basic	"Basic	Unit of	Unit of
Session	Session	"Regular	"Premium
Rate"	Rate"	Overtime"	Overtime"
3 Hour	4 Hour	(1½ time	(double
Session	Session	pay)	time)
$116.60	$155.46	$29.15	$38.86

(7) *Premium Rates* (Symphonic):

With respect to sessions (other than location recordings made during public performance) held between (i) midnight and 8:00 A. M.

(i) On Saturdays or Sundays if either day is a regular day off by contract or custom (which shall not be changed during the term of this agreement), or

(ii) On any of the holidays listed below, one and one-half (1½) times the basic session rate shall be paid for the first two hours, one and one-half (1½) times the regular overtime rate shall be paid in respect of the next four (4) hours and one and one-half (1½) times the premium overtime rate shall be paid in respect of all recording time in excess of six (6) hours:

In the United States

New Year's Day	Labor Day
Washington's Birthday	Thanksgiving
Memorial Day	Christmas
Independence Day	

In Canada

New Year's Day	Dominion Day
Good Friday	Labour Day
Easter Monday	Thanksgiving
Victoria Day	Christmas

Each of these holidays shall be observed on the day on which it is observed by employees of the United States Government or of the Government of Canada.

(8) *Health and Welfare Fund Contributions*
(Symphonic—"Extra Musicians")

Extra musicians, if not covered by an applicable Orchestra Health and Welfare Plan, shall be treated in accordance with the applicable provisions of I A (6) on page 12 in the case of instrumentalists, or II D on page 30 in the case of copyists.

C. *Leaders and Contractors*

The leader and contractor shall receive not less than double the applicable sideman's scale, but in any event, the scale for any one person shall not exceed double sideman's scale.

If twelve or more sidemen are employed for any session, a contractor shall be employed in respect of said session. The contractor shall be in attendance throughout the session for which he is employed. The contractor may be one of the sidemen at the session.

At each session one person shall be designated as leader but in the event only one person performs the musical service at a session, only that person can be designated as leader.

D. *Dismissal and overtime*

Musicians shall be dismissed upon completion of performances for which they have been engaged whether or not the full session has expired. Musicians may record at any time during the session for which they have been engaged.

No musician shall be required to remain longer than one-half hour overtime unless a longer time requirement was specified at the time he accepted the engagement.

E. *Advance notice of sessions and contract information*

When the company has prior knowledge of a session it will give advance notice to the appropriate Federation Local.

Where the Company employs an independent producer, the Company shall seek to include in the contract with such producer a provision which obligates such producer to notify the appropriate Federation Local in advance of recording sessions called by the producer. The Company will provide to the Federation a list of such producers who will provide to the Federation a list of such producers who do not agree to include such provision in their contracts with the Company.

If a session is called to add to existing musical tracks the Company will, at the request of the Local having jurisdiction in the area where the session is called, provide the Local with dates, places and contract numbers of prior sessions on the basis of Form B contracts in the Company's files.

The Company will notify the Federation and the appropriate Local of any change in title of a song listed on a Form B contract.

F. *Cancellation*

A session, once called, shall not be cancelled, postponed, or otherwise rescheduled less than 7 days prior to the date of the session. In the event of an emergency, a session may be cancelled, postponed or otherwise rescheduled upon shorter notice with the consent of the office of the Federation President.

G. *Doubling*

(1) When a musician plays one or more doubles during any session or during any unit of overtime or both, he shall be paid an additional 20% of the applicable session rate and the overtime related thereto for the first double and an additional 15% of such rate for each double thereafter.

(2) Instruments within the following respective groups are not construed as doubling:

(a) Piano and celeste (when furnished).

(b) Drummer's standard outfit consisting of bass drum, snare drum, cymbals, gongs, piatti, small traps, and tom toms when used as part of a standard outfit.

(c) Tympani.

(d) Mallet instruments: xylophone, vibraharp, bells and marimbas.

(e) Latin rhythm instruments: Any Latin instrument when used in less than eight bars in connection with any other instrument or used not in a rhythm pattern shall not in any event be a doubling instrument.

(3) Fretted instruments: Performance on more than two instruments within group (a) below or performance on any one instrument in group (a) together with any one instrument in group (b) below shall be treated as doubling. Performance of two or more instruments within group (b) below shall be treated as doubling:

(a) 6-String rhythm guitar
6-String electric guitar
"Combo" guitar (rhythm and electric combined)
6-String (steel) round hole guitar
6-String (nylon) classic guitar
12-String acoustic guitar
12-String electric guitar

(b) 6-String bass guitar
Tenor banjo
Plectrum
5-String banjo
Mandolin
Ukulele
Sitar

(4) Electronic devices: If an electronic device (e.g. multiplex, divider, maestro, multiplier of octaves) is used to simulate sounds of instruments in addition to the normal sound of the instrument to which such electronic device is attached or applied, such use of the electronic device shall be treated as a double.

(5) A special fee of $3 shall be paid for each additional instrument requiring a doubling fee which the musician is directed to bring to the engagement if such instrument is not actually used.

H. *Location recordings*

The Company shall give prior notice to the Office of the Federation President and to the Local of the Federation involved prior to making any recording on location during public performance. Location recording work shall be paid for at the rate of one basic session for each day of recording (from noon to the following noon). During any such day, no more than a total of three hours of performance shall be recorded. If more than fifteen minutes of recorded music is released for sale from each such three hours of recorded performance, the Company shall make additional payments equal to the regular hourly rate of pay for each additional five minutes of recorded music (or fraction thereof) released for sale. The Company agrees to send to the Office of the Federation President at the time of first release a copy of every album resulting from any such location recording.

The Company shall list the musical selections recorded at a location session from the tapes delivered to the Company by the producer and shall furnish to the Federation a copy of such list.

I. *Cartage*

The Company shall pay for actual cartage at the following rate, except that in lieu thereof the Company shall pay the submitted bills of a public carrier when any of these instruments are delivered by such carrier and such public carrier shall be used when it is the only practicable method of transportation.

Harp—$24; Accordion, String Bass, Tuba, Drums, all Amplifiers, Baritone Saxophone, Bass Saxophone, Cello, Contrabassoon, Contra Bass Clarinet—$5 each.

J. *Payment*

(1) Payment to instrumental musicians

The Company shall make the payments set forth in Exhibit A to each leader, contractor, and sideman employed at a recording session, through such agency or agencies of the Federation as may be designated from time to time by the Federation, within 15 days (excluding Saturdays, Sundays and holidays) after the date of receipt from the contractor, if any, or the leader of the recording session of a completed Form B and all completed W-4 forms.

(2) Payment to arrangers, orchestrators, or copyists

The Company shall make payment to arrangers, orchestrators, or copyists for work performed under the terms of this agreement, through such agency or agencies of the Federation as may be designated from time to time by the Federation, within 15 days (excluding Saturdays, Sundays, and holidays) after the date of receipt of their completed billings and all necessary and completed W-4 forms.

(3) (a) A penalty of 5% of the above-mentioned amount due and unpaid if the delinquent payment is made within 5 days (excluding Saturday, Sunday and holidays) after payment was due.

(b) A penalty of 7½% of the above-mentioned amount due and unpaid (excluding the penalty in 3a above) if the delinquent payment is made between the 6th and 10th business days excluding Saturday, Sunday and holidays) after payment was due.

(c) A penalty of 10% of the above-mentioned amount due and unpaid (excluding the penalties in 3a and b above) if the delinquent payment is made between the 11th and 15th business days (excluding Saturday, Sundays and holidays) after payment was due.

(d) A penalty of 15% of the above-mentioned amount due and unpaid (excluding the penalties in 3a, b, and c above) if the delinquent payment is made between the 16th and 30th business days (excluding Saturday, Sunday and holidays) after payment was due.

(e) A penalty of 20% of the above-mentioned amount due and unpaid (excluding the penalties in 3a, b, c, and d above) if the delinquent payment is made between the 31st and 50th business day after the payment was due.

(f) Payments made after such 50th business day shall require in lieu of the said additional 20% payment, the payment of an additional amount equal to 50% (fifty per cent) of the initial amount payable plus an additional 10% payment for each thirty days after the 50th day in which payment is not made. Such 50% and 10% payments shall not be required unless written notice had been given (which may not be given before the 31st day after the date of receipt of their completed billings and all necessary and completed W-4 forms) that the employer is delinquent and the employer has not made the payment within 15 business days after receipt of such notice.

(g) The above delinquent payment penalties shall not apply to payments which have not been made by the Company by reason of

(i) A bona fide dispute as to the amount due and payable notice of which shall be filed within five business days following receipt of bills with the local of the Federation in whose jurisdiction the work was performed.

(ii) Emergencies beyond the control of the Company.

(iii) Where the Company inadvertently makes a less than full payment and presentation of the claim for the remainder is deliberately delayed in an attempt to collect a penalty.

K. *Regulations Relating to Overdubbing, Tracking, Sweetening, Multiple Parts, etc.*

(a) Except as is specifically permitted below, nothing contained in this agreement shall be deemed to permit dubbing or tracking. The dubbing or tracking specifically permitted hereunder shall relate only to recordings made under, and during the term of, this agreement, subject to paragraph (g) on page 23.

(b) During a session the Company may add live performances to a recording made at the same session without notice and without any additional payment to the musicians employed for the session.

(c) After the completion of an original session the Company may add vocal performances to the recordings made at that original session without any additional payment to the musicians employed at the original session for their services thereat.

(d) At a session subsequent to the completion of the original session at which music was first recorded, the Company may add additional instrumental performances to such recorded music without any additional payment to the musicians employed at the original session for their services thereat.

(e) If a musician performs multiple instrument parts (other than doubles), or the same part of the musician is recorded in order to create the sound of additional instruments, he shall be paid the total of all payments which would otherwise have been payable had separate musicians been used for those parts.

(f) The following special provisions relate solely to "royalty artists" as such term is defined below:

(i) The rates set forth in sub-division (ii) below shall apply to each musician who is a "royalty artist," whether such musician plays multiple parts, doubles, over-dubs, or "sweetens." A "royalty artist" is a musician (a) who records pursuant to a phonograph record contract which provides for a royalty payable to such musician at a basic rate of at least 2% of the suggested retail list price of records sold (less deductions usual and customary in the trade) or a substantially equivalent royalty, or (b) who plays as a member of (and not as a sideman with) a recognized self-contained group as defined in sub-division (iii).

(ii) For the first session at which such royalty artist performs in respect to each selection he shall receive the basic session rate and related overtime rate.

(iii) A "recognized self-contained group" is:

(a) two or more persons who perform together in fields other than phonograph records under a group name (whether fictional or otherwise); and

(b) the members of which are recording pursuant to a phonograph record contract which provides for a royalty payable with respect to the group at a basic rate of at least 3% of the suggested retail list price of records sold (less deductions usual and customary in the trade) or a substantially equivalent royalty; and

(c) all of the musicians of which are or become members of the American Federation of Musicians as provided in this agreement.

Replacements of or additions to members of a recognized self-contained group shall be subject to the provisions of subdivision (i) and (ii) above, if they qualify under items (a), (b) and (c) of this subdivision (iii).

(iv) This subsection (f) shall not be applicable to any musician who himself is not a "royalty artist" but who nevertheless performs hereunder with such royalty artist or royalty artists.

(v) The provisions of this sub-paragraph shall not be applicable unless the contract between the royalty artists and the Company and all amendments thereto have been filed with the Office of the President of the Federation.

(g) The tracking permitted by the foregoing provisions of this agreement does not apply to recordings by symphonic orchestras. As to such recordings the Federation agrees to grant waivers which will permit tracking in any case needed to meet unusual situations subject only to the following procedures: (i) waiver requests will be made in advance of the intended use when it is known that tracking will be employed; and (ii) if not so requested, prompt notice of such use will be given to the Federation after the event. It is the specific understanding of the parties that tracking will continue to be permitted in those situations where tracking under prior agreements has heretofore been practiced.

L. *Certain Persons Not To Be Placed On Form B Contract*

A producer or any other person who acts in a Company capacity can be placed on the Form B contract only if he actually performs a musical service on that contract which is covered by this agreement. No contractor shall serve as an engineer, producer, or in any capacity representing the employer with respect to the session on which he is the contractor.

II
ARRANGERS, ORCHESTRATORS, COPYISTS
Arrangers, orchestrators and copyists shall be paid not less than the rates set forth below and the conditions set forth shall apply:
A. *Arrangers*
(1) Definition — Arranging is the art of preparing and adapting an already written composition for presentation in other than its original form. An arrangement shall include reharmonization, paraphrasing and/or development of a composition so that it fully represents the melodic, harmonic and rhythm structure and requires no changes or additions.
(2) Credits — Unless barred by a legal obligation undertaken by an arranger, he shall receive name credit on all seven-inch "pop-single" records and on all tapes and cartridges in respect of which the number of arrangers used is six or less. Without such request and if no legal obligation undertaken by him prevents the use of his name by the Company, the arranger shall receive name credit on all albums. Such credit may appear either on the record label or jacket, or on the tape or cartridge label or package.
(3) Minimum Rates — Since arranging represents highly individual creative skills, the wages paid for arranging are left to the discretion of the person doing the work, provided, however, that the wages shall never be less than provided for in paragraph B. (3). Arranging shall be paid for in addition to orchestrating where the same person performs the work of the two classifications. Payment for making and orchestrating an arrangement shall cover both the minimum for arranging and orchestrating.

130

B. *Orchestrators*

(1) Definition — Orchestrating is the labor of scoring the various voices and/or instruments of an arrangement without changing or adding to the melodies, counter-melodies, harmonies and rhythms.

(2) Times rates for orchestrators — May be used only on takedowns, adjustments, alterations, additions and in other situations where page rates are impractical. The hourly rates for time work shall be $13.65.

(3) Page rates for orchestrators [subject to the rules of paragraph "B. (4)"].

    (a) For not more than ten lines per score page:

        (i) Making an arrangement (which may include orchestrating) $8.97.

        (ii) Orchestrating an arrangement with no arranging, or revoicing a score, $4.51.

    (b) For each additional single line in excess of ten lines per score page, $.39.

    (c) For adding lines to a score already orchestrated (other than revoicing a score) (regardless of who the orchestrator was), per score page, per line, $.44.

    (d) For adding piano part, per score page, $1.65.

    (e) Orchestrating the parts (without score), the combined rate for orchestrating and copying.

    (f) For scoring a piano part from a lead or melody sheet, per piano page, $8.97.

    (g) For scoring a two-line or three-line full piano part from an orchestral score (or parts) or for scoring for solo piano, accordion, harp, etc., for individual performances, per piano page, $16.66.

    (h) For scoring page (choral) voices (a page consisting of four voices, including piano part, four bars per page, with come sopras being paid for), per page, $3.96, with payment for additional voices being the same as for additional instrumental lines.

(4) The following rules shall apply to page rates:

    (a) A score page consists of four bars and shall be computed on the basis of a minimum of ten lines.

    (b) Double staff parts shall count as two lines.

    (c) Each line of a divisi part shall count as one line.

    (d) A pick-up shall be computed as a full measure.

    (e) Come sopras shall be paid for.

    (f) Repeats shall not be used within a chorus to reduce the wage paid (but repeats, del segno, and the like, which appear in the composition are permissable).

    (g) The last page may be paid for on a half-page basis.

    (h) The page rates do not include proofreading service.

    (i) Voice and conductor lines written into a score shall be treated as instrumental lines.

    (j) The word "piano" shall be deemed to include organ, harp, celeste, harpsichord, accordian, cymbalum, etc., when written on two staves.

C. *Copyists*

(1) Time rates for copyists — May be used only on pasting, cutting, production lines, and in other situations where page rates are impractical. The hourly rates for time work shall be $7.05.

(2) Page rates for copyists shall be as follows (subject to the rules set forth in paragraph "C. (3)"):

INSTRUMENTAL PARTS:
  1. a. Single stave parts: single notation .... $ 1.38
     b. Single stave parts: chorded and/or divisi............................ 2.42
         (Chorded: Guitar, banjo, vibraphone and similar parts)
         (Divisi: When more than 50% of page)
  2. a. Double stave parts: chorded piano, organ, harp, celeste, etc. 2.42
     b. Rhythm piano parts: chord symbols and bass line 1.87
  3. a. Piano with vocal melody cued (no lyrics—full chords) 3.19
     b. Rhythm piano with vocal melody cued (no lyrics—chord symbols) 2.53
     c. Piano with orchestral cues (Piano-Conductor) 3.91
  4. a. Piano-Vocal: 3 staves with lyrics (one set) and full chords 3.74
     b. Rhythm Piano-Vocal: 3 staves with lyrics (one set) and chord symbols 3.03
     c. Piano-Vocal and orchestral cues/with lyrics (Piano-Conductor) 4.18
  5.   Lead Sheet: single melody line with lyrics (one set) and chord symbols 5.61
  6.   Concert score parts where transposition is necessary
         (no additional charge to be made for transposition) 2.15

VOCAL PARTS:
  7. a. Single voice line with lyrics (one set) 2.15
     b. Foreign language lyrics, extra per page .... .50
  8. a. Choir parts with lyrics (one set) 6.33
     b. Foreign language lyrics, extra per page .... .39

CONDUCTOR PARTS:
     (Piano-Conductor), Production, Control, etc. (one or more staves)
  9. a. Lead lines with notated instrumental cues .... $ 7.70
     b. (+) Harmonically complete 10.51
         (+) NOTE: If 12 stave paper is used in this category, not more than
         3 braced systems per page shall be allowed.
 10.   Adding lyrics (or words) per set, per page:
     a. Single stave parts .... .50
     b. Multiple stave parts .... .39
     c. Foreign language .... .77
 11.   Numbering bars, per page (no charge for normal use of rehearsal letters) ..... .22
 12.   Chord symbols (when added, per page):
     a. Single stave parts .... .50
     b. Multiple stave parts .... .22
 13. a. Single stave part for SOLO PERFORMANCE .... 50% additional
     b. Solo piano, classical, concert, symphonic or similar parts 4.18
 14.   MASTER COPY FOR REPRODUCTION: Copying or extracting parts
         to be duplicated by any process—Double all applicable rates ....
         (except items 5, 8 a and b, 9 a and b above which shall be paid at the single rate)
 15.   Adding symbols (other than chord symbols) for Electronic Instruments or Devices:
     a. Single stave parts .... .83
     b. Multiple stave parts .... .44

(3) The following rules shall apply to page rates:

(a) For duplicating orchestra and band scores (note for note), the minimum rate shall be one-half of the orchestrating rate for scoring same.

(b) For remaking a score from regular parts, the minimum rate shall be one-half of the orchestrating rate for scoring same.

(c) Modulations, new introductions, endings and interpolations from piano shall be paid for at orchestrating rates.

(d) Symphony, opera, cantata, oratorio, ballet or any other standard or classical music (copies, transcriptions, extractions) shall be paid for at one-third more than the rates listed.

(e) Special routine work (writing only) where two or more scores or orchestral parts must be used or referred to in constructing overtures, selections, finales, etc., shall be paid for at fifty (50%) per cent more than the rates listed, provided, however, that no extra charge shall be made for transposition.

(f) The contracting copyist shal be designated as a supervisor copyist and he shall be paid for his services 25% more than the wage scale for the work with respect to which he acts (including copying done by him) under the following circumstances:

(i) when he is required by the Company to give out or collect work and to supervise and give instructions with respect to the assignments, or

(ii) when the conditions of the job require the services of more than one copyist and the contracting copyist has notified the Company that more than one copyist will be required. Such notice, however, shall not be required when the copyist has received the work less than 72 hours prior to the recording session.

(g) When two or more copyists are required to split scores for the convenience of the Company, each copyist shall be paid at page and half-page rates for the section copied by him, but not less than the applicable hourly rate.

(h) Rates for copying do not include any proofreading services. Proofreading, if required by the Company, shall be paid for at the rate of $10.18 per hour, with no minimum call to be applicable to such rate.

(i) Editing shall be paid for at the copying rate plus 50%.

(j) Rates shall be computed on the basis of ten stave paper except that parts requiring three or more braced staves shall be written on twelve stave paper, unless impractical.

(k) Rates shall be computed on page and half-page rates except that the first page shall be paid in full rather than pro-rated.

(l) An average of four bars per stave shall be secured, if possible, and two staves of the first page (or any following pages, if necessary) shall be used for titles or other written items.

(m) The copyist who prepared the original part shall be paid the listed rate for any reproductions thereof by any mechanical means whatsoever except where a master copy was previously paid for at the rate listed.

(n) All paper and necessary working material shall be supplied by the Company or furnished by the copyist at cost.

(o) Transposition of all parts shall be paid for at fifty (50%) per cent more than the listed rates.

(p) Use of rehearsal letters every two, three or four bars or to circumvent payment for numbering shall not be deemed normal use.

D. *Health and Welfare Fund Contributions*

For each Arranger and Orchestrator the Company will contribute to any existing lawful Health and Welfare Fund of any Federation Local and commencing thirty days after notice in writing to any such lawful Fund as may be established hereafter by any other Federation Local, the sum of $2.15 for each original composition as to which services are performed on non-symphonic records performed within the jurisdiction of such Federation Local by each arranger and orchestrator covered by this agreement but not to exceed $6.50 for any individual for all music services performed in respect to any one Form B contract.

For each Copyist the Company will contribute to any existing lawful Health and Welfare Fund of any Federation Local and commencing thirty days after notice in writing to any such lawful Fund as may be established hereafter by any other Federation Local, for work on non-symphonic records performed within the jurisdiction of such Federation Local by each copyist covered by this agreement, the sum of $2.50 per day, but not less than $3.25 for each original service, with a maximum of $12.50 per week.

With respect to any such composition as to which services are performed within jurisdiction of a Federation Local where no such Fund is established, the Employer shall make the applicable payment to each such arranger, orchestrator, and copyist.

No such Health and Welfare Fund contribution whether paid to any Fund or paid directly to an arranger, orchestrator, and copyist shall be considered wages or the basis for computing the applicable AFM-EPW contribution or any other payments under this agreement such as overtime, premium pay, etc.

E. *General rules applicable to arrangers, orchestrators, copyists and librarians*

(1) The arranger or orchestrator shall deliver to the copyist a full score. A full score is a visual representation of parts to be performed by instruments and/or voice of a musical ensemble systematically placed on a series of staves, one above the other, and in which no

other than two instruments are combined on a single staff. Abbreviations by come sopra and/or col indications within the same score may be used.

(2) Arrangements, orchestrations and parts previously made for a use other than phonograph records shall be paid for hereunder when first used for phonograph records. Arrangements, orchestrations and parts made initially for phonograph records shall not be used in any other field either by the Company or with its authorization unless the rate applicable to such purposes is paid.

(3) Arrangers, orchestrators and copyists shall stamp the first and last pages of all arrangements and scores and the first page of all parts with their official union stamp. Card number, local and year must be written on deshon master copy.

(4) In cases where an hourly rate is applicable the minimum call shall be four hours, provided, however, that in the case of copyists the minimum shall be $35.

(5) Orchestrators and copyists shall receive the following premium rates:

(a) For work from 6:00 P.M. to 12 midnight, the listed rate plus one-half.

(b) For work on Saturdays from 9:00 A.M. to 6:00 P.M., the listed rate plus one-half.

(c) For work in excess of eight hours in one day and until midnight, the listed rate plus one-half.

(d) For work from 12 midnight until dismissed, and after 6:00 P.M. on Saturdays, double the listed rates.

(e) For work performed on the same job at anytime following a call-back less than eight hours after prior dismissal during premium pay hours, double the listed rates.

(f) For work on Sundays and the following holidays: New Year's Day, Lincoln's Birthday, Washington's Birthday, Memorial Day, Independence Day, Labor Day, Thanksgiving Day and Christmas Day double the listed rate.

Each of these holidays shall be observed on the day on which it is observed by employees of the United States Government or of the Government of Canada.

(6) (a) If the Company requests an orchestrator or copyist to work in a city other than the one in which he resides, work done out of town or en route shall be paid for at the listed rate plus 25%. In the case of an orchestrator, the Company shall guarantee a minimum of $45.00 per day plus $35.00 for personal expenses. In the case of a copyist, the Company shall guarantee a minimum of $35.00 plus $35.00 for personal expenses.

(b) Round-trip first class transportation, with sleeper for overnight travel, shall be furnished by the Company.

(7) Pick up and messenger service will be paid for by the Company.

(8) The rates specified herein relate to arranging orchestrating and copying services of every nature as utilized in connection with phonograph records and no other rates shall be applied for any such services.

(9) Copyists and librarians who are required by the Company to attend recording sessions shall be paid at the page rate or at the hourly rate, whichever is larger.

(10) The leader or arranger shall collect and return musical parts and scores to the Company representatives at the end of each recording session, provided however, that the Company shall not be liable for the leader's or arranger's failure to collect such parts and scores if it did not interfere with his efforts to do so.

EXHIBIT B

PENSION WELFARE FUNDS

1. The Company shall contribute an amount equal to ten per cent (10%) of the earnings of persons covered by this agreement (except for the payments made in lieu of Health and Welfare Fund contributions under Exhibit A, I, A (6) and II, D, above, and under the Special Payments Fund Agreement attached as Exhibit C) computed at the minimum rates set forth in Exhibit A as follows:

(a) For services performed in the United States to the American Federation of Musicians' and Employers' Pension Welfare Fund created by the Trust Indenture dated October 2, 1959, as heretofore or hereafter amended.

(b) For services performed in the Dominion of Canada to the American Federation of Musicians' and Employers' Pension Welfare Fund created by the Agreement and Declaration of Trust dated April 9, 1962, as heretofore or hereafter amended.

It is understood that, under the terms of said trust agreements, the employees (in addition to musicians as therein defined) on behalf of whom contributions to the aforesaid Funds may be made by other employers include the following:

(i) full-time employees of the Funds themselves,
(ii) full-time office and clerical employees of the Federation and any of its affiliated Locals, and
(iii) duly elected officers and representatives of the Federation and of any of its affiliated Locals.

2. The Company shall make such payments to such place as the Trustees of the Funds may designate, upon the filing of a Form B contract.

3. The Company shall submit reports in such form as the Trustees may reasonably require; and the Company shall be subject to such reasonable audit by the Trustees as the Trustees may require.

4. The Federation and said Trustees, or either of them, may enforce any provision of this Exhibit B.

EXHIBIT C

PHONOGRAPH RECORD MANUFACTURERS' SPECIAL PAYMENTS FUND AGREEMENT

(November, 1975)

AGREEMENT, made and delivered in the City and State of New York, on the date set forth below, by and between the undersigned and such others as shall hereafter agree to contribute to the fund referred to hereafter (individually called "first party" and collectively "first parties"), the undersigned Administrator ("Administrator"), and The American Federation of Musicians of the United States and Canada ("Federation").

WITNESSETH:

(a) Each first party has executed and delivered this agreement pursuant to its undertaking so to do as provided by the Phonograph Record Labor Agreement (November, 1975), simultaneously herewith entered into with the Federation.

(b) Each first party by executing and delivering this Agreement assumes the duties and obligations to be performed and undertaken by each such first party hereunder. The Administrator has been designated collectively by the first parties, who have requested it to assume and perform the duties of Administrator hereunder, and it is willing to do so in the manner prescribed herein.

NOW, THEREFORE, in consideration of the premises, of the mutual covenants herein contained, of the undertakings assumed by each first party, and of the undertakings herein by the Administrator at the request of the first parties, it is agreed as follows:

1. (a) There are incorporated herein and made part hereof, as though fully set forth herein, Addendums A and B.

(b) Subject to paragraph 2(d) hereof, each first party to this Agreement shall make the payments to the Administrator called for in Addendum A hereto, to provide for

(i) said First Party's contribution to the musicians' share of the Fund as defined under paragraph 2(b) hereof, and

(ii) any employment taxes or insurance premiums which may be owing by the First Parties with respect to the distribution of the musicians' share of the Fund.

(c) Within forty-five (45) days after the end of each calendar half-year (that is within forty-five (45) days after December 31 and June 30th in each year), each first party will pay to the Administrator such portion of the aforesaid payments as may have accrued hereunder during the preceding half-year, provided that the Administrator may agree with any first party that semi-annual payments be made with respect to other half-yearly periods ending on dates satisfactory to the Administrator. Each payment hereunder shall be accompanied by a statement, certified by the Treasurer, Controller, or other authorized officer or representative of the first party making such payment, containing such information as may reasonably be required to ascertain the correctness of the payment made. If such payments are not made when due hereunder, the same shall bear interest at the rate of six per cent (6%) per annum from the date when such payment was due.

(d) Each first party at all times, without limitation to the duration of this Agreement, shall keep full and accurate records and accounts concerning all transactions on which payments to the Administrator are based pursuant to this Agreement, in convenient form and pursuant to approved and recognized accounting practices. The Administrator shall have the right from time to time, without limitation to the duration of this Agreement and at all reasonable times during business hours, to have its duly authorized agents examine and audit such records and accounts, and such other records and accounts as may be necessary, such examination and audit to be made for the purpose of verifying any statements made hereunder by each first party, or due from such first party, during a period not exceeding four (4) years preceding such examination and of determining the amount of payments due to the Administrator pursuant hereto. It is agreed that the four year period provided herein shall not effect the operation of the applicable statute of limitations. Each first party agrees to afford all necessary facilities to such authorized agents to make such examination and audit and to make such extracts and excerpts from said records and accounts as may be necessary or proper according to approved and recognized accounting practices. Examinations and audits made pursuant hereto shall be coordinated, to the extent practicable, with examinations and audits made under the Phonograph Record Trust Agreements to which first party is signatory so that inconvenience to the first party may be minimized.

(e) Any sale, assignment, lease or license of, or other transfer of title to, or permission to use any device covered by Addendum A to this Agreement whether by operation of law or otherwise, shall be subject to the rights and duties established by this Agreement. The Administrator shall be advised monthly of each purchaser, assignee, lessee, licensee, transferee or user and of the identity of the phonograph record (as defined above) involved. No sale, assignment, lease, license, transfer or permission shall be made or granted by any first party to any person, firm or corporation doing business within the United States, Canada or Puerto Rico, unless and until such purchaser, assignee, lessee, licensee, transferee, or user, shall become an additional first party hereto. No other sale, assignment, lease, license, transfer or permission shall be made or granted unless such purchaser, assignee, lessee, licensee, transferee, or user, shall promise to make such first party the payments required by this Agreement, which said the extent that such first party has received such payments (i) in the United States or Canada, or (ii) in United States or Canadian currency or in a currency convertible into United States or Canadian currency, or (iii) in a currency not convertible into United States or Canadian currency, of which such first party has made beneficial use, or (iv) in an asset other than currency. No such first party will, without the consent of the Administrator and Federation forgive or compromise such obligation.

(f) All payments and other communications for each first party to the Administrator shall be made to the Administrator at its office which shall be located in New York, N.Y.

2. (a) The Administrator accepts the duties hereby assigned to it, and shall establish the proper administrative machinery and processes necessary for the performance of its duties hereunder. The Administrator shall as soon as practicable after May first of each year distribute as herein provided the "musicians' share of the Fund," as defined in paragraph 2(b) hereof. Each musician, as collectively referred to in paragraph 1 of the Phonograph Record Labor Agreement (November, 1975), shall receive as a special payment a fraction of the total distribution which shall be determined as follows: the numerator of said fraction shall be a sum determined by adding the scale wages payable to such musician by all First Parties hereto (i) during the immediately preceding calendar year weighted or multiplied by 5, (ii) during the immediately preceding calendar year less one weighted or multiplied by 4, (iii) during the immediately preceding calendar year less two weighted or multiplied by 3, (iv) during the immediately preceding calendar year less three weighted or multiplied by 2, and (v) during the immediately preceding calendar year less four weighted or multiplied by 1; the denominator of said fraction shall be a sum determined by adding the scale wages payable to all such musicians during the same calendar years as aforesaid by all said First Parties hereto similarly weighted or multiplied as set forth above. In the case of arrangers and orchestrators scale wages for all purposes of this paragraph 2(a) shall be deemed to be 150% of the scale wages paid to an instrumentalist for each tune on which the arranger or orchestrator performed services hereunder.

By way of illustration but not limitation:

Example 1:

If the scale wages payable to a musician participating in the 1971 distribution have been $50 in 1970 and $100 in 1969 and the total scale wages payable to all musicians during the same two years have been $10,000 in 1970 and $9,000 in 1969 the fraction of the distribution payable to that musician would be determined as follows:

Musician's scale wages	*Total scale wages*
Year	
1970— $ 50 × 5 = $250	$10M × 5 = $50M
1969— 100 × 4 = 400	9M × 4 = 36M
$650	$86,000

The musician's 1971 special payment would be 650/86000 of the "musicians' share of the Fund."

Example 2:

If the scale wages payable to a musician participating in the 1975 distribution have been $50 in 1974, $100 in 1973, $70 in 1972, none in 1971, and $30 in 1970 and if the total scale wages payable to all musicians during the same five years have been $10,000 in 1974, $9,000 in 1973, $7,000 in 1972, $5,000 in 1971 and $5,000 in 1970, the fraction of the distribution payable to that musician would be determined as follows:

Musician's scale wages	*Total scale wages payable to all musicians*
Year	
1974 — $ 50 × 5 = $250	$10M × 5 = $ 50 M
1973 — 100 × 4 = 400	9M × 4 = 36 M
1972 — 70 × 3 = 210	7M × 3 = 21 M
1971 — 0 × 2 = 0	5M × 2 = 10 M
1970 — 30 × 1 = 30	5M × 1 = 5 M
$890	$122,000

The musician's 1975 special payment would be 890/122,000 of the "musicians' share of the Fund."

(b) For purposes of this agreement, the "musician's share of the Fund" shall be an amount equal to:

(i) all sums received by the Administrator up to May first of the year of distribution, with respece to sales of phonograph records made:

(A) during the preceding calendar year, or,

(B) at any time prior to the preceding calendar year, if the payment with respect to such sales, was received by the Administrator after May first of the preceding calendar year.

(ii) less:

(A) all expenses reasonably incurred in the administration of the Fund, including the compensation of the Administrator herein provided, and appropriate bonding premiums.

(B) amounts reasonably reserved by the Administrator as an operating Fund, and for contingencies, and,

140

(C) an amount (hereinafter referred to as the "manufacturers' share of the Fund") equal to the total of any social security tax, Federal and/or State Unemployment Insurance Tax, other employment taxes, Disability Insurance premiums, and/or Workmen's Compensation premiums, which may be owing by the First Parties, individually or collectively, and/or by the Administrator, as employer or employers, with respect to the distribution of the musicians' share of the Fund.

(c) The First Parties, individually and collectively, hereby irrevocably designate the Administrator as their agent to pay from the manufacturers' share of the Fund, any social security tax, Federal and/or State Unemployment Insurance Tax, other employment taxes, Disability Insurance premiums, and/or Workmen's Compensation premiums, which may be owing by the First Parties individually and/or collectively, as employer or employers, with respect to the distribution of the musicians' share of the Fund.

(d) Notwithstanding any other provisions of this agreement, a First Party may, at the time it makes its annual payment to the Fund, request that the Administrator refund to it such proportion of such payment as:

(i) the total of any taxes and insurance premiums which may be payable under Paragraph 2(b) (ii) (C) hereof, with respect to the distribution of the musicians' share of the Fund in the year of payment, bears to
(ii) the total payments made to the Fund by First Parties in said year.

Any such refund shall be made by the Administrator to the First Party requesting the refund not later than September first of the year of payment.

If a refund is made to a First Party under this sub-paragraph, the Administrator shall not be responsible in said year, for payment of said First Party's share of any taxes and insurance premium payable under Paragraph 2(b) (ii) (C) hereof, with regard to the distribution of the musicians' share of the Fund.

(e) The Federation has agreed to furnish to the Administrator, and to cause its local unions to furnish to the Administrator, all data in the possession or subject to the control thereof which is necessary and proper to assist in the orderly and accurate distribution to musicians as provided herein and to request the Trustees of the American Federation of Musicians and Employers' Pension Welfare Fund to do likewise upon reimbursement of all costs reasonably incurred thereby in so doing.

(f) The Administrator shall indemnify and hold the First Parties harmless out of the Fund against any liability for making any of the payments to the musicians under paragraph 2(a) hereof or any payments of employment taxes and insurance premiums which may be required to be made by the Administrator under paragraph 2(c) hereof, it being the express intent of the parties that all such payments are to be made out of the Fund with no further costs or expense of any whatsoever to the First Parties. Without limitation of the foregoing, the Administrator also shall furnish a surety bond with a responsible surety company satisfactory to the First Parties and to the Federation, to guarantee the full and faithful performance of its duties as herein described.

(g) In making distribution to musicians hereunder, the Administrator shall clearly and legibly display the following legend on all checks, vouchers, letters or documents of transmittal: "This is a special payment to you by all of the Phonograph Record Manufacturers who are operating under the Phonograph Record Labor Agreements negotiated by the American Federation of Musicians."

(h) In the event of the death of a musician entitled to a distributive share hereunder, the Administrator shall distribute such share to the beneficiary designated by such musician pursuant to the AFM-EPQ Pension Welfare Fund; and if no beneficiary be so designated, then to the surviving spouse of such musician; and if there be no such person, to the musician's estate.

3. (a) In the event that any First Party shall default in the payment of any sums to the Administrator when the same shall become due pursuant to this Agreement, the Administrator shall have the duty, right and power forthwith to commence action or to take any other proceedings as shall be necessary for the collection thereof, including the power and authority to compromise and settle with the Federation's consent. The Administrator's reasonable expenses, attorney's fees and other disbursements incurred in the collection of any such overdue sums shall be paid to the Administrator by the First Party so defaulting and such payment shall be added to the special payment fund.

(b) Nothing contained herein shall create any cause of action in favor of any musician as defined in the Phonograph Record Labor Agreement (November, 1975) against any First Party but the Federation may enforce distribution of the musicians' share of the Fund in behalf of the individual musicians.

(c) The Administrator shall deposit all money and property received by it, with or without interest, with any bank or trust company, insured by the Federal Deposit Insurance Corporation and having capital, surplus and undivided profits exceeding $5,000,000; provided, however, that in the event that Canadian dollars are receivable by the Administrator and it is not feasible or desirable to convert such Canadian dollars into the United States funds, such Canadian funds and any securities purchased therewith may be deposited in a Chartered Bank of the Dominion of Canada, anything herein to the contrary notwithstanding. Except as modified by the provisions of paragraph 3(d) hereof, the Administrator shall have the right and power to invest and reinvest the said money and property only in bonds and other direct obligations of the United States of America and of the Dominion of Canada, without regard to the proportion which any such investment or investments may bear to the entire amount of the Fund and to sell, exchange and otherwise deal with such investments as the Administrator may seem desirable.

(d) In connection with the collection of any sums due to it hereunder, the Administrator may consent to and participate in any composition of creditors, bankruptcy, reorganizaion or similar proceeding, and in the event that as a result thereof the Administrator shall become the holder of assets other than money, obligations to pay money conditioned only as to the time of payment, or property of the class specified in paragraph 3(c) hereof (which assets are in this subsection (d) called "property"), the Administrator may consent to and participate in any plan of reorganization, consolidation, merger, combination, or other similar plan, and consent to any contract, lease, mortgage, purchase, sale or other action by any corporation pursuant to such plan and accept any property which might be received by the Administrator under any such plan, whether or not such property is of the class in which the Administrator by paragraph 3(c) hereof, is authorized to invest the Fund; the Administrator may deposit any such property with any protective, reorganization or similar committee, delegate discretionary power thereto, and pay part of its expenses and compensation and any assessment levied with respect to such property; the Administrator may exercise all conversions, subscription, voting and other rights of whatsoever nature pertaining to any such property, and grant proxies, discretionary or otherwise, in respect thereof and accept any property which may be acquired by the Administrator by the exercise of any such rights, whether or not such property is of the class in which the Administrator, by paragraph 3(c) hereof, is authorized to invest the Fund. Anything to the contrary contained in this paragraph 3(d) notwithstanding, the Administrator shall reasonably endeavor to dispose of any such property in order that the Fund, to the fullest extent possible, at all times shall be comprised as specified in paragraph 3(c) hereof.

(e) Parties dealing with the Administrator shall not be required to look to the application of any moneys paid to the Administrator.

(f) The Administrator has consented to act as Administrator hereunder upon the express understanding that it shall not in any event or under any circumstances be liable for any loss or damage resulting from anything done or omitted in good faith, and further, that this understanding shall not be limited or restricted by any reference to or inference from any general or special provisions herein contained or otherwise. In particular, and without limiting the foregoing, the Administrator shall not be subject to any personal liability for moneys received and expended in accordance with the provisions hereof.

(g) Within ninety (90) days after the end of each calendar year, the Administrator shall furnish a statement for such calendar year of its operations to each First Party hereto making payments to the Administrator and to the Federation. Such statements shall set forth in detail the properties and moneys on hand and the operations of the Administrator during the immediately preceding calendar year, including without limitation the details of any compromise or settlement made by the Administrator with any First Party, and such other information and data as shall be appropriate to inform fully the recipients of such statements and shall be certified by independent certified public accountant.

(h) The Administrator, at all times without limitation to the duration of this Agreement, shall keep full and accurate records and accounts concerning all transactions involving the receipt and expenditure of moneys hereunder and the investment and reinvestment thereof, all in convenient form and pursuant to approved and recognized accounting practices. Each First Party and the Federation shall have the right from time to time, without limitation to the duration of this agreement, and at all reasonable times during business hours, to have their respective duly authorized agents examine and audit the Administrator's records and accounts for the purpose of verifying any statements and payments made by the Administrator pursuant to this Agreement, during a period not exceeding two (2) years preceding such examination. The Administrator shall afford all necessary facilities to such authorized agents to make such examination and audit and to make extracts and excerpts from said records and accounts as may be necessary or proper according to approved and recognized accounting practices.

(i) The Administrator shall recognize and honor lawful assignments to the Federation of a portion of the payments to which any musician shall become entitled hereunder.

4. The compensation of the Administrator shall be as set forth in Addendum B hereto attached, and shall be paid out of the funds and property in the hands of the Administrator.

5. (a) The Administrator may resign at any time by thirty (30) days written notice to the First Parties and the Federation. A successor Administrator shall thereupon be appointed by the Secretary of Labor of the United States.

(b) The Administrator shall be subject to removal as provided below, if an individual, the Administrator shall become unable to perform his duties hereunder by reason of illness or other incapacity or if the Administrator shall be guilty of malfeasance or neglect of duty hereunder. Any demand for the removal of the Administrator for the reasons aforesaid shall be submitted by any two or more of the First Parties hereto who have made individual payments hereunder to the Administrator during the calendar year immediately preceding the date of such submission aggregating $50,000 or more, together with the Federation, the the American Arbitration Association in New York, N.Y. The determination of whether the Administrator shall be removed for the reasons aforesaid shall be made in New York, N.Y. by three (3) Arbitrators selected from panels of the American Arbitration Association in accordance with the Rules thereof and judgment upon the award rendered by the Arbitrators may be entered in any court having jurisdiction thereof.

(c) In the event of the death of the Administrator, if an individual, or the removal of the Administrator, a successor Administrator shall be appointed in the manner designated in paragraph 5(a) hereof.

(d) No Administrator under this Agreement shall be a representative of labor, or of any union, or of employees within the meaning of Section 302(b) of the Labor Management Relations Act, 1947.

6. Any person, firm, corporation, association or other entity may apply to become an additional First Party to this Agreement by executing and delivering to the Administrator three (3) counterparts of Schedule 1 hereto attached. The Administrator shall indicate acceptance of such application by appropriately completing such application, executing such three

(3) counterparts, and delivering one (1) such counterpart to such additional First Party at the Administrator's office in the City of New York and one (1) such counterpart to the Federation. The Administrator shall forthwith advise the Federation of the execution and delivery of such agreement, and shall regularly advise all other First Parties thereof.

7. This Agreement shall be governed, construed and regulated in all respects by the laws of the State of New York.

IN WITNESS WHEREOF, each First Party, the Administrator and the Federation have hereunto set their respective names and seals, or have caused these presents to be executed by a duly authorized officer or officers thereof and their corporate seals affixed thereto as of the date set forth below.

Date	*Signatory*

ADDENDUM A

1. For the purposes of this Agreement, the terms "phonograph record" and "record" shall include phonograph records, wire or tape recordings, or other devices reproducing sound, and the term "master record" shall include any matrix, "mother," stamper or other device from which another such master record, phonograph record, wire or tape recording, or other device reproducing sound, is produced, reproduced, pressed or otherwise processed.

2. Each First Party shall make payments to the Administrator in the amounts computed as stated below, with respect to the sale during the period specified in 6 below of phonograph records, produced from master records containing music which was performed or conducted by musicians covered by, or required to be paid pursuant to, a collective bargaining agreement with the Federation known as Phonograph Record Labor Agreement (November, 1975) (but specifically excluding services solely as arranger, orchestrator or copyist) where such phonograph records are sold during said period by such First Party, or, subject to the provisions of paragraph 1(e) of the main text of this Agreement, by purchasers, lessees, licensees, transferees, or other users deriving title, lease, license, or permission thereto, by operation of law or otherwise, by, from or through such First Party.

3. The payments to the Administrator shall be computed as follows:

(a) .6% of the manufacturer's suggested retail price of each record, when such price does not exceed $3.79.

(b) For records where the manufacturer's suggested retail price exceeds $3.79, .58% of the manufacturer's suggested retail list price and for wire or tape recordings or other devices .5% of the manufacturer's suggested retail price.

With respect to a phonograph record produced after October 31, 1975, both from master records described in paragraph 2 of this Addendum A and recorded under Phonograph Record

Labor Agreement (November, 1975) for which payments are due hereunder and from other master records, First Party shall pay that proportion of the amount provided for above as the number of such master records recorded under said Agreement bears to the total number of master records embodied in the phonograph record.

4. For the purpose of computing payments to the Administrator,

(a) Each First Party will report 100% of net sales;

(b) Each First Party will have a packaging allowance in the country of manufacture or sale of 15% of the suggested retail list price for phonograph records (other than for records where the manufacturer's suggested retail list price is $3.79 or less, and other than for singles in plain wrapping or sleeves) and 25% of the suggested retail list price for tapes and cartridges.

(c) Each First Party will have an allowance, with respect to "free" records, tapes and cartridges actually distributed, regardless of mix, (except for record clubs which are dealt with separately below), or up to 20% of the total records distributed;

(d) With respect to its record clubs, if any, each First Party will have an allowance of "free" and "bonus" records, tapes and cartridges actually distributed of up to 50% of the total records, tapes and cartridges distributed by or through the clubs; and with respect to such "free" and "bonus" records, tapes and cartridges, distributed by its clubs in excess thereof, each First Party will pay the full rate on 50% of the excess of such "free" and "bonus" records, tapes and cartridges so distributed.

5. Schedules of current manufacturer's suggested retail prices for each record in each First Party's catalogue shall be furnished by each First Party to the Administrator upon the execution and delivery of this Agreement and amendments and additions thereto shall be so furnished as and when established. For the purposes of determining the amounts payable hereunder, such suggested retail price shall be computed exclusive of any sales or excise taxes on the sale of phonograph records subject to this Agreement. If any First Party discontinues the practice of publishing manfacturers' suggested retail prices, it agrees that it will negotiate a new basis for computing payments hereunder which shall be equivalent to those required above.

6. The payments provided for in this Agreement shall be made with respect to the sales of any phonograph record produced from a master record described in paragraph 2 of this Addendum A which take place during the period commencing with the calendar year during which a phonograph record produced from such master record is first released for sale and terminating at the end of the tenth calendar year thereafter. The year of such release shall be counted as the first year of the ten years. (By way of illustration but not limitation, if a phonograph record produced from a master record made pursuant to Phonograph Record Labor Agreement (April, 1969), is first released for sale in May, 1969, payments shall be made with respect to sales of said record which take place during the calendar years 1969-1978 inclusive. If said phonograph record is first released for sale in February, 1972, payments shall

be made with respect to sales of said record which take place during the calendar year 1972-1981 inclusive.)

7. The report to the Administrator required in paragraph 1(c) of the main text of this Agreement shall show the number of phonograph records, tapes and other devices subject to payment under this Agreement which have been sold during the period to be covered by the report, the dates of initial release for sale thereof, the manufacturer's suggested retail price thereof and of the component units thereof and the excise and sales taxes, if any, borne by the First Party thereon.

8. Despite anything to the contrary contained in this Agreement, it is specifically agreed that the First Party reserve the right, by written notice to the Administrator, effective with the effective date of any termination, modification, extension or renewal of the said Phonograph Record Labor Agreement (November, 1975), to terminate or change any of the terms of this Special Payments Fund Agreement, but no such termination or change shall be effective unless the First Party has secured the prior written approval thereto by the Federation. It is agreed, however, that no such change may have any retroactive effect.

9. Anything to the contrary herein contained notwithstanding, it is agreed that if the Phonograph Record Labor Agreement (November, 1975), or any successor agreement is not renewed or extended at or prior to its expiration date, and if a work stoppage by members of the Federation ensues, then all payments otherwise due to the Administrator based on sales for the period of such work stoppage, and only for such period, shall not be made to the Administrator. In lieu thereof, equivalent amounts shall be paid by each First Party as an additional contribution to the Trustee under the Phonograph Record Trust Agreement (November, 1975) unless otherwise determined as a condition for the cessation of such work stoppage.

ADDENDUM B

Administrator's Compensation

The total compensation of the Administrator for services rendered pursuant to this agreement and pursuant to similar agreements with producers and/or distributors of phonograph records and/or electrical transcriptions shall be at the total rate of Ten Thousand Dollars ($10,000) per annum.

SCHEDULE 1

Date: _____ , 19 ____

The undersigned, desiring to become an additional First Party to the within Agreement, does hereby adopt the declarations of the First Parties set forth therein, does hereby make the request made by the First Parties therein, and in consideration of the undertakings assumed therein by each First Party and of the undertakings assumed therein by the Administrator at the request of the First Parties, does hereby request the Administrator to accept the under-signed as an additional First Party to such Agreement, and does assume and agrees to be bound by the terms, covenants and conditions to be performed thereunder.

_____
(Name of Company or Individual Signatory)

By _____
(Signature of Officer and Title)

Address: _____

_____

ACCEPTED:
United States Trust Company of New York

By _____
Vice-President
Administrator

(If executed in the Province of Quebec this Agreement shall be properly notarized and otherwise executed according to the laws of the Province.)

PHONO-RECORDING SCALES: EFFECTIVE NOVEMBER 1, 1979—OCTOBER 31, 1980

NO RECORDING IS PERMITTED WITHOUT THE USE OF A VALID A. F. OF M. RECORDING AGREEMENT

ALL SESSION-AFM-EPW FUND CONTRIBUTION-10%, OF GROSS SCALE
(including overtime and doubling)

LOCAL 47 H & W FUND—$3.75 per session for each original service
ARRANGERS/ORCHESTRATORS- $2.60 per tune
Maximum 7.80 per Form B Contract
COPYISTS   - $3.00 per day, but not less than 3.75 per original service
Maximum 15.00 per week or 3.75 per session, per service

3 HOURS		15 MIN. MUSIC		NO. SIDES	
Basic Session		Ldr/Ctr	274.42	Basic-Unlimited	
		Sideman	137.21	Sweetner-4 Sides	
½ hour o. t.			45.74		
¼ hour o. t.			22.87		
1st double		(20%)	27.44		
2nd & each thereafter		(15%)	20.58		
EPW - 10% . . . Sideman 13.72 . . . Leader 27.44					

3½ HOURS	20 MIN. MUSIC	NO. SIDES	4 HOURS	MIN. MUSIC	NO. SIDES
Ldr/Ctr	365.90	Basic-Unlimited	Ldr/Ctr	457.38	Basic-Unlimited
Sideman	182.95	Sweetner-5	Sideman	228.69	Sweetner-6
1st Double	36.59	(20%)	1st Double	45.74	(20%)
2nd Double	27.44	(15%)	2nd Double	34.30	(15%)
EPW - 10%	Sideman 18.30	Leader: 36.59	EPW - 10%	Sideman 22.87	Leader: 45.74

4½ HOURS	30 MIN. MUSIC	NO. SIDES	5 HOURS	35 MIN. MUSIC	NO. SIDES
Ldr/Ctr	548.86	Basic-Unlimited	Ldr/Ctr	640.34	Basic-Unlimited
Sideman	274.43	Sweetener-7	Sideman	320.17	Sweetner-8
1st Double	54.89	(20%)	1st double	64.03	(20%)
2nd Double	41.16	(15%)	2nd Double	48.03	(15%)
EPW - 10%	Sideman: 27.44	Leader: 54.89	EPW - 10%	Sideman: 32.02	Leader: 64.03

LEADERS AND / OR CONTRACTORS:
1. Sessions must be reported in advance.
2. Contracts must be completely made out.
3. The leader or contractor must, within 72 hours of the session, turn in B-4 contract with completed W-4's for all personnel to the company and have the representative of the company accepting the contract initial and date it to acknowledge receipt of same. If the contract and W-4's are mailed to the company, they must be sent by certified mail, return receipt requested.

FOLLOWING HOLIDAYS - DOUBLE SCALE
New Year's Day, Washington's Birthday, Memorial Day, Independence Day, Labor Day, Thanksgiving, Christmas.

149

PREMIUM RECORDING SCALES—150% OF REGULAR SCALE

3 HOURS	15 MIN. MUSIC	NO. SIDES	3½ HOURS	20 MIN.MUSIC	NO. SIDES
Ldr/Ctr	411.66	Basic-Unlimited	Ldr/Ctr	548.88	Basic-Unlimited
Sideman	205.83	Sweetener-4	Sideman	274.44	Sweetener-5
½ hour o.t.	68.61		1st Double	54.89	
1st Double	41.17		2nd Double	41.17	
2nd Double	30.87				
EPW-10%	Sideman: 20.58	Leader: 41.17	EPW-10%	Sideman: 27.44	Leader: 54.88

4 HOURS	25 MIN. MUSIC	NO. SIDES	4½ HOURS	30 MIN. MUSIC	NO. SIDES
Ldr/Ctr	686.10	Basic-Unlimited	Ldr/Ctr	823.32	Basic-Unlimited
Sideman	343.05	Sweetener-6	Sideman	411.66	Sweetener-7
1st Double	68.61		1st Double	82.33	
2nd Double	51.45		2nd Double	61.75	
EPW-10%	Sideman: 34.31	Leader: 68.61	EPW-10%	Sideman: 41.17	Leader: 82.33

SESSIONS WHICH INCLUDE PREMIUM TIME

Premium Rates Apply as Follows:
 Weekdays: After 12:00 AM midnight
 Saturday: After 1:00 PM
 Sunday: All day

9:30 PM- 12:30 AM	Ldr/Ctr	297.30
or	Sideman	148.65
Saturday	1st Double	29.73
10:30 AM- 1:30 PM	2nd Double	22.30
EPW-10%	Sideman:14.87	Leader: 29.73

10:00 PM- 1:00 AM	Ldr/Ctr	320.18
or	Sideman	160.09
Saturday	1st Double	32.02
11:00 AM- 2:00 PM	2nd Double	24,01
EPW-10%	Sideman: 16.01	Leader: 32.02

10:30 PM-1:30 AM	Ldr/Ctr	343.04
or	Sideman	171.52
Saturday	1st Double	34.30
11:30 PM- 1:30 PM	2nd Double	25.73
EPW-10%	Sideman: 17.15	Leader: 34.30

11:00 PM- 2:00 AM	Ldr/Ctr	365.90
or	Sideman	182.95
Saturday	1st Double	36.59
12:00 PM- 3:00 PM	2nd Double	27.44
EPW-10%	Sideman: 18.30	Leader: 36.59

11:30PM-2:30 AM	Ldr/Ctr	388.78
or	Sideman	194.39
Saturday	1st Double	38.88
12:30 PM 3:30 PM	2nd Double	29.17
EPW-10%	Sideman: 19.44	Leader: 38.88

SPECIAL SESSION SCALES — SWEETENING IS NOT PERMITTED

1½ HOURS	7½ MIN. MUSIC	NO. SIDES	2 HOURS	7½ MIN. MUSIC	NO. SIDES
Basic Session:			Ldr/Ctr	241.48	2 Sides
Ldr/Ctr	181.12	2 Sides	Sideman	120.74	
Sideman	90.56		1st. Double	24.15	
1st Double	18.11		2nd Double	18.11	
2nd Double	13.65				
½ hour o.t. (max)	30.20				
¼ hour o.t. (max)	15.10				
EPW-10%	Sideman: 9.06	Leader: 18.11	EPW-10%	Sideman: 12.07	Leader:24.14

F. Session Calls and Cancellations

A session, once called, shall not be cancelled, postponed, or otherwise rescheduled less than 7 days prior to the date of the session. In the event of an emergency, a session may be cancelled, postponed or otherwise rescheduled upon shorter notice with the consent of the office of the Federation President.

APPENDIX D
American Federation of Television and Radio Artists National Code of Fair Practice for Phonograph Recordings

(1) UNION SECURITY

On the thirtieth (30th) day following the effective date of this provision or on the thirtieth (30th) day following the first engagement of an artist, whichever is later, membership in the union shall be required of each artist as a condition of engagement, provided however, that when a recording is produced in an area where AFTRA then does not have a bona fide Chapter or Local, (or, having a Chapter or Local, AFTRA does not warrant that it represents a majority of artists in that area), then the provisions of this clause shall not apply to artists engaged in making recordings in that area; it being understood however the other provisions of this Code shall apply to such artists.

(2) NO STRIKE, NO LOCKOUT

The Company shall not engage in any lockout and AFTRA, its representatives and members shall not cause, authorize, give leadership to or take part in any strike or other curtailment or restriction of work, pending arbitration as herein agreed to, provided, however, that the failure of a party to comply with any Arbitration Award made against such party, shall release the other party from its obligations under this paragraph.

(3) ARBITRATION

All disputes and controversies of every kind and nature whatsoever between any Company and AFTRA or between any Company and any member of AFTRA, arising out of or in connection with this Code, and any contract or engagement made or extended on or after April 1, 1977 (whether overscale or not, and whether at the minimum terms and conditions of this Code or better) in the field covered by this Code as to the existence, validity, construction, meaning, interpretation, performance, non-performance, enforcement, operation, breach, continuance, or termination of this Code and/or such contract or engagement shall be submitted to arbitration in accordance with the following procedure and such arbitration shall be conducted under the Voluntary Labor Arbitration Rules then obtaining of the American Arbitration Association except as otherwise provided herein:

(a) AFTRA, the Company concerned, or (with the written consent of AFTRA endorsed upon the demand for arbitration) the artist concerned, may demand such arbitration in writing, which demand shall include the name of the arbitrator appointed by the party demanding arbitration. Within three (3) days after such demand, the other party shall name its arbitrator, or in default of such appointment, such arbitrator shall be named forthwith by the Arbitration Committee of the American Arbitration Association. The two arbitrators so appointed shall select a third within a period of five days, from a panel submitted to them by the American Arbitration Association and in lieu of their agreement upon such third arbitrator, he shall be appointed by the Arbitration Committee of the American Arbitration Association. Each party shall bear his own arbitration expense and one-half the expense of the third arbitrator.

(b) The hearing shall be held on two (2) days' notice and shall be concluded within fourteen (14) days unless otherwise ordered by the arbitrators. The award of the arbitrators shall be made within seven (7) days after the close of the submission of evidence. An award agreed to by a majority of the arbitrators so appointed shall be final and binding upon all parties to the proceedings during the period of this agreement, and judgment upon such award may be entered by any party in the highest court of the forum, state or federal, having jurisdiction.

(c) The parties agree that the provisions of this Paragraph shall be a complete defense to any suit, action or proceeding instituted in any Federal, State or local court or before any administrative tribunal with respect to any controversy or dispute which arises during the period of this agreement and which is therefore arbitrable as set forth above. The arbitration provisions of this agreement shall, with respect to such controversy or dispute, survive the termination or expiration of this agreement.

(d) AFTRA shall be an ex officio party to all arbitration proceedings hereunder in which any artist is involved, and AFTRA may do anything which an artist named in such proceeding might do. Copies of all notices, demands, and other papers filed by any party in arbitration proceedings, and copies of all motions, actions or proceedings in court following the award, shall be promptly filed with AFTRA.

(e) Nothing herein contained shall be deemed to give the arbitrators the authority, power or right to alter, amend, change, modify, add to or subtract from any of the provisions of this Code or of any contract or engagement between the Company and an artist.

The arbitrators in making an award with respect to any claim hereunder may, in the light of all the facts and circumstances involved in connection with such claim, in their discretion: (1) make their award effective as of the date when payments were first due, or (b) make their award effective as of the date of the award, or (c) make their award effective as of any intermediate date.

Notwithstanding anything to the contrary which may be contained herein, it is agreed that in any instance where the Company has a written contract providing for the exclusive services of an artist, and the Company has reason to believe that the artist has recorded or contemplates recording in violation of said contract, the Company shall have the right to apply to any court having jurisdiction, for injunctive and other relief arising out of the act which gave rise to the complaint.

(4) FAVORED NATIONS CLAUSE

AFTRA shall not enter into any agreement with, or issue a Code to, any producer of phonograph records, which is more favorable to such producer than this Code without offering to producers who are signatories to this Code the benefits of such agreement or Code entered into with such other producer, subject to the same obligations. Any more favorable terms or conditions given to other persons, firms or corporations producing phonograph recordings will be made available by AFTRA to producers who are signatory to this Code to the extent given such other persons, firms or corporations and AFTRA shall give notice of any such more favorable terms to all signatories of this Code. This does not apply to waivers given by AFTRA in special instances if such waiver be given in good faith and without intent either to evade this clause or give an unfair competitive advantage.

(5) DUBBING, MULTIPLE TRACKING, AND CONVERSIONS

(a) Performances of artists rendered for use in any other medium (such as, but not limited to, radio, transcriptions, television or motion pictures) may be dubbed, re-recorded or otherwise transferred or converted for use as phonograph recordings so long as the Company gives notice thereof to AFTRA, on behalf of all such artists, pays the AFTRA scale to such artists and obtains the consent of any "star or featured or overscale artist," if any, and in addition, in such case where an artist performs the vocal sound track for the "star or featured or overscale artist," obtains the consent of such artist. The Company will furnish to AFTRA, upon request, a copy of the warranty or such other evidence in its possession which it relies upon as assurance of such consents having been obtained. Nothing herein contained shall mean that AFTRA itself has given or can give any consent on behalf of its members hereunder. All checks for services performed under this paragraph shall be mailed to the local AFTRA office.

(b) MULTIPLE TRACKING. When an artist participates in multiple tracking (i.e., sings again to the original track at the same session) he shall be paid for the session as if each overtracking were an additional side.

(6) MINIMUM RATES

The following minimum compensation shall be paid to artists for making phonograph recordings:

(a) SOLOISTS AND DUOS who are engaged to perform on phonograph records shall receive a minimum of $90.00 per person per hour or per side, whichever is higher.

(b) GROUP SINGERS

No. of Singers in Group	Rate Per Person Per Hour or Per Side Whichever Is Higher	Minimum Call
3 to 8	$35.50	$71.00

9 to 16	28.50	57.00
17 to 24	25.00	50.00
25 to 35 (Non-Classical)	21.25	42.50
36 or more (Non-Classical)	18.00	36.00

In the event payment on the hourly basis is more favorable to the artist, such payment may be computed in quarter-hour periods, i.e., payment shall be made on the basis of one fourth of the hourly rate for each quarter-hour or part thereof.

In addition to the above compensation each singer shall receive premium pay in an amount equal to $5.00 per hour for each hour of part thereof worked between 1:00 a.m. and 6:00 a.m. Monday thru Friday and for all hours worked on Saturday and Sunday, New Year's Day, Memorial Day, July 4th, Labor Day, Thanksgiving Day, and Christmas.

(c) CLASSICAL RECORDINGS

(i) When a singing group of 25 or more is engaged to record classical music in conjunction with an orchestra, the following rates and conditions shall apply:

$46.00 effective April 1, 1977; $48.00 effective April 1, 1978; $50.00 effective April 1, 1979. These rates apply for a 3 hour minimum call for up to 20 minutes of recorded music.

Overtime—$14.50 per hour or per side, whichever is higher.

(ii) Similar groups performing acapella (no orchestra or instrumental accompaniment) shall be paid $14.50 per hour or per side, whichever is higher, with a minimum call of 2 hours.

(iii) Coach rehearsal for such groups need not be contiguous to the recording session. Minimum call for coach rehearsal shall be 2 hours in length and shall be within 48 hours of the recording session. The rehearsal fee shall be $7.00 per hour.

(iv) In order to avail itself of this provision for coach rehearsal in connection with classical recordings, the Company shall submit a request to the AFTRA Local office and AFTRA shall determine whether or not the recording falls within the classical classification. Not more than four (4) days after the Company's request (excluding Saturdays, Sundays and holidays) AFTRA shall advise the Company of its determination, and in the absence of such advice the request shall be deemed granted. Except as provided in this subparagraph, all other rehearsal shall be computed at the per person per hour or per side rates provided in the schedules above.

(d) RECORDING OF LIVE PERFORMANCES (Concerts, Nightclubs, etc.)

In every instance in which there is a recording of an artist's live performance in concert (excluding festivals), or in a night club or the like (but excluding those recordings which are the subject of the provisions in Subparagraph (g) of this Paragraph 6), each artist shall be paid an amount equal to a minimum call of two hours for all performances recorded during any particular 24 hour period, whether or not any sides are released. If any side so recorded is released, the artist shall then receive the difference, if any, between the amount paid him under this provision (6) (d) and the applicable minimum scale payments hereunder.

(e) "STEPPING OUT"

(i) If out of any group, a soloist or duo steps out and sings 16 or more cumulative bars on a particular side, then each of the singers so stepping out shall be paid for that side at the soloist and duo rate in paragraph 6(a) above, in lieu of the group rate. This provision shall not apply to groups of 5 or less where the terms of such engagement include any royalty payment. In any case in which payment shall be required pursuant to this subparagraph (i), the provisions of the three following sub-paragraphs shall not be applicable.

(ii) In out of a group of 9 or more singers called for a particular side, less than the number called steps out for 8 or more successive bars or 16 or more cumulative bars, the smaller group shall be paid for that side the minimum compensation applicable to a group of that size. A solo or duo stepping out for 8 or more successive bars but less than 16 cumulative bars shall be paid $35.50 for that side in addition to the group fee for the group called.

(iii) If out of a group of 8 or less called for a particular side, one singer steps out for 8 or more successive bars but less than 16 cumulative bars, then that singer shall be paid $35.50 for the side in addition to the group rate; if 2 singers step out for 8 or more successive bars but less than 16 cumulative bars, then each shall be paid $23.75 for that side in addition to the group rate; if 3 or more singers step out for 8 or more successive bars but less than 16 cumulative bars as soloists or duos, then each shall be paid $17.75 for that side in addition to the group rate. This provision shall not apply to groups of 5 or less where the terms of such engagement include any royalty payment.

(iv) Any bar or bars sung on a particular side by such "step-out" after 8 or more successive bars or 16 or more cumulative bars, whether immediate to or not, requires the applicable payment hereinabove provided.

(f) ACTORS, NARRATORS AND ANNOUNCERS

The minimum rate applicable to actors shall be $59.75 and to narrators and announcers $67.50 per hour or per side, whichever is higher, and the minimum call in one session for actors, narrators and announcers shall be at least the equivalent of the rate for two sides. There shall be no doubling on any side without additional compensation equivalent to the full minimum fee per part played. In the event an actor plays 3 or more roles, his minimum fee shall be $179.25 per hour or per side, whichever is higher. A singer who speaks incidental lines in character or an actor who sings in character shall receive not less than the higher of the two fees. It shall be considered doubling if a singer speaks lines not in character or an actor sings lines not in character and both applicable fees shall be paid in such cases. Participation in crowd noises shall not be considered doubling.

(g) MINIMUM RATES—ORIGINAL CAST SHOW ALBUMS

With respect to the recording of musical original cast show albums, all persons in the show with a voice part shall be compensated at the rates enumerated above but in no case shall the minimum fee be less than $300.00 per person or per side or per hour rate, whichever is greater, provided that in the case of off-Broadway musical shows the minimum shall be $220.00 per person or per side or per hour rate, whichever is greater. Company shall not require any person in the show to work beyond 6:30 p.m. on any show day. Performers who are not in the cast shall be paid in accordance with the applicable provisions of the Code, and be paid in accordance with the number of singers added to the cast. Participation in crowd noises shall not be considered a voice part.

With respect to the recording of original Industrial cast albums of a show, done in the manner of an original cast show, all persons in the show with a voice part shall be compensated at the rates and under the conditions as specified above for minimum rates for off-Broadway musical shows. However, with respect to the recording of an Industrial show album done in any other manner all persons with a voice part shall be compensated at the rates and under the conditions as otherwise specified in this Code.

The premium pay provision of paragraph 6 (b) hereof shall not be applicable to recordings made under this sub-paragraph (g).

In the event that the Union having original jurisdiction of the musical show or off-Broadway musical show shall negotiate a higher rate than the above rates for the recording of original cast show albums, that higher rate shall be paid. For purposes of Contingent Scale Payment, rates shown above, including any higher rates as negotiated by the Union having original jurisdiction, shall be the "applicable minimum scale" for the purpose of applying Contingent Scale Payment provisions.

(h) SOUND EFFECTS ARTISTS

The minimum rate applicable to sound effects artists shall be $59.75 for the first hour and $22.75 for each additional half-hour or less. Sound effects artists performing vocal sound effects shall be paid the actors' minimum rate.

(i) LIMITATION OF PAYMENTS—SELF CONTAINED GROUPS

Notwithstanding the foregoing, as to Artists (including Contractors) in self contained groups of two or more who are engaged for performing on phonograph records, where the terms of such engagements include royalty payments, such royalty artists shall be paid the minimum scale payments for each side recorded but in no event shall such royalty artists be entitled to more than three times the minimum scale payments per side regardless of the number of times such side is recorded or the number of hours required to record such side.

(j) CONTINGENT SCALE:

In addition to the minimum compensation due an artist as provided in the preceding sub-paragraphs of this Paragraph 6, certain additional payments ("contingent scale") may be applicable under Appendix A.

(7) COMPENSATION (No fees or compensation due an artist for performing services in any other media covered by a collective bargaining agreement may be credited against such artist's royalties.)

Artists shall be paid not less than the minimum fee applicable in legal tender of the United States and not later than twenty-one (21) calendar days after the time specified for performances. The mimimum fees specified in this Code shall be net to the artist and no deductions whatsoever may be made by Company from such fees except for such taxes and withholdings as are required by law which shall be deducted and paid by the Company to the appropriate authority(ies). In cases where performances in one media are transferred or converted for use as phonograph records as provided in Paragraph 5, the date of such release shall be the time specified for performance for purposes of this paragraph; provided, however, that the penalty for late payment as hereinafter provided shall not apply if notwithstanding the Producer's reasonable efforts (including notice to AFTRA prior to such release that an issue of identity exists) he is unable to ascertain the name of a performer entitled to the payment required by

Paragraph 5. When the performer's identity has been ascertained the provision for penalty shall apply.

Company agrees to furnish each artist or the contractor on behalf of the artist represented by him, a statement specifying the name of employer, the dates of performance, the amount of payment, and of each deduction, and all other pertinent information which may be necessary for tax purposes. Such statement may be on check vouchers, or in any other convenient form which may be retained by the artist. In states which have State Disability Insurance Laws requiring deductions, such deductions shall likewise be noted on the check or statement. The statement should also include the employer's name or registration number in those states where unemployment insurance laws require that such information be given to the employee by the employer. All session payments for any services rendered to the Company pursuant to this Code shall be in the form of checks issued in favor of the individual performers concerned and mailed to the local AFTRA office for distribution. Such checks must be for not less than the minimums required by this Code nor may payments of any nature to the performers concerned be deducted from such minimum checks except royalties, advances and loans and deductions required by applicable law.

Penalty For Late Payment

The following cumulative payments shall be added to the compensation due and payable to the performer for each day, beginning with the day following the day of default, on which payment remains not made. Three Dollars ($3.00) for each day's delinquency up to 30 days (excluding Saturday, Sunday, and holidays which the company observes). Thereafter, the penalty payment shall cease unless either AFTRA or the member gives written notice by registered mail to the Company of non-payment. In the event such notice is given and full payment including accrued penalties is not made within 10 working days thereafter, the penalty payment shall be resumed on the 11th day and continues without limitation. The above such payments shall be in addition to any and all remedies which AFTRA or the performer may have against the producer under the Code. The above cumulative payments shall not apply in the following cases:

(a) A bona fide dispute as to the amount due and payable concerning which AFTRA has been notified promptly;

(b) Force majeure;

(c) Where there is no contractor, and an artist has failed to furnish to the Company pertinent information required on Schedule B, and all W-4 forms (provided, however, that Company has made such forms available at the recording date);

(d) Where there is a contractor, and he has failed to furnish to the Company his W-4 form, (provided, however, that Company has made such forms available at the recording date);

(e) Where the artist, having been furnished his engagement contract on or before session day, fails to return the signed engagement contract promptly.

Liquidated Damages Defined

Wherever in this agreement there is provision for a fee or penalty arising out of the Producer's failure to comply with the terms of this agreement relating to payment to Performer on time, the amount set forth in this agreement as a fee or penalty for such breach is an amount agreed upon between the parties hereto, which is presumed to be the amount of damage

157

sustained by reason of the breach, because from the nature of the situation it would be impracticable or extremely difficult to fixe the actual damage.

(8) DEFINITION OF "SIDE"

(a) Re: Singers

A side shall be deemed to be one song or a bona fide medley on a single record, the playing time of which shall not exceed 3½ minutes, and for each 60 seconds or portion thereof in excess of 3½ minutes, an additional 50% of the applicable per side unit shall be paid. In the case of long playing or extended play records or other micro groove recordings or tape or any other similar or dissimilar device now or hereafter devised, of longer duration than the single side established above, payment shall be made in accordance with the per hour or per side rate in musical selection units of 3 minutes and 30 seconds or less. With respect to long playing records containing selections of 1½ minutes or less in length, the total playing time of such selections shall be paid for in units of 3½ minutes, and any remaining selections thereon which exceed 1½ minutes shall be paid for as separate selections. In the case of classical recordings the above scales shall be predicated upon recording ten minutes of finished recorded music in a two-hour session; fifteen minutes in a three-hour session—or an average of not more than five minutes of finished recorded music for each hour of the session. When in the case of classical recordings the finished recorded music within a two or three hour session exceeds these limits, the artist shall receive one-fourth hour's pay for each additional 1¼ minutes of finished recorded material or part thereof. NOTE: See paragraph 6(c), page 4, for additional provisions concerning classical recordings.

(b) Re: Actors, Announcers and Narrators

A side shall be deemed to be a narration, dramatic reading, poetry, monologue or dialogue, on a single record, the playing time of which shall not exceed 3 minutes and 30 seconds, and for each 60 seconds, or portion thereof in excess of 3 minutes and 30 seconds an additional 50% of the applicable per side rate shall be paid. In the case of performances of such material embodied on long playing or extended play records or other micro groove recordings or tape or any similar or dissimilar device now or hereafter devised of longer duration than the single side established above, artists shall be paid at the per side rate for each 5-minute segment on which they respectively perform, or at the per hour rate, whichever is higher, provided, however, that when in any one day (not exceeding eight hours of recording within a consecutive nine hour period, one hour of which shall be a meal period assigned no later than the fourth or fifth hour of recording) any artist has performed on eight 5-minute segment on which he performs, or at the per hour rate, whichever is higher. If performer is not informed of total number of sides on which he will appear at the time of his call he shall be paid on the basis of the number of hours worked, sides rehearsed or recorded, whichever is greater, whether or not final recording actually includes such performance but in no case less than two sides.

In the case of original cast show albums of such material, the minimum fee shall be not less than $300.00 per performer, or the per side or per hour rate whichever is greater except for off-Broadway shows where such minimum fee shall be $220.00 per performer, or such higher rate as might be required under paragraph 6(g), or the per side or per hour rate whichever is greater. Notwithstanding anything to the contrary which may be contained hereinabove, it is agreed that when any artist has performed eight hours of recording in any one day, he shall be paid for any subsequent recording services on that day in accordance with the above provisions of this subparagraph (b), as if said subsequent services were rendered on a separate day, including the provisions for the applicable minimum of $300.00 or $220.00 or such higher rate as might be required under paragraph 6(g). Company shall not require any artist having a conflicting engagement to work beyond 6:30 p.m. of any day of which engagement artist has notified Company at the time of call.

(9) CONTRACTORS

(a) Group Singers

Contractors shall be those artists who perform any additional services, such as contacting singers, pre-rehearsing, coaching, or conducting singers, arranging for sessions or rehearsals, or any other similar or supervisory duties, including assisting and preparing of production memorandum. In all cases the contractor shall be a member of AFTRA and a performing member of the singing group, except in those cases where the sex of the group precludes the utilization of the contractor's singing services. A contractor shall be required on all engagements of group singers consisting of 3 or more. The contractor shall be present at all times during the session. In addition to his fee as a singer, the contractor for group singers shall receive, in the case of groups of 3 to 8, $17.75 per side or per hour, whichever is higher; in the case of groups of 9 to 16, he shall receive $22.25 per side or per hour, whichever is higher; in the case of groups of 17 to 24, he shall receive $26.50 per side or per hour, whichever is higher; in the case of groups of 25 to 35, he shall receive $32.50 per side or per hour, whichever is higher; and in the case of groups of 36 or more, he shall receive $38.50 per side or per hour, whichever is higher. A contractor who does not perform at the session shall be paid either the applicable contractor's rate or the rate for the largest group performing at the session, whichever is higher.

(b) Original Cast and Industrial Show Albums

The Company shall give the Local office of AFTRA nearest to the location at which an Original Cast or Industrial Show Album is recorded 7 days advance notice of said recording. In the event Company does not itself have notice 7 days in advance, it will notify the AFTRA office promptly upon receiving it.

A contractor shall be required on all Original Cast Show Albums employing a singing group of 3 or more. Such contractor shall be a member of AFTRA in good standing who is a member of the singing group or a contractor who is a member of AFTRA in good standing not a member of the singing group. Such contractor's duties shall be: 1) act as a liaison between producer and cast and must be present at all times when 3 or more members of the said group are working; 2) responsible for the deportment and cooperation of the cast and assist the producer in the performance of his duties, as: calling rest periods, meal breaks, informing cast about rehearsal schedule and required duties, keeping accurate tally of rehearsal hours and notifying producer of AFTRA provisions pertinent to the session; 3) responsible for the completion of all appropriate forms and the filing of the same with AFTRA within 48 hours; 4) mandatorily notify AFTRA immediately of any violation or abuse of the terms and conditions of this Code or of any dispute arising at, or out of, the session. For the performance of services set forth above the contractor

159

shall be paid at least the applicable minimum rates specified above. Said payment shall be in addition to whatever fees he may earn as a performer on the album.

(10) WAIVERS

Upon written application by the Company for waivers from this Agreement, the National Board of AFTRA agrees to consider giving waivers in each and all of the following cases:

(a) Persons engaged because of reputation acquired in fields other than those covered by the Associated Actors and Artistes of America, insofar as the first side, record, or album for which they were originally engaged by the Company because of said reputation is concerned.

(b) Singing groups such as glee clubs, choirs and Choruses of bona fide philanthropic, educational or religious organizations. In respect to groups of 50 or more covered by this paragraph, if AFTRA grants a waiver request, the Company will pay at least $24.00 to each member of the group for his services at each recording session of three hours at which is produced not more than 60 minutes of recorded music.

Requests for waivers shall be made by the Company in writing and must be confirmed in writing by AFTRA within 4 days of receipt excluding Saturdays, Sundays and legal holidays. In the absence of written confirmation, all terms and conditions of this Code shall apply. Such waivers shall not be used by the Company to extend its present practices in these fields in a manner calculated to evade the obligations of this Agreement.

AFTRA agrees to consider waivers of other persons and groups, when requested by the Company, within the spirit of this Agreement.

(11) REST PERIODS

There must be a rest period of five minutes in each hour of any recording session. It shall be the contractor's or leader's responsibility (or that of a deputy appointed by the singing group if there is no contractor or leader) to request such rest period.

(12) PRODUCTION MEMORANDUM AND MEMBER REPORT

(a) Production Memorandum

Company agrees to furnish AFTRA with a production memorandum of each individual recording session, signed by an authorized agent of the Company. The production memorandum shall give full and specific information sufficient to permit computation of the performer's fee with respect to the services rendered by the performer and the gross fee paid. Where the artist is engaged on a royalty basis, the production memorandum shall so indicate. The form shall be as set forth on Schedule "A". The procedure for having these reports filed by the Company shall be as follows: It shall be the duty and responsibility of the contractor to fill out the pertinent information required on the form supplied by AFTRA, as set forth in AFTRA MEMBER CONTRACTOR STANDARD REPORT FORM and then deliver such form to the authorized representative of the Company who in turn will fill out whatever additional information is necessary and then file Schedule "A" form with the AFTRA office within 21 calendar days after the engagement. Where no contractor is engaged, it shall be the sole duty and responsibility of the Company to fill out the pertinent information required in the form and deliver such form to AFTRA within the time specified above.

(b) AFTRA Member Report

The Company has notice of the AFTRA rule requiring an actor, announcer, narrator, sound effects artist, soloist, or a member of a duo, or the contractor for singing groups of three or more to report on a form furnished by AFTRA, information regarding all phonograph recording engagements. The Company or producer agrees to initial such report indicating that the recording engagement has in fact been held. It is, however, the duty and responsibility solely of the AFTRA member to fill out properly and file the report with AFTRA.

(13) UNFAIR STUDIOS

The Company under this Code acknowledges that it has notice that under AFTRA's rules, no member of AFTRA may render services or give a performance for recording purposes in any recording studio or use the recording facilities of any recording studio declared unfair by AFTRA or where AFTRA has declared a strike or where AFTRA members have been locked out or where AFTRA has established an authorized picket line. The Company is not bound by such rules of AFTRA but neither AFTRA nor AFTRA members shall be subject to action for breach of contract or otherwise for complying with or enforcing such rules.

(14) ENGAGEMENTS

The artist shall have notice of date, time and place of recording, estimated number of sides and time required for rehearsal and recording, and to the extent practicable, such notice shall be given at the time of call. Compensation shall be computed from the time specified in the call or from the time the artist's services commence in the studio, whichever is earlier, provided, however, that if any AFTRA member engaged to perform under this Code is late in reporting for the call, then compensation for all other AFTRA members so engaged shall be computed from the time all AFTRA members scheduled to perform in that session are ready to perform, but in no event later than 30 minutes after the time of call. Where an artist has a bona fide engagement which will require him to leave the recording session any time after 30 minutes beyond the estimated closing of the recording session, Company agrees that if it is advised of such conflict at the time of the call but at least 48 hours excluding Sundays prior to the first scheduled session, then artist's attendance at such conflict shall not be considered a breach of contract.

(15) CANCELLATIONS

(a) Cancelled Session:

Where the recording session is cancelled by the Company, the artist shall, nevertheless, be paid no less than his minimum call, unless he shall have been notified of the cancellation at least 24 hours in advance of the first scheduled call.

(b) Cancelled individual engagements:

In the event the artist's engagement for the session is cancelled by the Company, the Company agrees to pay the artist his minimum call or his contract price if there is an applicable individual contract, whichever is higher, except where cancellation is for gross insubordination, or misconduct. Company agrees that after the engagement is made, the risk of the artist's competence is assumed by it.

(16) EXISTING CONTRACTS WITH ARTISTS
No provisions in existing contracts between the Company and artists which are more favorable to the artists than the provisions herein specified, shall be deemed modified by this Code.

On and after the effective date of this Code, the Company shall pay not less than the minimum rates specified herein, notwithstanding the provisions of existing contracts.

(17) CONTRACTS WITH ARTISTS
Every contract (whether written or oral) hereafter made between the Company and any artist must contain and shall be deemed to contain the following clause:

"Notwithstanding any provision in this contract to the contrary, it is specifically understood and agreed by all parties hereto:

(1) They are bound by all the terms and provisions of the AFTRA Code of Fair Practice for Phonograph Recordings.

(2) That should there by any inconsistency between this contract and the said CODE OF FAIR PRACTICE, the said CODE OF FAIR PRACTICE shall prevail, but nothing in this provision shall affect terms, conpensation or conditions provided in this contract which are more favorable to members of AFTRA than the terms, compensation and conditions provided for in said CODE OF FAIR PRACTICE.

(3) If the term of this contract is of longer duration than the term of the said Code, then from and after the expiration date of the Code: (a) the provisions of this contract shall be deemed modified to conform to any agreement or modifications negotiated or agreed to in a renewal or extension of the Code; and (b) while no code is in effect the existence of this contract shall not prevent the artist from engaging in any strike or work stoppage without penalty by way of damage or otherwise to the artist of AFTRA. In the event artist engages in such strike or stoppage the Company may suspend this contract for the duration of the strike or stoppage and may have the option of estending the term of this contract for a period of time equal to the length of such strike or stoppage which option must be exercised by written notice given to the artist within 30 days after the end of the strike or stoppage.

(4) The artist is or will become a member of AFTRA in good standing, subject to and in accordance with the union security provisions of said Code of Fair Practice.

(5) The artist is covered by Par. 34 of said Code entitled "AFTRA PENSION & WELFARE FUNDS."

(6) Compensation to artist as provided herein for the recording session, which shall in no event be less than the minimum fees set forth in said AFTRA CODE OF FAIR PRACTICE, shall be paid in legal tender of the United States of America not later than twenty-one (21) calendar days after the time specified for performance by artist.

(7) If this contract provides for royalty or other compensation (other than contingent scale payments) to be payable to artist on the basis of the number of units sold, Company agrees to furnish artist at least semi-annually and to AFTRA upon request (with regard to agreements effective on or after April 1, 1968) so long as there shall be sales, a full and

proper accounting in order to correctly ascertain the amount of royalty or other compensation due artist."

AFTRA reserves the right to require the Company to file with the local AFTRA office a copy of all such individual contracts subsequent to the execution thereof.

(18) PROHIBITED PAYMENT

If the artist performs services in any media covered by a collective bargaining agreement, the artist shall not pay to the Company or a subsidiary or an employee of the Company, nor may the Company require or accept, any portion of the fees paid to the artist in accordance with the terms of such collective bargaining agreement, except that nothing herein contained shall prohibit the repayment by the artist from such fees of a bona fide obligation then owed by artist to the Company or a subsidiary, nor the division of such fees paid to the artist among the artist performing as a group.

(19) ADDITIONAL SERVICES

No service of the artist is contracted for except as specified herein. This paragraph is not intended to prevent the artist from contracting for services of a kind not covered by the Code by individual contract at such rates of pay and under such conditions as the Company and the artist shall agree, provided that it shall not be in conflict with this Code.

(20) PRODUCTION PROSECUTED

In the event that the recording for which an artist is engaged by the Company is complained of because of the nature of the material, and a suit civil or criminal, private or governmental, shall follow, the Company agrees at its expense, to defend the artist and to pay all judgments and reasonable expenses and charges properly incurred in connection with the defense. This paragraph does not apply to a case where the action is in respect of material furnished by the artist or acts done by the artist without authorization of the Company.

(21) BONDS

AFTRA reserves the right in its sole discretion to require the posting in advance of an adequate bond, cash or other security.

(22) LEGISLATION AND/OR INTERNATIONAL CONVENTION

In the event that, during the term of this Agreement, new Federal domestic legislation is enacted into law and/or, during said term, the International Convention for the Protection of Performers, Producers of Phonograms and Broadcasting Organizations, dated October 26, 1961, becomes effective, which legislation or Convention creates new rights for performing artists with respect to their performances on phonograph records which are used directly for broadcasting or for any communication to the public, and, as a result of such enactment of legislation or the said Convention becoming effective, remuneration is in fact received by the Company, the Company and AFTRA will, on thirty (30) days' written request of either party to the other after March 31, 1974, negotiate in good faith how much of said remuneration shall be paid to the performers covered by the AFTRA Code who after March 31, 1974 will be engaged in the recording of the records involved for any such public performances. If such Convention or legislation shall provide for separate payments to performers, by reason of such public performance, none of the foregoing provisions of this paragraph shall apply. Nothing in this paragraph shall be construed as any indication that the Company favors the Convention or any legislation of the type or scope referred to in this paragraph.

It is specifically agreed that the principle hereinabove enunciated shall be contained in the next succeeding Code.

(23) COMPANY'S DUTIES
The Company agrees that:

(a) It will not enter into any agreement with or engage any artist for phonograph recordings covered hereby, upon terms and conditions less favorable to the artist than those set forth in this Code.

(b) No waiver or release by any artist of any provisions of this Code shall be effective unless the written consent of AFTRA to such waiver is first had and obtained.

(c) Nothing in this Code shall be deemed to prevent any artist from negotiating for and/or obtaining better terms than the minimum terms provided for herein.

(d) No waiver or release, whether oral, written, or endorsement on a check or otherwise, shall be effective to deprive an artist of his rights under this Code.

(24) OVER MINIMUM CONTRACTS
Any artist who is engaged to perform services at a scale, or under terms or conditions over and above the minimum scales, terms or conditions provided for in the Code, shall nevertheless have the protection and benefit of all other provisions and conditions set forth in this Code. If the compensation of the artist for any engagement is above the minimum specified herein, additional services at applicable minimum fees for such engagement may be credited by the Company up to the full amount of the compensation paid to such artist if there is a specific provision to such effect in the artist's written contract, or if in the case of verbal engagement, it is specifically agreed at the time the verbal engagement is entered into that the Company is entitled to such credit.

(25) ADMITTANCE
An authorized representative of AFTRA shall be admitted to the premises of the Company or where the rehearsal or recording takes place, at any reasonable time, to check the performance by the Company of this Code: but such checking shall be done so as not to interfere with the conduct of the Company's business.

(26) NO DISCRIMINATION
The parties to this Code reaffirm their long-established and prevailing policy against discrimination as set forth in the Joint Industry-AFTRA Statement of Policy, of which a copy is filed with AFTRA, and also agree not to discriminate against any artist because of race, sex, creed, color, age, or national origin.

(27) SEPARABILITY
If any clause, sentence, paragraph, or part of this Code or the application thereof to any person or circumstances, shall for any reason be adjudged by a court of competent jurisdiction to be

invalid, such judgment shall not affect, impair, or invalidate the remainder of this Code, or the application thereof to any person or circumstances, but shall be confined in its operation to the clause, sentence, paragraph, or part thereof directly involved in the controversy in which such judgment shall have been rendered and to the person or circumstances involved. It is hereby declared to be our intent that this Code would have been accepted even if such invalid provisions had not been included.

(28) CAST CREDITS

Cast Credits shall be listed on the album jackets for all performers playing major parts in a dramatic production (whether or not "Original cast"), except in the case of Broadway or off-Broadway shows where the Independent Producer of the show has specifically prohibited the same.

(29) MODIFICATIONS

Except by mutual agreement to the contrary, or unless this Agreement specifically provides otherwise, each party agrees that the other, for the life of this Agreement, shall not be obligated to conclude an agreement with respect to any subject pertaining directly or indirectly to the engagement of any artist in the phonograph record field, whether or not such subject is covered by this Agreement.

(30) UNFAIR PRODUCERS

This Code represents the minimum terms and conditions of recording artists. Anyone engaging artists in this field who breaches or violates any terms or conditions of the Code may be regarded as unfair, and artists may be instructed without injury or damage to artists or AFTRA, not to work on recordings covered by this Code for anyone who is unfair.

(31) INDEPENDENT CONTRACTORS

The Company agrees that in every agreement that it makes with an independent contractor (and the term "independent contractor" as used herein shall be deemed to mean all persons or entities with whom the Company enters into any relationship which includes the employment or performance for the Company of artists covered by this Code, in recordings, whether or not the relationship is one of sale and purchase, lease of masters, or sales and distribution of phonograph records on the Company's or the independent contractor's label, or any other label), it will include a provision expressly for the benefit of AFTRA and AFTRA members, requiring such independent contractor to sign, adopt and conform to the 1977-1980 AFTRA CODE OF FAIR PRACTICE FOR PHONOGRAPH RECORDINGS, and provided further that a signed copy of the Code is delivered by the Company or the independent contractor to AFTRA prior to the recording engagement. In the event Company fails to deliver to the AFTRA office prior to the recording engagement, or within 48 hours subsequent thereto, copies of the Code signed by the Independent Contractor then the Company will be obligated to make the minimum scale payments referred to in this Code with any applicable contributions thereon to AFTRA Pension and Welfare Funds.

(32) PURCHASED MASTERS

The Company agrees that if it purchases and/or leases any demonstration, presentation, audition or other master recordings recorded in the recording territory during the term of this Agreement for use in connection with the manufacture and sale of phonograph records, it will obtain from the seller and/or lessor thereof, the following warranty and representation for the direct benefit of AFTRA and all artists performing on the recording:

"That all artists whose performances embodied thereon were recorded in the recording territory, have been paid the minimum rates specified in the 1977-1978 AFTRA CODE OF FAIR PRACTICE FOR PHONOGRAPH RECORDINGS or the applicable Code then in effect at the time the recording was made, and that all payments due to the AFTRA PENSION AND WELFARE FUNDS have been made."

Company agrees to furnish to AFTRA on a form (Schedule "D") supplied by AFTRA the warranty and representation when masters are purchased from third parties or in the absence of the warranty the Company will execute Schedule "A" listing performers and proper payment by the Company.

The requirements of this Paragraph (32) shall be deemed to mean and include any instance described above in this Paragraph (32) in which the Company acts as the sales agent or distributor for another person or entity either on the Company's label, the label of the other person or entity, or any other label, and whether or not the Company is compensated on a royalty or commission basis.

If the warranty set forth in this Paragraph (32) shall be false, and if the seller, lessor, person or other entity controlling the said master recording was not a signatory to an AFTRA PHONOGRAPH RECORDING CODE at the time the recording was made or at the time of the purchase, lease or any other arrangement as defined herein, then the Company shall be obligated to make the minimum scale payment required together with any applicable contributions thereon to the AFTRA PENSION AND WELFARE FUNDS.

(32) (a) TRANSFERS OF TITLE FOR BENEFIT OF CREDITORS, ETC.

In addition to the provisions set forth above, and not in limitation or derogation thereof, it is further agreed that:

The transferee of title to or rights in a "master" recording, whether such transfer is effected by sale, assignment, pledge, hypothecation, or other transfer, or by attachment, levy, lien, garnishment, voluntary bankruptcy, involuntary bankruptcy, arrangement, reorganization, assignment for benefit of creditors, probate, or any other legal proceeding involving the Producer or the Producer's successors in interest, shall be responsible (after default by the Producer in the Producer's royalty obligations to any Artist whose performances are embodied in the "master" and receipt by the transferee of written notice from the Artist specifying the default) for the payment of all royalties due to the Artist, in accordance with the Artist's contract with the producer, accruing by virtue of sale by the transferee or under license by him of phonograph records derived from such "master" after the receipt by the transferee of such notice, which shall be accompanied by due proof of the Artist's royalty arrangements. Any transferee becoming responsible for obligations to an Artist pursuant to this section shall remain responsible to the Artist with regard to such sales by a successor in interest of the transferee, unless such successor has been accepted by AFTRA as a signatory to the then current AFTRA National Code of Fair Practice for Phonograph Recordings. When a successor is such a signatory all prior transferors other than the Producer shall no longer be responsible for such sales by further successors.

Every transferee of title to or rights in a "master" recording who is not a signatory to the then current AFTRA National Code of Fair Practice for Phonograph Recordings, shall sign an agreement with AFTRA assuming the obligations set forth in the immediately preceding paragraph.

Every Producer hereunder agrees to incorporate the terms of this entire paragraph 32 (A) in any transfer of all or part of his interest in a "master" recording as well as a provision requiring the same undertaking to be incorporated in all such subsequent transfers.

In the event a transferee in addition to acquiring title to or rights in a "master" recording also acquires from the Producer or the transferor finished goods or inventories of phonograph records derived from such "master" recording, the transferee shall also pay to the Artist under the conditions as set forth above, all royalties accruing by virtue of sales of such finished goods or inventories by the transferee to third parties including subsidiaries or affiliates of the transferee, and also incorporate the same undertaking in any subsequent transfer by him of the "master" recording concerned, where such transfer includes such finished goods or inventories previously acquired by transferee but not theretofore sold by transferee.

The provisions of this paragraph 32 (A) shall apply only to such transfers made on or after April 1, 1968.

(33) CATALOGUES AND RETAIL PRICE LISTS
The Company shall promptly furnish to the American Federation of Television and Radio Artists, upon request, a copy of all of the Company's record catalogues and a schedule of its manufacturer's suggested retail prices for each record in its catalogue and thereafter from time to time a schedule listing all amendments and additions thereto as and when established.

At the end of each calendar month, the Company shall advise the American Federation of Television and Radio Artists of all recordings made by the Company during said month, the serial or other number thereof, and any additional information in connection with such recording which AFTRA may reasonably require. Upon request by AFTRA, the Company shall promptly furnish to it a copy of any such recordings. The Company shall respond promptly to reasonable request by AFTRA for information relating to the Company's performance of the terms and conditions of this Code.

(34) AFTRA PENSION AND WELFARE FUNDS
SECTION 1. (a) Subject to the limits hereafter provided, the Company shall make to the American Federation of Television and Radio Artists Pension and Welfare Funds (hereinafter referred to as the AFTRA Pension and Welfare Funds), a payment equal to 7¾% of the gross compensation actually paid to an artist by the Company, in respect of services (including rehearsal) rendered by him or contracted by him under this Code on and after April 1, 1974, and regardless of the commencement date of any existing contract between the artist and the Company, said payment to be made to the AFTRA PENSION & WELFARE FUNDS not later than three weeks following date of performance. The term "gross compensation" as used hereinabove includes but is not limited to all forms of payment of any kind or nature whatsoever (but without any recoupment, deductions, set-offs, etc., except as otherwise specifically provided herein), including salaries, earnings, royalties, fees, advances, guarantees, deferred compensation, proceeds, bonuses, profit-participation, shares of stock, bonds, options and property of any kind or nature whatsoever paid to the artist directly or indirectly or to any other person, firm, entity or corporation on his behalf, and/or whether paid during the term of this Code or the artist's individual agreement with the Company regardless of the continued existence of this or successor Code.

(b) Notwithstanding anything to the contrary hereinabove provided, said 7¾% payment shall be applicable only as follows:

(1) In the case of an individual artist—to the first $100,000 of gross compensation paid to the artist in respect of any calendar year regardless of time or method of payment.

(2) In the case of a group of artists under a group contract with the Company—to the first $100,000 of gross compensation paid to the group in respect of any calendar year regardless of the time or method of payment, it being understood and agreed that each member of the group shall be entitled to his aliquot portion of the gross compensation or as provided in his agreement with the Company or his agreement with the other members of the group. Where the membership of the group is changed by reason of death or replacement of a member or members in any year the Company's maximum liability in respect of the group shall not be increased thereby.

(c) Irrespective of any agreement between the artist and the Company which permits the Company to recoup, set-off, or deduct recording costs before payment to the artist, and without in any way affecting or modifying any such agreement, the 7¾% Pension & Welfare payment shall be computed on the basis of the payment made to the artist less union minimum scale fees or fees based upon such minimum scale actually paid by the Company in respect of musicians (including leaders, instrumental musicians, orchestra contractors, copyists, orchestrators, and arrangers) employed in connection with the artist's such services.

(d) In the case of a deceased individual artist the 7¾% payment to the AFTRA Pension and Welfare Funds shall be applicable to the artist's gross compensation in respect of the year of death and subsequent years, whether paid to the artist or to his personal representatives, but only up to an aggregate of $100,000. In the case of a deceased member of a group of artists the same limit shall be applicable except that such limit shall be computed by reference to the artist's aliquot share of the group's gross compensation.

(e) The aforementioned sum shall be used solely (i) for the purpose of providing pension benefits for artists (eligible employees) under this Code, (ii) for the purpose of providing welfare benefits for artists under this Code and, at the discretion of the Trustees, for artists (eligible employees) within AFTRA's jurisdiction and, at the further discretion of the Trustees, for their families, and (iii) for the incidental expenses connected with the establishment and administration of the AFTRA Pension and Welfare Funds. The aforementioned sum may also be used to provide occupational disability benefits to artists (performers) who suffer disability arising out of or in the course of employment in rendering services within the jurisdiction of AFTRA. The Trustees of the AFTRA Welfare Fund are directed to continue such benefits to artists (performers), whether or not eligible for other benefits of the AFTRA Welfare Fund, so long as the Trustees determine in their discretion that such benefits can be provided to such artists (performers) without impairing the financial capacity of the AFTRA Welfare Fund to continue or expand the existing plan of benefits.

(f) Nothing in this Code shall be construed as suspending or modifying the prior AFTRA Code Pension and Welfare provisions applicable to services performed from October 1, 1959 to and including March 31, 1974 nor shall this Code be construed as requiring any duplication of payment under such prior AFTRA Code Pension and Welfare provisions.

Section 2. The AFTRA Pension and Welfare Funds shall be Trust Funds and shall be administered under the AFTRA Pension and Welfare Funds Agreement and Declaration of

Trust, dated November 16, 1954, which Agreement and Declaration of Trust is hereby ratified and confirmed, and is made a part of this Code with the same force and effect as though fully set forth herein. The said Agreement and Declaration of Trust shall provide, among other things:

(a) That the Pension and Welfare Funds be administered by twelve (12) named Principal Trustees, six (6) designated by the Producers and six (6) designated by AFTRA; and six (6) named Alternate Trustees are designated to serve in place or stead of the Principal Trustees in the event of death, disability, resignation or absence.

(b) That AFTRA may, at any time in its discretion on written notice to all the Trustees then in office, appoint a successor or successors for any one or more of the AFTRA Principal Trustees and Alternate Trustees named in said Agreement and Declaration of Trust. The written notice shall contain the names of the new Principal and/or Alternate Trustees and the names of the Principal and/or Alternate Trustees whom they replace. The Producers may, in a similar manner in their discretion, appoint successor Principal Trustees and Alternate Trustees for any one or more of the Producer's Principal Trustees named in said Agreement and Declaration of Trust. The Principal Trustees of the AFTRA Pension and Welfare Funds and any Alternate Trustee when acting as a Principal Trustee are herein referred to as the "Trustees." The Trustees shall act by majority vote.

(c) That the Trustees shall determine the form, nature, and amount of pension and welfare benefits and the rules of eligibility for such benefits, except as otherwise provided in this agreement. The welfare benefits shall include in the discretion of the Trustees any one or more of the following benefits (but none other): death, accidental death, dismemberment, hospitalization, surgical expense, medical expense, temporary disability.

(d) That employers having other collective bargaining agreements with AFTRA may, with the approval of the Trustees, become contributing Producers and parties to the Trust Agreement; and by agreeing to be bound by the Trust Agreement, such other Producers thereby appoint the Producers' Principal Trustees and Alternate Trustees named in the Agreement and Declaration of Trust and/or their successors.

(e) That the plan of pension benefits adopted thereunder shall be subject to the approval of the Internal Revenue Service as a qualified plan. If any part of the plan is not approved by the Internal Revenue Service the plan shall be modified by the Trustees, but subject to the limitations set forth in this agreement, to such form as is approved by the Internal Revenue Service.

(f) That no portion of the contribution may be paid or revert to the Company (Producer).

(g) That during the term of this Code, the said Agreement and Declaration of Trust shall not change or modify this paragraph 34.

SECTION 3. Each Company (Producer) shall furnish the Trustees the information pertaining to the names, job classifications, social security numbers and gross compensation up to the specified limits for all artists covered by this Agreement, together with such other information as may be reasonably required for the proper, low cost and efficient administration of the AFTRA Pension and Welfare Funds. Advances made to an artist will be reported to the appropriate office of the Pension and Welfare Funds on a quarterly basis if not reported earlier pursuant to the reporting obligations of Section 6. The Trustees and AFTRA represent, warrant, and covenant that all such information will be treated as confidential and will be used solely for purpose of administering the AFTRA Pension and Welfare Funds and for no other purpose except as may be required by due process of law.

SECTION 4. These provisions for the AFTRA Pension and Welfare Funds are in addition to (and not in substitution in whole or in part for) any existing pension and/or welfare funds covering any of the artists (performers) under this agreement; and no artist (performer) shall lose in whole or in part, any of his rights or privileges under such other pension and/or welfare funds by virtue of receiving or being entitled to receive benefits under the AFTRA Pension and Welfare Funds; nor may any payments, rights, or privileges available to an artist (performer) under the AFTRA Pension and Welfare Funds be credited to any payments, rights, or privileges under any other pension and/or welfare funds and vice versa.

SECTION 5. No part of the Company's (Producer's) contributions or the artist's (performer's) benefits from the Pension and Welfare Plans (a) may be credited against the artist's (performer's) overscale compensation or against any other benefits or emoluments whatsoever that the artist (performer) may be entitled to, no matter what form such other benefits or emoluments may take, or (b) are subject to any talent agency commission, or other deduction.

SECTION 6. With respect to the payments required pursuant to sub-paragraph (b) of Section 1 hereof, the Company agrees to furnish a combined Pension & Welfare Remittance Report and AFTRA Production Report, as set forth on Schedule "C". This supplemental report will be used for each contract artist or group under contract wherein gross compensation paid includes form of payment (in addition to scale) as set forth in Paragraph 34, Section 1 (a) of this Code. Additional supplemental reports will be filed periodically until the amount set forth in Paragraph 34, Section 1 (b) of this Code has been paid with a final complete Report due on or before April 30 of each year for the preceding calendar year.

SECTION 7. The Producers and AFTRA hereby ratify and confirm the action of the Trustees of the AFTRA Pension and Welfare Funds in amending the existing Agreement and Declaration of Trust, dated November 16, 1954 to provide coverage for the benefit of AFTRA employees and employees of the AFTRA Pension and Welfare Funds upon terms and conditions established by the Trustees.

SECTION 8. Wherever the phrase "Agreement and Declaration of Trust" is used in this paragraph 34, the Trustees shall have the right in their discretion to construe said phrase as also meaning the plural.

AMERICAN FEDERATION OF TELEVISION AND RADIO ARTISTS (AFTRA)

(Affiliated with the American Federation of Labor and the Congress of Industrial Organizations)

1977-1980 AFTRA CODE OF FAIR PRACTICE FOR PHONOGRAPH RECORDINGS

Minimum Terms and Conditions for Phonograph Recording Artists

AGREEMENT made this .... day of ...., 19......, between American Federation of Television and Radio Artists (herein called "AFTRA") and the undersigned producer of phonograph records (herein called the "Company"). It is agreed that the annexed Code of Fair Practice contains the minimum terms and conditions for the engagement of actors, announcers, narrators, sound effects artists and singers (herein called "Artists") for the purpose of making phonograph recordings in the United States of America, its territories and possessions (herein called the "Recording Territory").

The phonograph recordings covered by this Agreement are herein called "recordings" and include single records, long playing or extended play records, or other micro groove recordings or tape or any other similar or dissimilar device now or hereafter devised. The Company agrees not to make master tapes or portions of master tapes, including but not limited to the use of one to three tracks of a four track tape, or one to seven tracks of an eight track tape, available for use of any kind or nature whatsoever in any other medium; but the foregoing prohibition shall not apply to the Company's use of the said tape or portions thereof in connection with the Company's normal phonograph record operation including but not limited to Company sales meetings, intra-Company promotions, and for file purposes. In addition, the Company may make available to a signatory of AFTRA's then current National Code of Fair Practice for Network Television Broadcasting an incomplete track or portion of a master tape, for use on television, but it shall be the Company's responsibility to ascertain that the intended user is a signatory to said Code.

AFTRA warrants, represents and agrees that it represents for collective bargaining purposes a majority of the artists engaged by the Company for recordings and will for the period of this Agreement continue to represent such majority in the Recording Territory. The bargaining unit is a national unit. The Company recognizes AFTRA as the exclusive bargaining agency for all artists engaged by the Company directly or indirectly or through its agents or representatives for the making of recordings in the Recording Territory.

AFTRA agrees and represents that it is and will continue to be an open union, and will admit to and retain in membership all eligible artists engaged under said Code.

The Company agrees that it will not for the purpose of evading performance under this Code, (1) sublet or transfer responsibility hereunder to any third person, or (2) transfer its operations to any other place of origin.

This Agreement becomes effective as of April 1, 1977 and ends at midnight March 31, 1980. It will automatically renew itself for one-year periods unless terminated by either party giving the other party at least 60 days' written notice prior to the expiration of any contract period. In the event such notice is given, AFTRA and the Company agree to commence negotiations in good faith immediately with respect to a new agreement.

IN WITNESS WHEREOF, AFTRA and the Company have signed this Agreement on the day and year above stated.

AMERICAN FEDERATION OF
TELEVISION AND RADIO ARTISTS

By:_____

Signature

_____
National Executive Secretary

_____
Print or type signature

_____
Address

_____
City

171

Phonograph Record Sessions Report _____   Schedule A & B
and P & W Report

Company Name

Address

P&W Account No:_____   Job Number

American Federation of Television and Radio Artists

1350 Avenue of the Americas	1717 No. Highland Avenue	It is the responsibility of the Member to file a pink
New York, NY 10019	Hollywood, CA 90028	copy of the report with the AFTRA Local Office
Tel - (212) 265- 7700	Tel - (213) 461 - 8111	within 48 hours of the session and deliver all other
1012 17th Avenue South	307 N. Michigan Avenue	copies to employer at end of session.
Nashville, TN 37212	Chicago, IL 60601	
Tel - (615) 256 - 0155	Tel - (312) 372 - 8081	

Type of Recording		Single		Album		Classical		Other

Date of Employment   Recording Studio   Address

Featured Artist   Label

Producer   Address   Phone No.

Song No.	Record (Title)	Over Dub	Playing Time*	Song No.	Record (Title)	Over Dub	Playing Time*
1				5			
2				6			
3				7			
4				8			

* Give playing time only if over 3½ minutes on any side.

Featured AFTRA Artist Social Security Number	Name			Song No.	Time		No. of Sides	No. of Hours	Gross Compensation
	Last	First	Middle Initial		From	To			

Other Performers Social Security Number	Name			Song No.	Cate-gory	Time		No. of Sides	No. of Hours	Gross Examination
	Last	First	Middle Initial			From	To			

This Engagement governed by and subject to the applicable terms of the AFTRA National code of Fair Practice for Phonograph Recordings_____

Total All Gross Compensation _____

_____ 7 3/4% AFTRA Pension & Welfare Contribution _____

Company Name

Key To Category

Soloists - Duos	S	Groups 17 - 24	S17	Narrator	N	Contractor	C
Groups 3 - 8	S 3	Groups 25 - 35	S25	Sound Effects	SE		
Groups 9 - 16	S 9	Groups 36 +	S36	Step - Out	SO		

Additional Remarks

Signature of Employer or Representative   Signature of AFTRA Member   Phone No.   Date

RD 1645 5/75

APPENDIX E
Sample
Independent Record
Production Contract*

Agreement made this *1st* day of *January 1980*, between *Joe Producer's Co.* (hereinafter, you) and *The Great Record Co.* (hereinafter, *GRC*).

1. TERM

A. This agreement shall commence as of *January 1, 1980*, and shall continue in force for a term that shall consist of an initial period ending *12/31/1980* (unless extended or suspended as provided herein [hereinafter, the Initial Period]) and the additional period or periods, if any, for which such term may be extended through *GRC's* exercise of one or more of the options granted to GRC in paragraph 1 B below.

B. You grant *GRC* two (2) consecutive options to extend the term of this agreement for additional periods of one (1) year each (hereinafter, the First Option Period and the Second Option Period, respectively) upon all of the terms and conditions herein contained. *GRC* may exercise each such option by giving you notice in writing at least thirty (30) days prior to the expiration of the then current contract period.

2. MINIMUM PRODUCING COMMITMENT

A. During each of the three contract periods described in Article 1 above, you will furnish the services of *Joe Producer* (hereinafter, the Producer) as independent producer(s) in connection with Master Recordings embodying the performances of such recording artists upon whom you and we shall mutually agree (hereinafter, the Artist or Artists) sufficient to constitute *20* sides but for not more than *4* Artist(s).

*For purposes of clarity, blanks in this contract form have been filled in with fictitious names, numbers, and dates. All such insertions have been italicized.

B. The Producer's obligations under this agreement are joint and several, and all references to the Producer herein shall apply to the Producers collectively where this is applicable and to each of them individually.

3. RECORDING PROCEDURE

A. The Producer will follow the procedure set forth below in connection with Master Recordings made hereunder:

(a) Except as expressly noted otherwise in this agreement, prior to the commencement of recording in each instance he shall obtain the approval of GRC of each of the following, in order, before proceeding further:

(1) Selection of material, including the number of Compositions, to be recorded. GRC shall not be deemed to be unreasonable in rejecting any request to record an Album consisting of more than one (1) twelve (12)-inch 33-⅓ rpm Record. The Producer shall advise GRC of the content of all medleys prior to the recording thereof.

(2) Specification of accompaniment, arrangement, and copying services.

(3) Selection of dates of recording and studios where recording is to take place, including the cost of recording therein. The scheduling and booking of all studio time will be done by GRC. To the extent of GRC's union and other requirements, GRC's facilities and the services of its engineers will be used in all recordings made hereunder.

(4) (a) A proposed budget on GRC's then current recording authorization budget form (which the Producer will fill out and submit to GRC sufficiently in advance of the planned commencement of recording to give GRC a reasonable time to review and approve or disapprove it at least fourteen (14) days before the planned commencement of recording).

(4) (b) The Producer shall notify the appropriate Local of the American Federation of Musicians in advance of each recording session.

(4) (c) As and when required by GRC the Producer shall aloow GRC's representatives to attend any recording sessions hereunder.

(4) (d) The Producer shall timely supply GRC with all of the information it needs in order (1) to make payments due in connection with such recordings; (2) to comply with any other obligations GRC may have in connection with the making of such Master Recordings; and (3) to prepare to release Phonograph Records derived from such Master Recordings. Without limiting the generality of clause (2) of the preceding sentence, the Producer shall furnish GRC with all information it requires to comply with its obligations under its union agreements, including, without limitation, the following:

(i) If a session is held to record new tracks intended to be mixed with existing tracks (and if such information is requested by the American Federation of Musicians), the dates and places of the prior sessions at which such existing tracks were made, and the AFM Phonograph Recording Contract (Form B) number(s) covering such sessions.

(ii) Each change of title of any Composition listed in an AFM Phonograph Recording Contract (Form B).

(iii) A listing of all the musical selections contained in recordings made at location sessions and delivered to GRC hereunder.

(4) (e) The Producer shall submit to GRC fully edited Master Recordings, satisfactory for its manufacture and sale of Phonograph Records, and deliver to GRC all original and duplicate Master Recordings of the material recorded, together with all necessary licenses and appropriate permissions.

B. Nothing in this agreement shall obligate GRC to continue or permit the continuation of any recording session or project, even if previously approved hereunder, if GRC reasonably anticipates that the Recording Costs will exceed those specified in the approved budget or that the recordings being produced will not be satisfactory.

4. RECORDING COSTS

A. GRC will pay all talent costs (including, without limitation, all costs of instrumental, vocal, and other personnel and arrangements and copying specifically approved by GRC in respect of the recording of such Master Recordings), and all other amounts required to be paid by GRC pursuant to any applicable law or any collective bargaining agreement between GRC and any union representing Persons who render services in connection with such Master Recordings.

B. All amounts described in paragraph A above, plus all other amounts representing direct expenses paid by GRC or incurred in connection with the production of Master Recordings hereunder (including, without limitation, all studio and engineering charges, in connection with GRC's facilities and personnel or otherwise), are herein sometimes called Recording Costs and shall constitute Advances against the royalties payable with respect to the services of the Artist. The cost of metal parts and payments to the AFM Special Payments Fund and the Music Performance Trust Fund based upon record sales (so-called per record royalties) shall not constitute Advances. Any Recording Costs in excess of 110 percent of the amount approved by GRC will be your sole responsibility and will be promptly paid by you (or reimbursed by you if paid by GRC).

5. GRANT OF RIGHTS

A. All Master Recordings produced hereunder from the Inception of Recording thereof, and all Matrices and Phonograph Records manufactured therefrom, together with the performances embodied thereon, shall be the sole property of GRC, free from any claims whatsoever by you, the Producer, or any other Person; GRC shall have the exclusive right to copyright such Master Recordings in its name as the owner and author thereof and to secure any and all renewals and extensions of such copyright.

B. Without limiting the generality of the foregoing, GRC and any Person authorized by GRC shall have the unlimited right to manufacture Phonograph Records by any method now or hereafter known, derived from the Master Recordings made hereunder, and to sell, transfer, or otherwise deal in the same under any trademarks, trade names, and labels, or to refrain from such manufacture, sale, and dealing, throughout the world.

C. *GRC* and any Licensee of *GRC* each shall have the right and may grant to others the right to reproduce, print, publish, or disseminate in any medium your name and the name of the Producer, and the portraits, pictures, and likeness of the Producer and biographical material concerning him, as news or information, for the purposes of trade, or for advertising purposes, including but not limited to "institutional advertising" (i.e., advertising designed to create goodwill and prestige and not for the purposes of selling any specific product or service), provided, however, that no direct endorsement by the Producer of any product or service shall be used without his written consent.

D. Provided you and the Producer have fulfilled all of your obligations hereunder, *GRC* will accord the Producer the following credit as producer on the labels of single records and disc Album jackets prepared in connection with the initial release in the United States of Phonograph Records derived from Master Recordings produced exclusively by the Producer hereunder and in any full-page trade advertisements relating solely to such Records placed by *GRC* in the United States: "Produced by *Joe Producer* for *Joe Producer's Co.*" if *GRC* fails to comply with the preceding sentence in any instance(s), its sole obligation to you and the Producer by reason of such failure shall be to rectify the error in all such materials prepared after its receipt of notice thereof from you.

6. ADVANCES

A. All monies paid to you or the Producer on your or the Producer's behalf during the term of the agreement at your or the Producer's request, other than royalties paid pursuant to Articles 7 and 10 hereof, shall constitute Advances unless otherwise expressly agreed in writing by an authorized officer of *GRC*.

B. (a) *GRC* will make Advances (hereinafter, Basic Advances) to you in respect of each contract period hereof as follows:

Contract Period	Amount
Initial Period	$10,000
First Option Period	15,000
Second Option Period	20,000

(b) With respect to the *$10,000* Basic Advance to be paid to you during the Initial Period, you will be paid *$5,000* upon the commencement of said period and the balance of *$5,000* in three (3) equal installments on the first day of each of the third, sixth, and ninth months following commencement of the Initial Period.

(c) With respect to the *$15,000* Basic Advance to be paid to you during the First Option Period, if any, you will be paid *$7,500* upon the commencement of said period and the balance of *$7,500* in three (3) equal installments on the first day of each of the third, sixth, and ninth months following commencement of the First Option Period.

(d) With respect to the *$20,000* Basic Advance to be paid to you during the Second Option Period, if any, you will be paid *$10,000* upon the commencement of said Period and the balance of *$10,000* in three (3) equal installments on the first day of each of the third, sixth, and ninth months following commencement of the Second Option Period.

C. The Basic Advances described in paragraph 6B(a) are predicated on the Producer's producing at least *20* Sides during each of the three (3) contract periods hereunder. In the event the Producer produces more than *20* Sides during any of said contract periods, you will be paid an additional Advance in the amount specified below for each such Side, following the Delivery of all of the recordings to be made in connection with the recording project concerned.

Contract Period	Additional Advance per Side in Excess of *20*
Initial Period	$ *500 per side*
First Option Period	*750 per side*
Second Option Period	*1,000 per side*

7. ROYALTIES

You will be paid royalties on Net Sales of Records as hereinafter set forth:

A. (a) (1) *GRC* will pay you a basic royalty of 6% of the applicable Royalty Base Price in respect of Net Sales of Phonograph Records in disc form, consisting entirely of Master Recordings produced hereunder and sold by *GRC* or its Licensees through Normal Retail Channels for distribution in the United States (hereinafter, USNRC Net Sales).

(2) If *GRC* has released Albums that consist entirely of performances by the Artist concerned and have achieved average USNRC Net Sales of fewer than *50,000* units prior to the initial release by *GRC* of an Album produced by the Producer under this agreement, the basic royalty on the latter Album will be:

(a) *7%* rather than *6%* on all USNRC Net Sales of that Album in excess of *50,000* units and up to *500,000* units; and

(b) *8%* on all such USNRC Net Sales in excess of *500,000* units.

(3) If *GRC* has released Albums that consist entirely of performances by the Artist concerned and have achieved average USNRC Net Sales for the last two (2) Albums in excess of *50,000* units but fewer than *150,000* units prior to the initial release by *GRC* of an Album produced by the Producer under this agreement, the basic royalty on the latter Album will be *7%* rather than *6%* on all USNRC Net Sales of that Album in excess of the particular Artist's average USNRC Net Sales for the two (2) Albums prior to the release of the latter Album.

(4) If *GRC* has released Albums that consist entirely of performances by the Artist concerned and have achieved average USNRC Net Sales for the last two (2) Albums in excess of *150,000* units prior to the initial release by *GRC* of an Album produced by the Producer under this agreement, the basic royalty on the latter Album will be *7%* rather than *6%* on all USNRC Net Sales of that Album in excess of *150,000* units.

(b) No royalty shall be payable to you on Phonograph Records of performances by any Artist until *GRC* has recouped all Recording Costs in connection with that Artist's Master Recordings produced hereunder from royalties payable with respect to that Artist's services in connection with those Phonograph Records. After such recoupment, royalties shall be computed retroactively and paid to you on all such Records, from the first Record sold. For the purposes of computing such recoupment, such Recording Costs for each Side produced hereunder will be deemed to include *one-twentieth* of the Basic Advance payable under paragraph *6B(a)* for the contract period concerned.

B. (a) In respect of Phonograph Records sold through any Club Operation, the royalty rate shall be determined by multiplying the otherwise applicable royalty rate by a fraction, the numerator of which is 3 and the denominator of which is the basic royalty fixed in paragraph 7A, and such royalties shall be computed on the basis of 90% of Net Sales of such Records. Notwithstanding the foregoing, no royalty shall be payable to you with respect to (1) Phonograph Records received by members of any such Club Operation in an introductory offer in connection with joining it or upon recommending that another join it or as a result of the purchase of a required number of Records including, without limitation, records distributed as "bonus" or "free" Records, or (2) Phonograph Records for which such Club Operation is not paid.

(b) Notwithstanding clause (1) of the last sentence of paragraph 7B(a) at least *two-thirds* of all Phonograph Records distributed through any Club Operation during the term of this agreement will be deemed to have been sold. Such computation shall be made on an overall basis rather than at the end of each accounting period.

C. In respect of catalog Phonograph Records sold by *GRC* special products operations (hereinafter, *SPO*) to educational institutions or libraries or to other *SPO* clients for their promotion or sales incentive purposes (but not for sale to the general public through normal retail channels), the royalty shall be *one-half* of the royalty rate otherwise payable. In respect of noncatalog Phonograph Records created on a custom basis for clients of *SPO* the royalty rate shall be *one-half* of the royalty rate otherwise payable and shall be computed on the basis of *GRC's* actual sales price therefor (less all taxes and Container Charges). In respect of any Master Recording leased by *GRC* to others for their distribution of Phonograph Records in the United States, 50% of *GRC's* net receipts therefrom (after deduction of all copyright, AFM, and other applicable third party payments) will be divided among you and all Artists or other Persons entitled to royalties in respect of such Records, in the same ratio as that among your respective basic royalty percentage rates.

D. In respect of Phonograph Records sold in the form of prerecorded tape, the royalty rate payable to you therefor shall be the same applicable royalty rate that would have been payable to you if such Records were sold in disc form.

E. The royalty rate on any Budget Record, Record bearing a Reissue Label, or twelve (12)-inch "disco single" shall be *one-half* of the otherwise applicable royalty rate.

F. The basic royalty rate under paragraph 7A in respect of Phonograph Records sold by *GRC* or its Licensees for distribution outside the United States of America shall be *one-half*. Notwithstanding the foregoing, the basic royalty rate for Records sold by *GRC* or its Licensees in Canada shall be *two-thirds*. Such royalties shall be computed on the basis of 90% of Net Sales of such Records, but if any *GRC* Licensee accounts to *GRC* on the basis of more than 90% of such Net Sales, *GRC* will account to you on the same basis for the Records concerned.

G. In respect of Phonograph Records derived from Master Recordings leased or otherwise furnished by *GRC* Licensees to others for their manufacture and distribution of Records outside the United States, *GRC* will pay you *one-half* of the amount that would otherwise be payable to you if *GRC* or its Licensees manufactured and distributed such Records.

8. MISCELLANEOUS ROYALTY PROVISIONS

Notwithstanding anything to the contrary contained in Article 7 hereof:

A. There shall be no Jointly Produced Recording without your prior approval. Notwithstanding the foregoing, in the event of such a Jointly Produced Recording the royalty rate to be used in determining the royalties payable to you shall be computed by multiplying the royalty rate otherwise applicable thereto by a fraction, the numerator of which shall be one (1) and the denominator of which shall be the total number of producers entitled to receive royalties with respect to their services in connection with such recording.

B. With respect to a Phonograph Record embodying Master Recordings made hereunder together with other Master Recordings, the royalty rate payable to you shall be computed by multiplying the royalty rate otherwise applicable by a fraction, the numerator of which is the number of Sides contained thereon embodying Master Recordings made hereunder and the denominator of which is the total number of Sides contained on such Record.

C. No royalties shall be payable to you in respect of Phonograph Records sold or distributed by GRC or its Licensees as cutouts after the listing of such records has been deleted from the catalog of GRC or the particular Licensee, for promotional purposes, as "free," "no charge," or "bonus" Records (whether or not intended for resale), or to radio stations, or for use on transportation carriers and facilities to promote and stimulate the sale of Phonograph Records.

9. ROYALTY ACCOUNTINGS

A. GRC will compute royalties payable to you hereunder as of June 30th and December 31st for each preceding six (6)-month period during which Records as to which royalties are payable hereunder are sold and will render a statement and pay such royalties, less any unrecouped Advances, prior to each succeeding September 30th and March 31st, respectively.

B. Royalties for Records sold for distribution outside the United States (hereinafter, Foreign Sales) shall be computed in the national currency in which GRC is paid by its Licensees and shall be paid to you at the same rate of exchange at which GRC is paid. For accounting purposes, Foreign Sales shall be deemed to occur in the same semi-annual accounting periods in which Licensees account to GRC therefor. If GRC is unable, for reasons beyond its control, to receive payment for such sales in United States dollars in the United States, royalties therefor shall not be credited to your account during the continuance of such inability; if any accounting rendered to you hereunder during the continuance of such inability requires the payment of royalties to you, GRC will, at your request and if GRC is able to do so, deposit such royalties to your credit in such foreign currency in a foreign depository, at your expense.

C. (a) At any time within *2 years* after any royalty statement is due you hereunder you shall have the right to give GRC written notice of your intention to examine GRC's books and records with respect to such statement. Such examination shall be commenced within thirty (30) days after the date of such notice, at your sole cost and expense, by any certified public accountant or attorney designated by you provided he is not then engaged in an outstanding examination of GRC's books and records on behalf of a Person other than you. Such examination shall be made during GRC's usual business hours at the place where GRC maintains the books and records that relate to you and that are necessary to verify the accuracy of the statement or statements specified in your notice to GRC and your examination shall be limited to the foregoing.

(b) Notwithstanding the second sentence of paragraph 9C(a), if GRC notifies you that the representative designated by you to conduct an examination of GRC's books and records under paragraph 9C(a) is engaged in an examination on behalf of another Person (hereinafter, Other Examination), you may nevertheless have your examination conducted by your designee, and the running of the time within which such examination may be made shall be suspended until your designee has completed the Other Examination, subject to the following conditions:

(1) You shall notify *GRC* of your election to that effect within fifteen (15) days after the date of *GRC*'s said notice to you;

(2) Your designee shall proceed in a reasonably continuous and expeditious manner to complete the Other Examination and render the final report thereon to the client and *GRC*; and

(3) Your examination shall not be commenced by your designee before the delivery to *GRC* of the final report on the Other Examination but shall commence within thirty (30) days thereafter and shall be conducted in a reasonably continuous manner.

D. Your sole right to inspect *GRC*'s books and records shall be as set forth in subparagraph 9C(a) hereof, and *GRC* shall have no obligation to produce such books and records more than once with respect to each statement rendered to you. Without limiting the generality of the foregoing, *GRC* shall have no obligation to furnish you with any records that do not specifically show sales or gratis distribution of Phonograph Records as to which royalties are payable hereunder.

E. Unless notice shall have been given to *GRC* as provided in paragraph 9C hereof, each royalty statement rendered to you shall be final, conclusive, and binding on you and shall constitute an account stated. You shall be foreclosed from maintaining any action, claim, or proceeding against *GRC* in any forum or tribunal with respect to any statement or accounting due hereunder unless such action, claim, or proceeding is commenced against *GRC* in a court of competent jurisdiction within three (3) years after the due date of such statement or accounting.

10. MECHANICAL LICENSES

A. (a) (1) All Controlled Compositions are hereby licensed to *GRC* for the United States and Canada, at the royalty rate of two (2) cents per Controlled Composition on the basis of Net Sales of Phonograph Records, except that no copyright royalties shall be payable with respect to Records described in paragraph 8C. The royalty rate with respect to Records described in paragraph 7E or distributed through a Club Operation shall be 75% of said rate, and arranged versions of public domain Compositions that are claimed by you to be Controlled Compositions shall be licensed to *GRC* at 50% of said rate.

(2) Notwithstanding the foregoing, *GRC* shall not be required to pay an aggregate copyright royalty in excess of *$.20* for any Album or *$.04* for any single Record consisting of recordings made hereunder.

(b) Commencing on the effective date of any change in the statutory compulsory license mechanical copyright royalty rate in the United States or Canada:

(1) The rate fixed in the first sentence of section 10A(a)(1) will be changed to such new statutory rate (instead of two [2] cents), and

(2) The maximum aggregate royalties fixed in section 10A(a)(2) shall be changed to (i) the amount ten (10) times the new minimum statutory rate, in respect of Albums, and (ii) twice the new minimum statutory rate, in respect of single Records (instead of *$.20* and *$.04* respectively),

in respect of Net Sales in the country concerned of Phonograph Records consisting of recordings of Controlled Compositions recorded hereunder after such effective date.

(c) Accountings for such royalties shall be rendered quarter-annually, within forty-five (45) days after the end of each calendar quarter.

B. Any assignment made of the ownership or copyright in, or right to license the use of, any Controlled Compositions referred to in this paragraph shall be made subject to the provisions hereof.

C. The provisions of this Article 10 shall constitute and are accepted by you, on your own behalf and on behalf of any other owner of any Controlled Compositions or any rights therein, as full compliance by GRC with all of its obligations, under the compulsory license provisions of the Copyright Law, as the same may be amended, or otherwise, arising from any use by GRC of Controlled Compositions as provided herein.

D. If any recordings made hereunder contain one or more Compositions, other than Controlled Compositions, not in the public domain and not previously recorded in the United States by the owner of the copyright or with his permission, you will obtain, at GRC's election and for GRC's benefit, mechanical licenses covering such Compositions on the same terms applicable to Controlled Compositions pursuant to this Article 10.

11. WARRANTIES AND REPRESENTATIONS; RESTRICTIONS; INDEMNITIES

A. You warrant and represent:

(a) You have the right and power to enter into and fully perform this agreement.

(b) GRC shall not be required to make any payments of any nature for, or in connection with, the rendition of the Producer's services or the acquisition, exercise, or exploitation of rights by GRC pursuant to this agreement except as specifically provided herein.

(c) No Materials, as hereinafter defined, or any use thereof, will violate any law or infringe upon or violate the rights of any Person. Materials, as used in this Article 11, means all Controlled Compositions and all other musical, dramatic, artistic, and literary materials, ideas, and other intellectual properties, furnished or selected by you or the Producer and contained in or used in connection with any recordings made hereunder or the packaging, sale, distribution, advertising, publicizing, or other exploitation thereof.

B. During the term of this agreement, neither you nor the Producer will enter into any agreement that would interfere with the full and prompt performance of the Producer's obligations hereunder and the Producer will not produce or render any services for the purpose of producing or making Phonograph Records or Master Recordings for any Person other than GRC except for the following:

(a) The Producer may continue to render his production services with respect to a certain artist p/k/a/ (professionally known as) *another singer*.

(b) The Producer may continue to render his production services under an existing agreement with XYZ Records with respect to a certain artist p/k/a/*former commitment*.

(c) The Producer may produce two phonograph Albums pursuant to a certain existing agreement between the Producer and XXX Records.

C. The Producer's services are unique and extraordinary, and the loss thereof cannot be adequately compensated in damages, and *GRC* shall be entitled to injunctive relief to enforce the provisions of this agreement.

D. You will at all times indemnify and hold harmless *GRC* and any Licensee of *GRC* from and against any and all claims, damages, liabilities, costs, and expenses, including legal expenses and reasonable counsel fees, arising out of (a) the use of any Materials, as defined in this Article 11, or (b) any breach by you or any warranty or agreement made by you herein that has resulted in a judgment against *GRC* or its Licensees or that has been settled with your consent. You will reimburse *GRC* and/or its Licensees on demand for any payment made at any time after the date hereof in respect of any liability or claim in respect of which *GRC* or its Licensees are entitled to be indemnified.

12. DEFINITIONS

As used in this agreement the following terms shall have the meanings set forth below:

A. *Master Recording*—every recording of sound, whether or not coupled with a visual image, by any method and on any substance or material, whether now or hereafter known, which is used or useful in the recording, production, and/or manufacture of phonograph records. Notwithstanding the foregoing, *GRC* shall not record "sight and sound" performances hereunder without your prior consent.

B. *Inception of Recording*—the first recording of performances and/or other sounds with a view to the ultimate fixation of a Master Recording.

C. *Matrix*—any device now or hereafter used, directly or indirectly, in the manufacture of Phonograph Records and which is derived from a Master Recording.

D. *Person* and *Party*—any individual, corporation, partnership, association, or other organized group of persons or legal successors or representatives of the foregoing.

E. *Records* and *Phonograph Records*—all forms of reproductions, now or hereafter known, manufactured or distributed primarily for home use, school use, juke box use, or use in means of transportation, embodying (a) sound alone or (b) sound coupled with visual images, e.g., "sight and sound" devices.

F. *"Wholesale Price"*—(a) with respect to Records sold for distribution in the United States or Canada: (1) the average net price received by *GRC* from independent distributors for Phonograph Records during the six (6)-month period immediately preceding the accounting period concerned, calculated separately for each separately priced Record series manufactured and sold by *GRC*; or (2) if there are no applicable independent distributors, *GRC*'s published subdistributor price in effect as of the commencement of the accounting period concerned, less ten (10) percent. (b) With respect to Records sold for distribution outside the United States and Canada, one-half of the suggested or applicable retail list price in the country of sale.

G. *Royalty Base Price*—the applicable Wholesale Price of Phonograph Records less all taxes and less the applicable container charge.

H. *Container Charge*—(a) with respect to disc Phonograph Records, 10% of the applicable Wholesale Price of such Phonograph Records; and (b) with respect to Phonograph Records in nondisc configurations, 15% of the applicable Wholesale Price of such Phonograph Records.

I. *Net Sales*—gross sales less returns and credits.

J. *Club Operation*—any direct sales to consumers conducted on a mail order basis by *GRC* or its Licensees.

K. *Advance*—amount recoupable by *GRC* from royalties to be paid to you or on your behalf pursuant to this or any other agreement.

(b) Each Advance made under Article 6 will be recoupable only from royalties on Records of performances by the Artist to whose recordings such Advance is attributable. For the purposes of this paragraph, *one-twentieth* of the Basic Advance payable under paragraph 6B for the contract period concerned will be attributable to each Side produced under this agreement.

L. *Composition*—a single musical composition, irrespective of length, including all spoken words and bridging passages and including a medley.

M. *Controlled Composition*—a composition written, owned, or controlled by you, the Producer, and/or any Person in which you or the Producer has a direct or indirect interest.

N. *Album*—one (1) or more twelve (12)-inch 33-⅓ rpm records, or the equivalent thereof, sold in a single package. (A "disco single" shall not be deemed an Album.)

O. *Side*—a recording of sufficient playing time to constitute a single side of a 45 rpm record, but not less than two and one-quarter (2¼) minutes of continuous sound.

P. *Jointly Produced Recording*—any Master Recording produced by the Producer and by another producer with respect to whose services *GRC* is obligated to pay royalties.

Q. *Sales through Normal Retail Channels in the United States*—sales other than as described in paragraphs 7B, 7C, 7E, and 7F hereof.

R. *Licensees*—includes, without limitation, subsidiaries, wholly or partly owned, and other divisions of *GRC*.

S. *Delivery* or *Delivered*—when used with respect to Master Recordings means the actual receipt by *GRC* of fully mixed and edited Master Recordings, satisfactory to *GRC* and ready for *GRC's* manufacture of Phonograph Records, and all necessary licenses and permissions.

T. *Reissue Label*—a label used primarily for reissues of recordings released previously.

U. *Budget Record*—a record bearing a suggested retail list price at least two (2) dollars lower than the suggested retail list price used for the top line Phonograph Records embodying performances of pop artists released by *GRC* or its Licensees in the territory concerned.

13. APPROVAL AND CONSENT

A. As to all matters treated herein to be determined by mutual agreement, or as to which any approval or consent is required, such agreement, approval, or consent shall not be unreasonably withheld.

B. Your agreement, approval, or consent, or that of the Producer, whenever required, shall be deemed to have been given unless you notify *GRC* otherwise within ten (10) days following the date of *GRC's* written request therefor. *GRC* shall have the right to rely conclusively upon any such agreement, approval, or consent given by you on behalf of the Producer.

14. SUSPENSION AND TERMINATION

A. If at any time the Producer fails, except solely for *GRC's* refusal without cause to allow him to perform or *GRC's* failure to approve sufficient Artists to produce, to fulfill the minimum producing commitment within the time set forth herein, then, without limiting *GRC's* rights, *GRC* shall have the option, exercisable by notice to you, to:

(a) extend the expiration date of the then current contract period and/or to suspend

GRC's obligation to make payments to you hereunder for the period of the default plus such additional time as is necessary so that GRC shall have no fewer than sixty (60) days after completion of your Minimum Producing Commitment within which to exercise its option, if any, for the next following contract period, or

(b) increase the Minimum Producing Commitment in any subsequent contract period by the number of incompleted Master Recordings, in addition to the otherwise applicable Minimum Producing Commitment. No additional Advances will be payable under paragraph 6B for any recording comprised in such an increase. Each such recording will be deemed to have been made during the contract period in which it was originally required to be produced for the purposes of the last sentence of subparagraph 7A(b) and the second sentence of subparagraph 12K(b).

B. If because of act of God; inevitable accident; fire; lockout, strike, or other labor dispute; riot or civil commotion; act of public enemy; enactment, rule, order, or act of any government or governmental instrument (whether federal, state, local, or foreign); failure of technical facilities; illness or incapacity of any performer or producer; or other cause of a similar or different nature not reasonably within GRC's control; GRC is materially hampered in the recording, manufacture, distribution, or sale of records, then, without limiting GRC's rights, GRC shall have the option by giving you notice to suspend the then current contract period for the duration of any such contingency plus such additional time as is necessary so that GRC shall have no fewer than thirty (30) days after the cessation of such contingency in which to exercise its option, if any, for the next following contract period.

15. ASSIGNMENT

A. GRC may assign its rights hereunder in whole or in part to any subsidiary, affiliated, or controlling corporation or to any Person owning or acquiring a substantial portion of the stock or assets of GRC and such rights may be assigned by any assignee thereof; provided, however, that any such assignment shall not relieve GRC of any of its obligations hereunder. GRC may also assign its rights hereunder to any of its Licensees to the extent necessary or advisable in GRC's sole discretion to implement the license granted.

16. NOTICES

A. Except as otherwise specifically provided herein, all notices hereunder shall be in writing and shall be given by personal delivery, registered or certified mail, or telegraph (prepaid) at the respective addresses hereinabove set forth or such other address or addresses as may be designated by either Party. Such notices shall be deemed given when mailed or delivered to a telegraph office, except that notice of change of address shall be effective only from the date of its receipt. A copy of each notice sent to GRC shall be sent simultaneously to GRC's legal department.

17. MISCELLANEOUS

A. This agreement contains the entire understanding of the Parties hereto relating to the subject matter hereof and cannot be changed or terminated except by an instrument signed by an officer of GRC. A waiver by either Party of any term or condition of this agreement in any instance shall not be deemed or construed as a waiver of such term or condition for the future or of any subsequent breach thereof. All remedies, rights, undertakings, obligations, and agreements contained in this agreement shall be cumulative and none of them shall be in limitation of any other remedy, right, undertaking, obligation, or agreement of either Party.

B. Those provisions of any applicable collective bargaining agreement between *GRC* and any labor organization that are required, by the terms of such agreement, to be included in this agreement shall be deemed incorporated herein.

C. No breach by *GRC* of its material obligations hereunder will entitle you to recover damages, or affect any of your obligations hereunder, unless GRC has failed to remedy such breach within a reasonable time following receipt of your notice thereof.

D. This agreement has been entered into in the *State of New York* and the validity, interpretation, and legal effect of this agreement shall be governed by the laws of the *State of New York* applicable to contracts entered into and performed entirely within the *State of New York* with respect to the determination of any claim, dispute, or disagreement that may arise out of the interpretation, performance, or breach of this agreement. Any process in any action or proceeding commenced in the courts of the State of New York or elsewhere arising out of any such claim, dispute, or disagreement may among other methods be served upon you by delivering or mailing the same, via registered or certified mail, addressed to you at the address first above written or such other address as you may designate pursuant to Article 16 hereof. Any such delivery or mail service shall be deemed to have the same force and effect as personal service within the *State of New York* or the jurisdiction in which such action or proceeding may be commenced.

E. In entering into this agreement, and in providing services pursuant hereto, you and the Producer have and shall have the status of independent contractors and nothing herein contained shall contemplate or constitute you or the Producer as *GRC's* agents or employees.

F. This agreement shall not become effective until executed by all proposed Parties hereto.

G. Any and all riders annexed hereto together with this basic document shall be taken together to constitute the agreement between you and *GRC*.

By _____
    The Great Record Co. (GRC)

By _____
    Joe Producer

In order to induce *GRC* to enter into the foregoing agreement with *Joe Producer's Co.*, dated *January 1, 1980*, I hereby assent to the execution of such agreement and agree to be bound by the terms and conditions thereof including, without limitation, any provisions of such agreement relating to me and restrictions imposed upon me in accordance with the provisions of such agreement. I hereby acknowledge that GRC shall be under no obligation to make any payments whatsoever to me in connection with the services rendered by me and/or the fulfillment of my obligations pursuant to the foregoing agreement.

_____
                      Joe Producer

Joe Producer
555 Hit Boulevard
Hollywood, CA
January 1, 1980

A New Recording Artist
#1 Main Street
New York, N.Y.

Dear *New Recording Artist:*

The following will confirm the agreement reached between *Joe Producer* and the members of the group known as *A New Recording Artist*, which is as follows:

    1. The artist will enter into an exclusive recording agreement with *Joe Producer* for an initial period of 18 months, with two 18 month options, it being agreed that this recording contract with *Joe Producer* will terminate concurrent with the signing by *Joe Producer* and *A New Recording Artist* of a third party distributor agreement. This agreement is null and void in six months from the above date unless *Joe Producer* has entered into a recording agreement with a third party distributor.

    2. Any royalties received from a third party distributor will be split on a 60/40 basis with the *New Recording Artist* receiving 60%, but the artist will not receive less than 6% of retail and *Joe Producer* will never receive a royalty in excess of 4% of retail.

    3. The artist will receive advances for the first period of approximately $25,000.

4. A commitment for tour support will be secured to cover any deficit with no more than one-half recoupable in an amount of at least $30,000.

5. During the first period, the artist will have a firm commitment for two albums and there will be a two album minimum during each of the option periods with the provision for one additional album at third party distributor's request to fall somewhere during the second and third periods.

6. A mutually acceptable distributor will be secured and the rest of the terms shall be subject to mutual approval.

7. It is agreed that *Joe Producer* will produce all records recorded by the artist and that if *Joe Producer* should decide not to produce then he will receive no further royalty. If however the artist decides that *Joe Producer* will not produce, then *Joe Producer* will receive a 2% of retail override for the next two albums.

If the foregoing is in accordance with your understanding, please sign where indicated and return to me for counter signature.

Sincerely,

_____

Joe Producer

Agreed and accepted:

_____

A New Recording Artist

Glossary

A&R. Abbreviation for "Artist and Repertoire," a term used to signify record company personnel involved in signing artists and producers and casting the right songs for recording artists.

Acetate. A reference disc of recorded material.

Advance. Money paid to artists and producers by record companies before it is earned, or in advance of record royalties; if, for example, the advance to a producer were $5,000, the record company would retain the first $5,000 of the producer's royalties in order to recover, or recoup, its advance.

All-in production contract. Synonym for an overall production agreement whereby the artist and the producer receive a combined royalty.

Arranger: A person who arranges or orchestrates a song for performance by musicians on a recording session.

Assembling. The positioning of songs in the sequence that will be heard as side 1 and side 2 of a long-playing album.

Attenuator. A switch built into the mic/line circuit of a recording console and used to reduce overloading and distortion by reducing level; used when recording strong signals.

Baffles. Portable walls treated with sound-absorbing or sound-reflecting materials that help prevent leakage.

Basic tracks. Synonym for the rhythm tracks on a record.

Beats. Rhythmic pulses of equal time value associated with a bar or measure of music; the recording engineer will usually splice musical sections at the beginning of a beat.

Blank tape. Virgin tape used to create space between the bands on each side of an album; used in place of leader tape if the producer wishes a completely noiseless bridge between performances.

Block booking. An arrangement whereby a professional studio owner agrees to allow a producer to use a studio on a twenty-four-hour basis for the duration of recording; block bookings enable everyone to go home at night without having to break down the recording setup, or zero the recording console.

Blue box: A processing device that electronically adds octaves to the signal by doubling or halving the frequency cycle.

Board. Synonym for a recording console.

Bottom. Term referring to low frequency response or bass presence.

Bounce. Synonym for ping-pong.

Brightness. Term referring to the high frequency response.

Budget records. A product line whose retail list price is several dollars lower, or between 30 and 50 percent less, than a company's first-line product.

Bus. Industry slang for an output channel that carries recorded signals to a tape recorder.

Cardioid microphone. A mike that picks up in a heartlike pattern; radiating from a central point to an arc of approximately 90 degrees.

Charts. Musical arrangements that are written out for band members.

Clam. Slang for a mistake, i.e., a bad note.

Clean. Production slang for an uncluttered performance executed without flaw.

Close-miking. The current industry norm for recording instruments live; the microphone is placed from six to twelve inches away from the instrument or amplifier.

Compressor. A processing device that compresses the dynamic response of a particular sound and creates a more constant, even level.

Concept album. A recording with a musical or lyrical theme underlying the entire album.

Condenser microphones. Mikes that are excellent reproducers of high frequencies and are generally more sensitive than are dynamic microphones but require a separate power supply.

Container charge. An allowance for lowering the base price of an album for purposes of computing record royalties; the record company's argument is that the artist and the producer should be charged something for the design, fabrication, and printing of attractive album covers and inner sleeves that help sell their records.

Copyist. A person who takes the orchestration created by an arranger and copies it neatly into orchestral parts for each musician.

Cover. A new recording of a song already commercially released.

Crispy. Production slang for a tight snare drum sound.

Cross-collateralization. The right of a company to retain income under one agreement (such as a production deal) to pay back unrecouped expenses under another agreement (such as a publishing deal); from the producer's viewpoint, cross-collateralization is unfair and should be avoided at all costs.

Cue mix. A mono or stereo blend of musical performances that can be fed to a musician's left and/or right earphone during recording.

Cue system. A communications network built into the recording console whereby the producer and the recording engineer can talk to musicians in the studio through earphones and feed previously recorded performances or performances in progress to the musicians while they record.

Custom label. A minirecord company distributed by a larger, full-service company, which uses the label identification of the custom label owner (who many times is a superstar producer); custom label royalties are the highest production royalties in the industry.

189

Producing Hit Records

Cutoff. Production term that signifies the way singers close off words and end a performance together.

Cutouts. Product that has been deleted from a record company's catalog; no royalties are paid on cutouts.

Cuts. Synonym for tracks or individual selections.

Cutting. Industry slang for recording a performance (e.g., cutting four sides) or negotiating a deal (e.g., cutting a deal for the band).

DDL. Abbreviation for digital delay line.

Dead room. An acoustical environment that absorbs or lessens reverberation.

Decay. The time that elapses as a signal becomes inaudible.

Demo. Demonstration tape or record that presents a song or an artist not for commercial release.

Desk. Synonym for a recording console.

Digital delay line. A processing device that can vary the speed of reverb effects from a few milliseconds to about one second of delay.

Direct box. A piece of equipment used to match the impedance of electric instruments to the input of the recording console; direct boxes are used when a microphone is not employed.

Disco single. A record that for purposes of continuous dancing is powerfully rhythmic and of long duration; disco singles are sometimes longer than album versions of songs.

Double. A performance (e.g., a lead vocal) that is assigned two tracks and recorded twice in two separate passes.

Double-tracked. Production term for two separate but similar performances that are blended together.

Duplicating. The process of making multiple copies of a recording for purposes of evaluation, insurance from theft or damage, or compliance with the requirements for delivering product to a record company.

Dynamic microphones. Rugged, dependable, all-purpose mikes that can take bursts of power and high levels without causing too much distortion; they need no separate power supply.

Echo. A natural force in nature that causes sound to repeat itself; echo effects can be created in the recording studio by using various sound processing devices.

Echoplex. A reverb device that uses a tape loop to create repeat or delay effects.

Echo send. A recording console control used to direct signals to a reverb chamber.

Editing. The process of cutting or splicing taped performances so that the finished tape is either longer or shorter; also, the splicing together of two or more separate performances of the same music so that the edited performance sounds better than the separate performances.

EMT. An electronic stereo echo-producing device.

EQ. Abbreviation for equalization.

Equalization. Manipulation of frequency response to produce a desirable sound.

Executive producer. An executive (often the head of A&R) at a record company who functions primarily in an administrative capacity overseeing recording projects.

Extension or suspension. The stretching of an agreed term beyond the original date, usually caused by the failure of a producer to deliver his minimum recording commitment on time or to meet other contractual obligations to the record company.

Fader. A recording console control used to make changes in sound level.

190

Fat. Production slang for a full, big sound; also the unnecessary parts of a song or record that should be edited out.

Fixer. Production slang for a performance designed to repair or improve a substandard performance.

Flanger. A signal-processing device very similar to a phase shifter.

Flat. Using no equalization or without coloration.

Free goods. Records and tapes that are given away free to distributors and wholesalers as incentives to purchase the product, effectively lowering the per record price; no royalties are paid on free goods.

Gold record. An award issued by the Recording Industry Association of America for both 45 rpm records that sell in excess of one million copies and long-playing records that sell in excess of 500,000 units.

Graphic equalizer. A device that allows manual adjustment of a signal over a broad range of frequencies.

Guaranteed release. A provision in a contract that guarantees release of a product within a certain period of time by the record company.

Harmonizer. A processing device that creates delay effects and changes the pitch of a sound without affecting its tempo.

Headroom. Production term for the safety margin that allows peaks to record or reproduce without saturation or distortion.

High end. Production term for frequencies above 5,000 kHz.

Highly directional microphone. A mike that picks up in a relatively narrow arc and screens out neighboring sounds.

Hole. A momentary pause or space in a musical passage.

Hooks. Musical passages in a record that are repeated a number of times and literally "hook" the listener; infectious, memorable sections of a song.

Hotter. Term referring to more level.

Image. Synonym for the stereo panorama of a record.

Independent producer. A producer who works on a free-lance basis and as an independen contractor; as a rule, independent producers receive higher production royalties than do staff producers, who are employees of the company and receive company benefits.

Initial period. The first term of a contract, usually one year or a portion thereof.

Juice. Production slang signifying the desire for more energy in a performance.

Jumps out. Production slang for a sound that stands out well in context.

Kepex. A processing device that prevents extraneous noises below a threshold set by the recording engineer from triggering the output of the amplifier; a noise gate.

Lacquers. Discs (acetates) that when plated produce a series of stampers used to manufacture records.

Lay back. Production slang that means to relax during a performance so as not to rush the tempo.

Layering. Synonym for separation recording, or recording one track at a time.

Lazy. Production slang for a laid-back feeling.

Leader tape. White-paper tape used to create space between the bands on each side of an album.

Leakage. A condition caused when sound waves from one source spread and bounce over a large area of the recording studio and are picked up randomly by other microphones; leakage can be controlled by using baffles and by carefully selecting and positioning microphones.

LEDs.   VU meters that reflect transient peaks in sound level.

Letter of intent.   An informal document that can be just as binding as a formal contract; used very often by producers to sign artists prior to securing a recording commitment from a major record company.

Licks.   Production slang for the musical lines, or *hooks*, a producer wants to have orchestrated into a recording.

Limiter.   A processing device that reduces peaks but affects overall dynamics less than a compressor does.

Lip noise.   Extraneous sounds, such as lip smacking or teeth clicking, that the micriphone picks up during a vocal performance.

Live.   Production slang for ensemble recording as opposed to overdubbing (e.g., "We cut the tracks live.").

Live chamber.   Industry term for a specially treated recording room used to create reverb effects.

Live recording.   Recording every instrument in the band or orchestra at the same time; concerts are invariably live recordings, but the producer has much less control over a live recording situation than he has using separation recording techniques.

Live room.   An acoustical environment that produces a bright, reverberant sound.

Low end.   Production term for frequencies below 500 kHz.

Master.   A completed, professionally produced recording suitable for commercial release.

Mastering.   The process whereby information contained on a tape is transferred to a lacquer disc for the purpose of manufacturing records in great quantity.

Master purchase agreement.   A form of recording contract used by record companies to obtain exclusive rights in a master recording produced on spec by a producer.

Meat.   Refers to the fundamental sound of an instrument.

Minimum recording commitment.   The smallest number of sides that will be deemed to satisfy a contractual recording requirement of a record company.

Mix-down recorder.   A two-track tape recorder onto which will be recorded the fully mixed multitrack tape performance; the finished records will be made from the two-track tape.

Mixing.   The art of combining prerecorded tracks into a finished master recording that is customarily reduced to two-track stereo.

Monitors.   The expensive speakers used in a control room for evaluating recorded performances.

Muddy.   Production slang for a dull, uncrisp sound.

Multitrack tape recorder.   A machine that has the ability to record as few as two or as many as thirty-two individual channels of music, either one at a time or in any combination desired by the producer.

Noise-reduction equipment.   Electronic devices that improve the signal-to-noise ratio without adding significant coloration to the recorded sound.

Octave divider.   A manually operated electronic device that produces higher and lower octaves to a given signal. Similar to a blue box.

Omnidirectional microphone.   A mike that picks up from all sides.

On spec.   Producing records at your own financial risk.

On top.   Production slang for a performance with an aggressive attitude that anticipates the beat.

Option period.   The consecutive periods (often one year) for which a contract can be extended by a company in order to keep the artist and/or the producer performing under that contract.

Outboard equipment.   The electronic devices that can be patched into the recording console to create special effects.

Overbudget factor.   A financial cushion (15 percent is recommended) to be added to the estimated total cost of a master recording; always submit budgets to a record company with the overbudget factor included.

Overdub.   Any performance recorded after the first track is on tape.

Packing the tape.   Production slang for putting persistently high signal levels on the tape; causes overloading, distortion, and loss of transparency in the finished record.

Pan pot.   A recording console control and type of fader used to place a signal to the left, right, or center of the stereo image.

Parts.   Another term for lacquers used to manufacture records.

Phase cancellation.   The loss of frequency response caused by too many microphones picking up a common signal at slightly varying times; often an unpleasant phenomenon associated with recording the drums.

Phase shifter.   A manually controlled electronic device that creates an audible swirling effect by dividing and combining the signal to produce phase.

Ping-pong.   Production term used to signify the combining of several prerecorded tracks onto another track so that previously recorded tracks become available for new material.

Platinum record.   An award issued by the Recording Industry Association of America for both 45 rpm records that sell in excess of two million units and long-playing records that sell in excess of one million units.

Pop.   Term used to describe a musical component of a record that stands out.

Processed sound.   Production term signifying that the normal sound of an instrument has been changed by using a processor to create a special effect.

Processors.   Electronic devices (e.g., digital delay lines, reverb units, harmonizers, and kepexes) used to create special effects during studio recording and/or mixing.

Product.   Industry slang for phonograph records and tapes.

Promotional records.   Records that are given away free to critics, radio station personnel, and other parties who, in the opinion of the record company, should receive free demonstration records; no royalties are paid on promotional records.

Punch in.   To record a passage of music replacing the original performance while the tape is moving.

Punch out.   To go out of record at the completion of a performance while the tape is still moving.

Punchy.   Production slang for a tight, "popping" sound; usually refers to the acoustics and unique character of a particular studio and console; also refers to a specific instrument such as the drums.

Recording console.   A control board that has many input and output channels, as well as sound processing capability built into it; the brain of a recording studio through which all signals are routed.

Recording costs.   Overall term for the arranging, copying, talent, studio, engineering, transportation, and other costs involved in producing master recordings.

Recording engineer. The technical expert in charge of operating the equipment in the recording studio.

Records shipped. The number of records and tapes sent to wholesalers and dealers for possible sale but not yet sold.

Records sold. The actual number of records and tapes purchased by distributors and wholesalers for which the record company has been *paid*; also, product purchased by consumers through record clubs and direct mail campaigns.

Reference vocal. A vocal track used as a guide during the recording of instrumental overdubs.

Reissue records. A product line that specializes in releasing "golden oldies," or popular records from the past.

Relaxed. Production slang for a comfortable and confident performance.

Reserve account. An accounting procedure whereby over a period of time returns can be debited from the artist's or the producer's royalty account and records that are actually sold can be credited to the artist's or the producer's royalty account.

Reserves. An unspecified amount of product for which the record company will pay no royalties until sales and returns are finally calculated.

Returns. Phonograph records and tapes sent back to record companies by wholesalers and dealers or to wholesalers and distributors by retail accounts; no royalties are paid on returns.

Ribbon microphones. Extremely sensitive, rare, and expensive mikes.

Ride. To move a fader up and down to achieve the desired sound level.

Ride the vocal. Production slang for working the fader up and down to even out a vocal performance.

Roll off. To attenuate or take away.

Room mike. An omnidirectional microphone used to pick up the overall sound in a recording studio during a musical performance.

Royalty. A relatively small percentage of either the wholesale or the retail price of a product, used as the principal means for paying artists and producers.

Royalty accounting. The section of a recording agreement that specifies when the artist and the producer will be paid and the procedure for auditing the company's royalty statements.

Saturation. Distortion caused by too much sound level on the tape.

Sel sync. Production term used to signify the ability of a tape recorder to record one track at a time in synchrony with previously recorded tracks.

Separation recording. The most popular contemporary recording technique; the producer records a song in controlled segments, usually one track at a time, rather than live.

Sequencing. Synonym for assembling.

Singles version. A performance that for purposes of radio play is edited to be shorter than or different in some other way from the LP version.

Snaky. Production slang for funky; loose but appealing.

Splash. Production slang for an extreme pan of echo; used to create a special effect.

Stacking. A production technique whereby many tracks of the multitrack tape recorder are used to build up the sound of a performance, which is then ping-ponged to one track so that it eventually sounds bigger than life (e.g., hand claps).

Staff producer. A salaried employee of a record company who is assigned to produce artists through the company's A&R department.

Statutory rate. The amount of money that U.S. copyright law states should be paid to the publisher of copyrighted music for use of the publisher's song on a phonograph recording; currently the statutory rate is $.0275 per composition or $.005 per minute per composition, whichever amount is greater.

Step out.   Production slang for an instrument asked to play a solo on a recording.

Stereo panorama.   Industry term used to signify the placing of instruments extreme left, extreme right, or degrees of left, center, and right in the finished master; instruments placed extreme left will sound as though they're coming out of the left speaker of a stereo system, and so on.

Sweetening.   Overdubbing additional musical components onto an existing recording.

Taken direct.   Production slang signifying that an instrument is being recorded directly through the recording console, without a microphone.

Tight.   Production slang for a "together" sound, well executed by the ensemble.

Toys.   Production slang for the newest sound processing gadgets on the market; refers also to small percussion instruments of infinite variety.

Track.   Synonym for channel (a twenty-four-track tape recorder has twenty-four separate recording channels); refers also to a particular recorded side (e.g., "We cut three tracks.").

Transients.   Sudden changes in dynamics.

Transparent sound.   Clear sound; the listener has a sense of being able to "hear through" the recorded instruments.

Undirectional microphone.   Synonym for a cardioid microphone.

VU meter.   An electronic device used to indicate sound level; each channel on the recording console and each track on the multitrack tape recorder has its own VU meter, or LED.

Variable speed oscillator.   A feature on a professional tape recorder or an outboard device that enables the producer to adjust manually the speed of the tape recorder; used very often to create special effects.

Vocal.   Industry slang for a voice recording.

VSO.   Abbreviation for variable speed oscillator.

Wah-wah pedal.   A device that, when activated by the opening and closing of a pedal, electronically increases and decreases tonality; usually used with a guitar.

Washed out. Production slang signifying an overly reverberant sound that lacks definition.

Wetter sound.   Production slang for a more reverberant sound.

Wimpy.   Production slang for a thin, weak sound.

Wooden.   Production slang for a dull, dead, like wood sound (usually refers to the snare drum sound).

XY stereo microphone placement.   Two microphones crossing each other to form a stereo pattern that resembles the letters X and Y.

Zero the console.   Returning all functions to the off position.

Additional terms relating to recording contracts are defined in article 12 of the sample independent production agreement presented in appendix E.

Diary of a Hit

Demonstration material from the production and master tapes of
"Baby Come Back," performed by Player (courtesy RSO Records, Inc.)
Narrated by Dennis Lambert

Members of Player:
J.C. Crowley—keyboards, synthesizer, guitars, vocals
Peter Beckett—guitars, vocals
Ronn Moss—bass, vocals
John Friesen—drums
Wayne Cook—keyboards, synthesizer
"Baby Come Back" written by Peter Beckett and J.C. Crowley.
Copyright © Touch of Gold Music, Inc./Crowbeck Music/Stigwood Music, Inc.
Produced for Haven Records by Dennis Lambert and Brian Potter.

Side 1	*Side 2*
Introduction	Processed Guitar Sounds
Drums	Synthesizer
Bass Guitar	Percussion
Rhythm Guitars	Review
Keyboards	Completed Version (Excerpt)
Completed Rhythm Section	
Vocals	
Completed Vocals and Rhythm Section	